DANIEL KOLAK, SERIES EDITOR

Thomas Hobbes

Leviathan

EDITED BY MARSHALL MISSNER

UNIVERSITY OF WISCONSIN

PEARSON
Longman

New York • Boston • San Francisco
London • Toronto • Sydney • Tokyo • Singapore • Madrid
Mexico City • Munich • Paris • Cape Town • Hong Kong • Montreal

Editor in Chief:	Eric Stano
Senior Marketing Manager:	Ann Stypuloski
Production Coordinator:	Scarlett Lindsay
Text Design and Electronic Page Makeup:	Sunflower Publishing Services
Cover Designer/Manager:	John Callahan
Cover Illustration/Photo:	Courtesy of Getty Images, Inc.
Manufacturing Manage:	Mary Fischer
Printer and Binder:	R.R. Donnelley, Harrisonburg
Cover Printer:	Phoenix Color

Library of Congress Cataloging-in-Publication Data on file at the Library of Congress

Please visit us at www.ablongman.com

ISBN 0-321-27612-4

1 2 3 4 5 6 7 8 9 10-DOH-09 08 07 06

Contents

THOMAS HOBBES
Leviathan

PART I
Of Man
page 3

PART 2
Of Commonwealth
page 113

Editor's Introduction

I. INTRODUCTION

The Leviathan, a huge, sprawling, and powerful creature, is an apt metaphor for Thomas Hobbes' huge, sprawling, and powerful book. Leviathans are creatures that encompass a vast volume and cover great gobs of space, and the same is the case with this book. It not only provides a theory of political philosophy, clearly its main aim, but it also spouts forth ideas about Empiricism, Rationalism, Analytic Philosophy, Decision Theory, the Materialist and Computational theories of the Mind, Formal methods, Utilitarianism, Kantianism, Social Contract theory, Psychological Egoism, and legal theory. One can also find Hobbes engaging in the political and theological disputes of his day, as well as making witty and cynical observations about human behavior. This book is, in fact, much like its title immense, maddening, fascinating, somewhat frightening, sometimes out of control, and clearly, something to be reckoned with.

A. This Edition

This edition of *Leviathan* differs from the original in two particular ways. The first is that it contains only the first two parts of a book that is divided into four parts. The first two parts of the *Leviathan* are carefully studied today and are still the subject of a great deal of interest by those who are interested in political theory and by scholars in the history of modern philosophy. The last two sections are not included because they deal with issues that were much more specific to Hobbes' particular historical context. These latter sections concern what Hobbes called a "Christian Commonwealth" and his very harsh criticism of the Catholic Church. In the 17th Century, when *Leviathan* was written, England was engaged in some very bitter and violent sectarian conflicts, and these last two sections speak directly to these struggles. They are of interest to historians of that time, but for most current readers the issues involved have faded away.

The other major change requires more discussion. Although *Leviathan* was written in English, this particular edition is a quasi-translation of Hobbes' language into a somewhat more contemporary form. While Hobbes was a very forceful and talented writer, he did live and write a long time ago, and that means that the current reader of the original text has to struggle greatly with different conventions of spelling and punctuation, with a somewhat different vocabulary, and especially with a form of English syntax that varies greatly from ours.

First, the spelling of many English words was very different in the 17th Century than it is today, and furthermore, it had not yet become standardized. As a result there are many different spellings of the same word in the original text, and sometimes they occur in the very same sentence.

Second, the conventions of punctuation that Hobbes used were not the same as ours. He clearly had an inordinate love of commas, as they are sprinkled all over the book in places where we would find them unnecessary and superfluous. Semicolons and colons are also used in ways currently considered to be inappropriate, and there are no apostrophes to indicate possession. These differences do not make the original impossible to understand, but they soon become annoying, and do create a substantial obstacle to comprehension.

It is helpful that the vocabulary that Hobbes used did not contain an inordinate number of words that are unfamiliar to us. There are some, but in general the terms he used were ones we know. Unlike his near contemporary Shakespeare, there is certainly not the difficulty of being constantly confronted with exotic words that are not used anymore.

The most difficult aspect of reading Hobbes for the current reader is his syntax. Hobbes wrote in Latin as well as in English, as Latin was the scholars' common language in Europe at the time. One can see this Latinate influence in Hobbes' writing, and that is what makes his work so challenging for us to read. In the original edition of *Leviathan,* adjectives come after the nouns they modify as opposed to current English syntax, but that is not the main problem. In Latin nouns have case endings and verbs have many declensions, and that can be very helpful in determining the grammatical structure of sentences. In English, word order is much more important in forming grammatical structures, since verbs do not have that many different forms and case endings for nouns are minimal.

Sometimes in *Leviathan* one will come across long, complicated sentences, where the word order does not provide the clues one usually finds in English, but the noun and verb suffixes of Latin that would help sort things out are also missing. For this reason many of the very long sentences in the original text are like puzzles that one has to ponder for quite a while to deduce what pronoun goes with what referent.

The unfortunate consequence of the way that Hobbes wrote English is that many people find his work to be obscure and difficult to understand. Even worse, many feel overwhelmed and soon give up. To alleviate these problems I have endeavored to rewrite *Leviathan* in a way that preserves the flavor of the original as much as possible, while still making it comprehensible to current readers. In many editions this is done by modernizing the spelling and punctuation, but in this edition I have taken some further steps and have changed the vocabulary at points, and especially, I have tried to refashion the syntax. Some of the vocabulary changes are minor, such as using terms like 'seeks' instead of the old fashioned 'seeketh.' I also made some minor changes in the terms he used, but I tried to stay with Hobbes' original words, especially with the ones that I thought he considered to be important. When I thought some term of his had an obscure meaning for us, I have provided an explanatory footnote.

I have also tried to change Hobbes' syntax as little as possible, but in many cases substantial changes were necessary in order to improve clarity. I have moved phrases around, broken up long sentences into shorter ones, and provided explicit nouns instead of pronouns. My aims were to make the *Leviathan* easier to read, while still preserving every point that Hobbes wanted to express, and keeping his style intact as much as I could. I only made a change where I thought it would be helpful, but this turned out to involve changing almost every sentence in some way—sometimes just in minor ways, but sometimes quite substantially.

Ironically, if Hobbes has just written *Leviathan* in Latin, there would be no question of the appropriateness of an English translation, and the translation would be judged by its clarity and faithfulness to the original. But Hobbes also wrote an English version of his work, and many people think that if someone is an English speaker, that is what they should read. But Hobbes' English is not really our English, and so for those who are not prepared to struggle with the language itself, his writings will be lost. The aim of this particular edition is to present *Leviathan* in a way that its fascinating ideas, and even its vivid writing, will be available to a current reader.

B. Hobbes' Style

One unfortunate aspect of the change in English from the 17th Century to our day is that many people do not read one of the great writers of the English language. Hobbes is the only distinguished philosopher who wrote in English who also wrote a good deal of poetry. In the last decade of his life Hobbes produced verse translations of the *Iliad* and the *Odyssey*, and he also wrote an autobiography in rhyming couplets. While Hobbes' reputation as a writer does not rest on the quality of this poetry; nevertheless, Hobbes was a gifted wordsmith. There is no passage in all of English philosophy to match the power and punch of Hobbes' account of the state of nature in Chapter 13. This chapter is the culmination of the previous twelve chapters and is the main pivot of his argument about the basis of political order. To make the best case he could for this important point, Hobbes removed the constraints from his formidable rhetorical capacity. The result is a set of paragraphs that have a compelling effect on even the most skeptical reader of Hobbes' views.

Hobbes' flair for writing is evident all through the *Leviathan*. He had a talent for making memorable phrases, such as ". . . the life of man, [in the state of nature is] solitary, poor, nasty, brutish and short," which may be the most well-known sentence of philosophy written in English. That saying is from the famous 13th Chapter, but it is not difficult to find other examples that also stick in the mind. Another famous phrase also comes from the 13th Chapter that the "cardinal virtues of war are force and fraud." Here are two other examples that are written in the original way, just to give the reader a feeling what the original looked like. In Chapter 3 Hobbes described the pattern of thoughts of someone thinking of what will happen to a criminal. Such a person "re-cons what has seen follow on the like Crime before; having this order of thought, the Crime, the Officer, the Prison, the Judge, and the Gallowes." In Chapter 10 when Hobbes discussed the competitive nature of men, and especially military men, he said that such men are "enclined to continue the causes of warre; and to stirre up trouble and sedition: for there is no honour Military but by warre; nor any such hope to mend an ill game, as by causing a new shuffle."

Another aspect of Hobbes' writing prowess was his use of similes. Hobbes sometimes used an extended simile to make a point, and there is always the concern that the comparison will be difficult for a modern reader, because the basis of the simile is no longer familiar. But this is not a problem in reading Hobbes, as he seemed to have had a sense of what sorts of things would stay the same, and this served to render his similes understandable to his future readers. Here is an example of one of Hobbes' extended similes from Chapter 4. First I will present it in the original form, and then in the "translated form" of this edition. This will give the reader a chance to see the difference.

"From whence it happens, that they which trust to books, do as they that cast up many little summs into a greater, without considering whether those little summes were rightly cast up or not; and at last finding the errour visible, and not mistrusting their first grounds, know not which way to cleere themselves, but spend time in fluttering over their bookes; as birds that entring a chimney, and finding themselves inclosed in a chamber, flutter at the false light of a glasse window, for want of wit to consider which way they came in." (Original form)

"Those who trust books do the same thing as those that cast up many little sums into a greater without considering whether those little sums were rightly cast up or not. When at last these people find a visible error, they do not know how to correct it because they failed to mistrust the first grounds. They, thus, spend their time fluttering over their books like birds that enter a chimney, and finding themselves enclosed in a chamber, flutter at the false light of a glass window for the lack of wit to consider which way they first came in." (This edition)

Here is another striking simile that occurs in Chapter 5. Hobbes wrote, "And when men that think themselves wiser than all others, clamor and demand right Reason for judge; yet seek no more, but that things should be determined, by no other mens reason but their own, it is as intolerable in the society of men, as it is in play after trump is turned, to use for trump on every occasion, that suite whereof they have most in their hand." (Original form)

"When men that think themselves wiser than all others clamor and demand right reason to be the judge, they only seek that things should be determined by no other men's reason but their own. This is as intolerable in the society of men, as it is in a game, when after trump is turned, some people will use for trump on every occasion the suit they have most in their hand." (This edition)

Hobbes' tone was often contentious and biting, and he was often embroiled in controversies with other intellectual and religious personages of his day. In one way this is surprising because Hobbes claimed to be a very timorous person, and yet he often seemed to go out of his way to attack and criticize some very powerful people. Hobbes did not have a light touch in his criticisms, as he liked to portray those he disagreed with as stupid obfuscators or debased charlatans. An example of his scorn for pedants occurs at the end of Chapter 5: "And even of those men themselves, that in Councells of the Common-wealth, love to shew their reading of Politiques and History, very few do it in their domestique affaires, where their particular interest is concerned; having Prudence enough for their private affaires: but in publique they study more the reputation of their owne wit, than the successe of anothers businesse." (Original form)

"Very few of those men that love to show their reading of politics and history in councils of commonwealth, do the same in their domestic affairs where their particular interest is concerned. They have prudence enough for their private affairs, but in public they study more the reputation of their own wit than the success of another's business." (This edition)

Two of his main targets in this work were the Catholic Church and the Scholastic Philosophy of the Middle Ages that was based on theories of Aristotle. For those who have a taste for harsh put-downs, here is the kind of thing Hobbes had to say about the Scholastic philosophers. In Chapter 8 he quoted a sentence from a book by a 16th Century philosopher, Suarez, and after quoting it, Hobbes wrote, "When men write whole volumes of such stuff, are they not Mad, or intend to make others so?"

C. The Context of *Leviathan*

Leviathan was published in 1651 in the very middle of the 17th Century. During this century the pace of cultural, political, and intellectual change had increased dramatically. Copernicus' heliocentric theory, although proposed much earlier, was gaining adherents, and it was becoming clearer that Copernicus was right. It is difficult for us to imagine the shock that Copernicus' theory had on people of the 17th Century, since we take his view so much for granted. What was disturbing to the people of the 17th Century was not just that Copernicus' view conflicted with what the Bible supposedly said. That might be a matter of interpretation, but the view that the earth was moving around the sun indicated that our own senses were not that reliable. If there is one thing our senses tell us, as clearly as they tell us anything, it is that the earth is standing still. But if Copernicus' view were correct, then a belief that was taken to be certain was actually false. If a belief that seemed so true turned out to be false, then what else that was thought to be obvious might also be false?

The ferment in intellectual life in the 17th Century was stimulated by other developments in what was called then "natural philosophy" and which we now call "science." In Italy Galileo was casting doubt on the long-revered physics of Aristotle, and telescopes were revealing that the heavens were not exactly as the ancients had claimed. Hobbes' first mentor was Francis Bacon, who argued that the old methods of pursuing knowledge of the natural world had to be updated by methods that included experimentation as well as just observation.

There was another innovation that was developing at this time. Aristotle had argued that there were different approaches to understanding natural phenomena, but one essential point was to determine what is the goal of a natural object. He called this the final cause of an object, and he thought that all living as well as non-living things had a goal, or an end, that they were endeavoring to obtain. This approach to nature was becoming more and more obsolete in the 17th Century. Instead of considering the goal an object was pursuing, explanations were being framed more in terms of the mechanisms that controlled natural events. All of these changes are quite evident in Hobbes' various works, as he was one of the thinkers who was very taken with the new ideas, and who was ready to overthrow the long-established views of how we are to understand the world.

The prior century also was the time of the Protestant Reformation, and by the 17th Century religious and sectarian warfare was common all over Europe. Before the Reformation, there had been plenty of hostility and tension within the Catholic Church, but the struggles had always been internal, and there had been no challenge to the religious authority of the Church itself with Christendom. But Luther's challenge led to a period of great instability within Christianity and raised serious questions about what Christianity meant and what its role was to be in European society.

This became especially true in England at the end of the 16th Century. Henry VIII withdrew his allegiance from the Pope and the Vatican and set up his own Anglican Church. Henry's actions unleashed decades of turmoil in England—executions, torture, spying, conspiracies, confiscation of property, and what might be called general acts of terror. The Catholic Church did not just accept Henry's rebellion, and in the subsequent years there were attempts by Catholics to regain control over England. The sectarian and religious violence was Hobbes' experience of religion during the years of his life before he began to write anything.

And finally, in England itself, the 17th Century was a time of great political turbulence. Again, the prior history of England had not been one of peaceful acquiescence to the political authorities, as there had been periodic struggles among the claimants to the throne. But there had not been any challenge to the institution of monarchy itself. However, in the 17th Century, there was a rebellion against the King, a Civil War broke out, and the King was executed and Oliver Cromwell was installed as the ruler of the country, but not as its monarch.

These various kinds of change and instability formed the background of Hobbes' work. His main concern that was raised by the events of the day was the political one, and Hobbes being a royalist, fled England during the Civil War, and actually wrote *Leviathan* while he was in exile on the Continent. Hobbes wanted to once and for all determine the basis of political authority, but doing so would require that he also address the religious and scientific questions that were alive at the time. The distinctions between political, religious and scientific issues were not as distinct as they became later, and so a work that claimed to solve political problems would have to deal with religious and scientific ones too. The scientific controversies received some attention in the beginning of *Leviathan*, as Hobbes presented a sketch of his Materialistic views that he thought were the basis of everything that followed. But the main focus of the first two sections of this book was establishing the basis of political authority. Hobbes believed that his theory held the key for settling down the confusion and turmoil that were occurring in his country and in other places in Europe. But to be convincing and complete Hobbes realized that it would also be necessary to delve into the religious controversies that were an important part of the political tumult. This is the main reason that the last half of Hobbes' book on political philosophy concerned issues of ecclesiastical authority.

II. A VERY BRIEF BIOGRAPHY

Hobbes was born in 1588, and he claimed that his mother went into labor when she became frightened by reports that the Spanish Armada was approaching the English coast. He said that as a result, he and fear were born as twins, and that he became a fearful and anxious person for the rest of his life. He was born in the small town Malmesbury where his father was the deacon in a church. But if Hobbes was timorous by nature, his father seems to have been a rash and angry man, for he was forced to seek other employment after getting into a fight with some parishioners of his church.

Hobbes was a gifted young student, and as a young man, he studied at Oxford University. He was taught the old learning based on Aristotle and other Scholastics, and later in his life he claimed that his Oxford education was worthless. Interestingly enough, he never studied geometry until he was forty years old, but once being exposed to it, he was amazed. In a book by a contemporary, James Aubrey, the following anecdote is presented concerning Hobbes' initial reading of Euclid's book on geometry:

> He was 40 years old before he looked on Geometry; which happened accidentally. Being in a Gentleman's Library, Euclid's Elements lay open and 'twas the 47 El. libri I. He read the Proposition. By G__, said he (he would now and then swear an emphatical Oath by way of emphasis) this is impossible! So he reads the Demonstration of it, which referred him back to such a Proposition; which proposition he read. That referred him back to another, which he also read. Et sic deinceps [and so on] that at last he was demonstratively convinced of that truth. This made him in love with Geometry.

The effect of Euclid can be seen in Leviathan as Hobbes tried to present his political philosophy in the same manner. He wanted to start with basic axioms and definitions, and then build upon them in such a way that everyone would have to agree with the later theorems and principles.

Having graduated from Oxford, Hobbes became a secretary for Francis Bacon and then obtained employment as the tutor for the sons of various aristocrats. He accompanied them on their Grand Tours of Europe and this gave Hobbes a chance to meet some of the leading intellectuals of his day and to get immersed in the new scientific and philosophical issues that were being debated. But when he returned to England, he found that political and religious trouble was brewing, and this led to his writing some political tracts that described how he thought civil war could be avoided. However, Hobbes' writings did not calm the storms, and when the English Revolution began, Hobbes who supported the King against the rebels, fled to the Continent. He later boasted that he was the first to flee.

It was in Europe that he had a chance to work out his political views in their most developed form, and that became *Leviathan*. When the monarchy was restored after the Cromwellian Revolution, Hobbes returned to England and continued to contribute to the current intellectual debates. He claimed to be a timorous man, but Hobbes was very fierce in his polemics, and he acquired some very powerful enemies. He was called an atheist, maybe for good reason, and when the great fire of London occurred in 1666, some claimed that the fire was God's punishment for allowing Hobbes to live in London. Fortunately for Hobbes the King kept him from being delivered to his enemies, but he did forbid Hobbes from publishing any more works of philosophy in England. Until his death in 1679 Hobbes obeyed the King's order and contented himself with making verse translations of Homer.

Aubrey, who was a good friend of Hobbes, described him as friendly and witty, but not one to suffer fools. Other wits used to like to goad Hobbes to see him erupt. According to Aubrey it often was like the baiting of a bear. But in spite of his occasional bad temper, and his habit of acquiring enemies, Hobbes did have a social life, and as Aubrey says, he "did not hate women." In fact he was one of the few great philosophers of the modern period who deigned to participate in biological reproduction.

III. HOBBES' METHODS IN
LEVIATHAN

Like his famous contemporary, Rene Descartes, and other philosophers of the 17th Century, Hobbes had a great interest in matters of method. In order to find answers to an important question, Hobbes believed it was first necessary to have a conception of what would be the proper method to use for the particular issue. Finding the appropriate method was considered to be the most important, as well as the most difficult, part of an enquiry, for once the right method was obtained, it could be used it to generate the correct answer.

But there was another aspect to be considered in this matter of method. Hobbes realized that people not only have a variety of moral and theological views, but they also use very different ways of finding answers to questions. The methods that seem appropriate to some would seem crude to others, and the rigorous and technical methods that some people would be inclined to use would appear baffling and unnecessary to other people. People are very different in their sophistication and in their cultural and educational backgrounds, and this affects what methods they are willing to use. Hobbes knew that there is universal concern about the problems of war and peace, but even if he avoided moral and theological assumptions, he would not provide an answer to convince everyone if he just used the kind of method that appealed to just one group of people. To widen the range of those that would accept his views, he thought it was important to provide different kinds of arguments that would be suitable to different kinds of audiences.

In general, Hobbes developed two ways to support his views. One way was an intellectual method that he thought not everyone would be able to follow. He called this method "science." He called the other method "prudence," and it was based on ordinary experience

Before describing these two methods in a bit more detail, one qualification has to be made. Anyone who looks at *Leviathan* will notice that Hobbes frequently quotes the Bible in support of his views. The fact that he does so does not contradict the claim that Hobbes used just two methods in his political works to establish his conclusions. Hobbes lived in a time when the Bible was considered not to be just a religious book, but it was also thought to contain the most profound wisdom on all subjects. There is a good deal of doubt whether Hobbes believed this himself, but he realized that most of his contemporaries did hold this view. In order to convince them of his theories, Hobbes thought that it would be helpful to show that everything that he said was Biblically supported. Whether this was the case of the Devil quoting Scripture, as many of Hobbes' enemies said, is a legitimate question. But even if one grants that Hobbes sincerely thought that his views were compatible with the Bible, he clearly did not use the Bible in developing his ideas, nor did he think it was necessary to use the Bible in order to prove that his ideas were true. Science and prudence were the methods he would use for those two purposes. The quotations from the Bible were just a way to make his views more palatable and acceptable.

A. Science—The Intellectual Method

The method that Hobbes called "science" was based on Euclid's axiomatic method that Hobbes discovered in his middle age. What appealed to Hobbes was that Euclid used a method that compelled proof. One could present a statement, and if someone thought that the statement was not true, one could show how it followed from some more basic statement, and if questions were raised about the more basic statement, one could be referred to an even more basic statement. The result of all of this is a structure, where each level is supported by lower levels, and once the lower levels are accepted, then everything follows in a logical and rigorous way that cannot be denied.

It is obvious that in this kind of structure the soundness of the upper levels depends on the solidity of the foundation. If somehow one can begin with incontrovertible foundational statements and then build on them with careful reasoning, then like it or not, anyone capable of understanding will have to accept what is presented at the higher levels.

It was Hobbes' dream to develop a system of this kind to support his views, particularly about the causes of war and the way to achieve peace. His hope was that he could make an axiomatic system that would have the same power as Euclid's geometry. In geometry anyone capable of thinking and reasoning has to admit that Euclid's conclusions about triangles, squares, and circles have to be true. Once the initial premises are accepted, then any reader will, like it or not, have to accept the theorems based on them. Taking people by the scruff of the neck, and as it were, showing them that they have to accept Hobbes' conclusions was something that he tried to do in his own work. In the first few chapters of *Leviathan*, Hobbes attempted to provide the incontrovertible basis of his subsequent views. These chapters concern language, reasoning, and how we know about the external world. Hobbes' account is sketchy and vague on many particulars, but interestingly enough one can see that it contains the seeds of the philosophical theory of Rationalism—a theory about knowledge, language, and the world that was subsequently developed by some of the most distinguished philosophers of the Modern period.

B. Prudence—The Method of Experience

Hobbes was well aware that not everyone is an intellectual, or at least that not everyone has the capacity, the patience, or the inclination to follow a long train of complicated arguments. If Hobbes had just been interested in convincing his fellow philosophers of his conclusions, he might not have worried about this issue, but Hobbes thought that his views and conclusions were very important for everyone to know. He wanted to present his views in a way that would be understandable, and hopefully be accepted, by all. This meant that he could not simply use the intellectual way to prove his points, but he would also have to provide a method that was accessible to a wider range of people.

This second lower-level method relied on the experience that every person has, whether literate or not, whether philosopher, peasant, courtier or king. The account that Hobbes provided of how experience works contained the seed of another philosophical view that developed after him—the view of Empiricism.

Hobbes' account is based on the fact that events in the world impinge on us and set up a sequence of ideas inside of us. When we look at these sequences, we note certain patterns, and these patterns provide us with data that we use to form expectations about what will happen. In a simple example we all note the association of dark clouds with rain, and so when we see dark clouds coming toward us, we begin to look around for our umbrellas.

Sometimes, though, the dark clouds appear and then there is no rain This shows that the way of ordinary experience is not completely reliable. What happens in the past may be a pretty good guide to the future, but it is certainly not a perfect guide. Hobbes thought that the intellectual way was superior, because it was, if done correctly, a much more reliable guide than ordinary experience. Nevertheless, if the intellectual way is one that only a few people use, it is of little value when one wants to convince everyone.

In applying the method of prudence to the main questions Hobbes wanted to pursue in *Leviathan*, he realized that we are going to have to apply this method to discover some critically important facts about human beings. We should pay attention to the behavior of our species-colleagues and note that often we can often detect patterns in them too. When we examine our experience of other people, we can remember that their dark clouds were also followed by rain, thunder, and lightning. But again, not always.

However, there is an additional source of experience that a person can use in trying to understand others besides just observing behavior. This additional source is remembering the effects of our own internal states. We can remember various sequences of events that we were involved in ourselves, in which an internal state was followed by some behavior. For example, I remember a sequence in which I saw an apple on my neighbor's tree, desired to have it, and then made plans to steal it during the night, which I subsequently carried out. I have noted other such sequences in my behavior. Now I see a person watching me in the parking lot of the crowded mall, trying to make it look like he is not watching. I have packages in the car. Comparing myself to this other person and making allowances for the difference in circumstances, I can make a pretty good guess about what he is planning to do, and so I lock my car.

This method is one that can be called "qualified introspection" and it is a method for determining what other people are up to. Using oneself as a model, one compares oneself with others, and takes into account the different circumstances and on that basis, tries to determine what the other person is thinking. This is by no means a foolproof method, as Hobbes clearly realized, but he also thought that it was one of the most useful instruments that we have. In *Leviathan* the method of qualified introspection is presented in the Introduction to the work itself, and Hobbes made a special point of telling his readers at the very beginning that this is the method they should use to verify the claims he was going to make about humanity in his book. Hobbes did not expect that everyone would be able to follow the more intellectual methods that he presented; nevertheless, we can all determine whether what he says is really so. "Read yourself," he said in the Introduction of *Leviathan*, to see if his view of human nature is one that you will agree with.

IV. THE MAIN ISSUE IN *LEVIATHAN*

Hobbes began *Leviathan* with a discussion of the methods he will use to answer important questions, and once the methods are described, it is time to apply them to what Hobbes considered the most important matter facing himself and his fellow humans. That was the question of "Why can't we just get along together?" This was the question that was asked by Rodney King, over three centuries after Hobbes wrote *Leviathan*. Mr. King asked the question after Los Angeles exploded in riots in 1992 after an all-white jury acquitted some policemen who were videotaped viciously beating the African-American Mr. King.

It is an interesting question. Just why can't we all get along? Why are there all of the fights and beatings and death? Why do human beings continue to wage war and brutalize each other century after century? The benefits of peace seem so obvious and so desirable, and anyone can see that cooperation will make everyone better off. But yet it goes on—in every continent, in every country, in almost every neighborhood, and in many, many homes. The constant battle. Yet, we also have to admit that life is not a continual war. People do live in peace and they do cooperate in activities for mutual benefit, at least for a time. There is this strange cycle of fighting and cooperating—neither one being stable. Why is that?

While Hobbes discussed a number of matters in this book, the main question that *Leviathan* addressed is why humans just can't get along. It is one of the perennial problems of human life, and it was especially salient for Hobbes. He lived in a time of great turmoil, during a Civil War. He saw himself what happened when political authority breaks down, and he devoted a good deal of his life to developing a solution to the constant scourge of war. Hobbes wrote three different versions of his views during his life, and *Leviathan* was his latest and most detailed account.

A. Human Nature

The main cause of war according to Hobbes can be found in human nature. Hobbes used his two methods to determine the aspects of human beings that incline us to war. One of the most important is our emotions, and Hobbes presents an interesting analysis of emotions in Chapter 6. Hobbes thought that our emotions have a great deal more sway on us than does our reason, and so if we are going to understand why people do what they do, an understanding of the emotions is critical.

Our emotions move us either towards an object or away from it, and Hobbes used this general point to begin to classify all of the emotions. We move towards or away from something depending on whether we desire to have it, or are averse to it. Of course, different things affect different people in different ways, and also we ourselves sometimes desire to have an object, but then at other times do not want it at all. So understanding what emotion another person is having at a particular time is not an easy matter to discern.

But one emotion that is very powerful and can be seen to be common in all people is fear. We worry that something bad might happen to us in the future, and even if we have no experience with some particular object, according to Hobbes, we tend to fear the worst. There are a number of strands of evidence that Hobbes provided to support this point, and one of them occurs in Chapter 12. He claimed that religion can be found in every known society, and he defined the basis of religion as fear. Of all the emotions, fear is the most universal.

To protect ourselves, and also to gain the things that we want, people seek power. This follows from Hobbes' view of the emotions. We do not know what we will want in the future, and we know there may well be dangers, and so Hobbes says that all human beings are characterized by a restless and ceaseless attempt to gain more power that only ceases when they die. No one is really ever content, according to him, and no one can ever rest on his or her laurels. We are all anxious and worried, and for good reason. We do not know what will happen in the future, and there always may be some trouble lurking.

B. State of Nature

These are the elements that Hobbes used to provide a general explanation why people fight with each other. The elements are the methods we use to develop our ideas about what is going on in the world, the intellectual way and the way of ordinary experience, the definitions of different emotions, the account of power, and the evidence provided by religion. These materials are really quite few—a minimalist toolbox of concepts and points to be arranged and combined to lead to the result that Hobbes wanted to convince us to accept. The minimalism is important, for it means that Hobbes' arguments, if successful, should appeal to many different kinds of people with very different backgrounds. People with different religious views should not be put off by what Hobbes said, because he did not use any religious views in his arguments. The same goes for all the different moral views that people hold. Hobbes abstained from all of these. The question is whether he was able to successfully achieve his goal with these few materials.

Hobbes presented a synthesis of all of these elements in Chapter 13, the most famous chapter in the whole *Leviathan*. The first point of this synthesis is a startling claim given the time that Hobbes was writing. He says that all people are equal by nature. Hobbes wrote this statement more than a century before the American Revolution and its basic document that would claim that "all men are created equal." Also he was writing in England and Europe, in countries containing nobles, aristocrats, lords and peasants, where class divisions were very distinct and obvious in daily life

Even more startling is the sense in which Hobbes said that people are equal. Whenever someone claims that humans are equal, it always raises the question in what respect, because there are obvious differences between people. Hobbes said that all people are equal in two respects—strength and quickness of mind. But this seems to be manifestly preposterous. People are equal in strength—does this mean that anyone of us can be compared to some gigantic professional football player? And we are also equal in quickness of mind? What could he have meant by this?

Hobbes gave each one of these points a unique twist. As far as physical strength, we are all equal because the weakest can kill the strongest. No one is invulnerable. Many football players are mighty specimens all right, but even they have to sleep, and when they do, they are as vulnerable as anyone else. Even when they are awake, with all of their muscles, they cannot repel the bullet of a small handgun. All of us have our moments when we are not alert, and all of us are covered by very soft and permeable armor. Anyone can be hit from behind, and that includes the most powerful political authorities that command vast armies. This is the peculiar sense in which Hobbes said we are equal in strength. We are all equally vulnerable to being attacked, and the weakest can kill the strongest.

The argument for the equality of quickness of mind is more complicated and is also harder to accept. He said that quickness of mind involved the facility people have in using the two methods, the intellectual way and the way of ordinary experience. Since the intellectual way is so rarely used, it can just be dismissed, and that means that the relevant method for this point is the way of ordinary experience. But here there is obviously equality, for everyone piles up experience at the same rate, one experience a second or something like that. He also threw in the observation that the only reason that people do not think everyone is equal in quickness of mind is because they overrate themselves, but the real proof that this particular capacity is equally distributed is that everyone is satisfied with their share.

It is at points like this that it is sometimes difficult to understand Hobbes, because what he was saying seems to be so irrelevant to the point he is trying to make, or else to be so poorly argued. For example, even if everyone piles up experiences at an equal rate, some people still will have more experiences than others just because they are older. Another point—even if everyone is satisfied with their share, it does not at all follow that the shares are equally distributed. Was Hobbes just making foolish mistakes here, or is there some underlying point that is really worth considering?

If we read Hobbes generously, we can see what he is getting at. People generally do trust their cognitive abilities in the sense that they think they have enough to get what it is that they want. When people get frustrated, they rarely blame their own abilities to figure things out. Rather, it is much more common to attribute the problem to circumstances, fate, or other evil people. Thus, Hobbes' point can be recast into the view that most people are confident enough in themselves to think that, given a fair chance, they could get what it is that they desire. This can also be seen as a minimalist point that would be difficult for anyone to deny. When people have a desire, they generally believe that they have the capacity to do what is necessary to satisfy it. This is an important point in Hobbes' theory, and stated in this general way, it is not that controversial.

The next step in Hobbes' argument is that our human situation consists of living near a number of other individuals, who all have desires that they think they can satisfy. The difficulty arises when it becomes clear that there are scarce resources, and that for one person to be satisfied, another will have to lose. In the simplest of cases this is clearly true. If one person wants to possess a physical object and use it when she wants, and another person has the same desire, then neither of the two can satisfy their desires at the same time. But, one might object, couldn't the two share the object? There are grave problems with sharing, and Hobbes' basic concepts and premises provide the materials to construct an explanation of why this is so.

First, no one really wants to share. It is always a compromise. The best situation that we all want would be one where we could have the object to ourselves. However, that is not always possible, so if we do not want to fight for possession of the object, we have to share. But sharing can only take place when we can trust that the other person will not take advantage. Sharing is based on an agreement, but the question is how we know that the other person will not try to cheat on the agreement. Given the premise about the desire for power, we have reason to think that the other person also wants sole possession. Even so, it is possible that the other is an honorable person who will keep to the agreement to share. However, we cannot really know whether the other person is honorable or not, and since we do not know, we are suspicious of them. And this suspicion leads us to treat them in a certain way—maybe to cheat on them before they cheat on us. Of course, the other person may be thinking the same things about us—an implication of Hobbes' claim that people are equal in their quickness of mind. And since we know that they may be thinking this way about us, and therefore may not trust us, then it might be a good idea to strike first. Suspicion thus leads to conflict.

There are two things that would modify this problematic situation. The first is that there would be enough goods so that no one would need to share and everyone could have what they wanted. The second one would be that we could tell if the other person was really trustworthy or not. But unfortunately, neither of these conditions exists.

If we lived in the Garden of Eden where everyone could just pick what was wanted off the nearest tree, then one major source of conflict would be avoided. But even though there has been a material explosion since

Hobbes' time, we are still very far from paradise. Nature and technology are still quite stingy in what they provide for us. The commodities we need still cost money—there is no free lunch or free anything else, and that means that there is competition for material goods. When everything is free, we will know that there is enough so that competition will be unnecessary. That is not our situation, nor will it occur for as long as we can foresee.

But even if the material scarcity could be overcome, there is another kind of scarcity that would still plague us. People not only compete for material goods, according to Hobbes, they also compete for honor. People want to be esteemed, and esteem on his view is a necessarily scarce good. One can have Utopian fantasies about solving the problem of the scarcity of material goods, but the desire for esteem can never be solved for everyone, because not everyone can have high self-esteem. We get our esteem by winning competitions with others, but everyone cannot be a winner. Even children in kindergarten realize that when everyone receives a blue ribbon for their artwork, the blue ribbon means nothing, and they all want to know whose work is really the best. We all desire honor, glory, self-esteem, and reputation, but it is an unfortunate fact that the nature of these goods is that they are brutally and necessarily scarce. For us to get our glory, we will have to be better than others, and it would help if the others would admit it. But the others want their glory too, and they see us as standing in their way. So, for us to get what we want, we have to defeat them, and for others to satisfy their desires, they have to defeat us. Scarcity leads to conflict.

The result is without some intervention, we will live in a state of nature, which Hobbes says is a war of all against all. Our desires, our emotions, the scarcity of our environment, all contribute to this general state. Everyone is striving to increase their power to attain the satisfaction of their desires, and when everyone does this, competition ensues. This competition could be mediated if we could judge to what extent others would be willing to compromise on the pursuit of their desires, but we cannot reliably judge this matter about other people. We cannot tell if we can trust others to share or to agree to inhibit their desires, and so lacking this crucial knowledge of others, we are suspicious of them. This suspicion leads to us taking a defensive posture toward each other and even contemplating pre-emptive actions. Given all of these factors, conflict and war are inevitable.

The sources of conflict are the meagerness of the material world and the fact that we have to compete with others who are basically equal to us in order to get what we want. But the most critical factor in this whole account is that we cannot reliably judge what other people are up to. Maybe this view of Hobbes is exaggerated and it does not apply to everyone. But it definitely applies to some. There are clearly some people who are untrustworthy, and the problem is that we have trouble identifying those who would take advantage of us. If they just had some mark, we could avoid them, or the rest of us (for surely, *we* are trustworthy) could band together in mutual protection organizations, but the nightmare of the situation is that we cannot pick out the deceivers. So even if Hobbes' view is not universally true and everyone is not a demanding and devious non-compromiser, it definitely is true of some people. Combining this point with the fact that we cannot identify the nasties means there will be suspicion of everyone. Once the suspicion starts developing, it is difficult to stop. Any look, any little move, can begin the process that will lead to the malignant and consuming whirlpool that will drown everyone.

C. The Solution—Creating a Sovereign

But all is not lost. There is a solution. Two factors in human nature incline us towards the solution. The first is the emotion of fear and the second is reason.

First, fear. Fear is the emotion that we have already seen is powerful and universal. While Hobbes used skepticism about other people as a very important part of his argument about war, his skepticism was limited. We can know that people fear death and wounds, and are very anxious about their futures. The universality of religion is the evidence for that. While it is true that we are competitive and desirous and are constantly seeking power, at some point fear kicks in, especially when we realize, as we sometimes do, that our current course is going to lead to a disaster for ourselves.

But what can we do? How do we get out of the predicament where everyone is suspicious of everyone else? Reason comes to the rescue. It is not completely clear just what Hobbes meant by reason at this point in his argument, but the general point he was making is quite evident. He meant that we are capable of generating arrangements and ideas that will get us out of this trouble. However, it is one thing to think of a solution, and quite another to actually have the drive and energy needed to put it into practice. Reason, at least, can make suggestions, but again the emotions will be needed to move us to the desired result.

Hobbes' account of war and conflict was a structure built on certain basic elements. In developing his view concerning the solution to conflict, Hobbes again tried to provide a minimalist account—one that would just use uncontroversial notions that would convince anyone, no matter what other moral, religious, or political view they held. But there is also an important difference between his solution for peace and the account of war. In telling us why people fight, Hobbes was presenting a descriptive theory. He was not really offering any advice in that part; he was just stating what factors lead to conflict. The account of the solution is different, because Hobbes was not just describing how people come to be peaceful. On this matter he was an advocate. He wanted to convince people that there is a way to get to peace, and that it is something they should adopt. Further, he thought his solution was the only one that was likely to work, and since he was living in the very turbulent time of a civil war, he thought it was urgent that people adopt his proposal. His solution was a prescription of what we must do to save ourselves.

The main concepts of Hobbes' solution are the terms 'right of nature' and 'law of nature.' These terms are unlike the concepts he defined earlier when he was discussing the causes of war. In the previous case the main concepts were fear, desire, power, etc., and these are terms that we all use, and so we can see if what Hobbes said corresponds with our own usage. But we do not talk about rights and laws of nature, and so another approach is necessary to understand this part of Hobbes' theory.

Hobbes claimed that everyone has the right of nature to everything. By saying this, he was not reporting or describing human actions, but rather it is more helpful to see him as presenting a useful picture. Let us picture ourselves as one of a collection of human beings scattered on an isolated island. Each one of us wants to live, and each one will do what is necessary to achieve that goal. Each one will try to take whatever food is available, will take the materials needed for shelter, and if these objects are in the proximity of another person, each one will use stealth or strength to obtain them. No one, in this situation, will acknowledge any restrictions on what they can take. In this picture each individual has the natural right to everything on the island—which means that we will take what we think is necessary to maintain our own lives.

But we soon realize that when we all exercise our natural right to everything, war and our own destruction will ensue. But our reason also tells us there is a way to stop the self-destructive conflict. The way is to make an agreement to limit the exercise of our natural rights if others will do so too. It is really as simple as that. In the agreement in which we

stop the war, we also create the laws of morality that forbid killing, stealing, and slandering. It is not necessary to say that God wants us to obey
these laws. We can see ourselves that we have to give up our right to kill
and take from others if we are to avoid living awful lives and ultimately
our own destruction. Hobbes called this realization a law of nature—a
restriction our reason tells us that we must apply to ourselves in order to
achieve peace, as long as everyone else does so too. While we may not be
naturally peaceful creatures, we do have the capacity of reason that tells
us how to end our conflicts. Reason tells us to make agreements, to
establish laws, to enact restrictions, to bind ourselves to these laws and
restrictions, and thus to create duties and obligations for ourselves. Reason tells us, in other words, to create moral rules that will lead to our
own preservation.

Unfortunately, it is not all that simple. The agreement that has to be
made becomes very tricky to carry out, and Hobbes almost seemed to
take delight in raising problems and complications concerning this basic
agreement that establishes peace. Here is one problem. Hobbes said that
agreements made in the state of nature are void. To see what this means,
let us suppose that two people on our island have wearied of the constant
fighting and conflict and have decided to restrict their own natural rights
and make an agreement with each other that they will not take the
other's food anymore. But there is an obvious problem with this contract. It involves future behavior and it is based on trust, but neither
party has any basis for trusting the other. Oh yes, the other person said
that they will honor the agreement, but Hobbes was not impressed with
the mere utterance of some sentence. It is too easy to lie, or to change
one's mind when it becomes advantageous. Also, neither person can
really tell whether the other person will honor the contract just by looking at them and remembering past actions. Peoples' actions can be as
deceptive as their words, and also there is a mutability issue—while a
person may sincerely intend to keep an agreement today, there may be
very different intentions and desires tomorrow. We cannot be sure the
other will live up to an agreement, and then why should we live up to it,
and then why not get them before they get us, and off we go again.

This complication is intriguing and important in itself, but it also
points to the main issue for Hobbes. Suspicion is the cause of war, and
trust is what is needed for peace, but how can the trust be created? It is
not a natural faculty for people to trust each other; it has to be created
and for Hobbes that meant that it is artificial. But how does one create
trust? How can we have confidence that the other person will keep their

part of an agreement—that they will restrict their own rights in the future?

The solution is to create a power, a terrifying power, that will enforce the agreements by punishing those who do not keep their agreements. With such a power in force, we can have the requisite confidence in other people. But if there is no such power, all agreements are worthless.

The key mechanism in this whole business is fear. People will not keep their agreements unless they are afraid that breaking them will be disadvantageous. So we can trust others when we know that if they break their word, they will suffer some very severe penalty—something that they would certainly be afraid of happening to them. But this kind of trust depends upon our confidence that first, there is such a power, and second, that everyone would actually be afraid of it. Considering the second question, we have already seen that the universality of religion indicates that people are afraid of what will happen to them. If we did not know that fear was such a powerful force, there would be no solution to the problem. So at least we can know this much about our fellow species-members—they will adjust their behavior to avoid what they are afraid of.

D. Creating The Fearful Power—The Sovereign

The main question is, how do we create a fearful power that will make people keep their agreements. We can do this by agreeing with each other that we shall all restrict our natural rights, and then just let some individual or some group have all of the power over us. The person or group for whom we restrict our own rights will have the right to do anything they want, and we will not be able to interfere with them.

To illustrate this point, let us return to the island. We all can see that we will soon die if we do not do something to institute peace. Several individuals have already made weapons for their defense, and of course, these weapons can be used for attack too. There is only one possibility for us to get out of this predicament. We have to agree to give up our rights to just take what we want and need, but more importantly, we also have to give up our weapons. But still there needs to be some way to enforce the agreement. To this end we also agree to let one person, let us call him Mighty Joe, not be party to this agreement and that means that he will have all of the weapons we have given up. We say, "Mighty Joe, you will be the leader as we give you the power to rule us, to set the laws, and to enforce agreements. By giving up our weapons, we have made ourselves defenseless, and that means you can punish us in any way you see fit if we violate any of the laws you will set up. "

Now Mighty Joe is armed to the teeth, and we have nothing, but Mighty Joe has not really gained any rights that he did not previously possess. It is just that we have agreed not to get in his way. Mighty Joe is now a terrifying and overwhelming force compared to us, and he even has the power to kill us. In Hobbes' terms, Mighty Joe is the sovereign, and we are the subjects.

Before raising the obvious questions about the wisdom of granting Mighty Joe so much power, let us first consider some of the implications that Hobbes drew from his view about how the sovereign was created. It is important to note that Mighty Joe himself was not a party to the agreement. We did not make an agreement with him that we will obey his laws and rules as long as he does his part in enforcing our agreements. No such agreement would be possible according to Hobbes because once we have given him our weapons, there is no power to make sure that Mighty Joe keeps his part. So rather than us making an agreement with him, we are actually just making it with each other. That means, according to Hobbes, we can never protest that Mighty Joe is not keeping his word, or that he is not doing what he is supposed to do. Mighty Joe made no promises, made no agreements, and so there is no basis for any complaint.

Suppose that only a majority of us agreed to make Mighty Joe the sovereign. There are then some individuals who decided that they did not want to give up their weapons and obey the laws Mighty Joe proclaimed. Mighty Joe is not pleased with these individuals, and being now in the possession of all of our weapons, he begins to coerce these people to become subjects, like we are. According to Hobbes, these dissenters really have no basis for complaint, and certainly have no grounds for saying that Mighty Joe is unjust. After all, he made no agreement with them, and they made no agreement with anyone else. The dissenters are in that state of mistrust and suspicion that characterizes people who have not made any agreement with each other, and that means they just have to do the best they can to defend themselves. If someone comes along who is stronger than they are, too bad for them.

Mighty Joe is certainly in a very powerful position according to Hobbes. Since everyone has restricted their own rights, he can walk around like a king, or a god. He can decide whether to raise an army; he can make any laws that he desires; he can decide what doctrines people can talk about; he can make decisions about what religions they can practice; he can decide rewards and punishments; he can determine who shall be honored. All the while he himself cannot be punished. What a life Mighty Joe will have.

E. Why Create a Sovereign?

There is an obvious problem to be raised here, which is will we really be better off being defenseless in the face of sovereign power? Why would we restrict our own rights to give someone the power to exploit and even kill us? Hobbes' response is to consider the alternative, which he thought was having no political authority which was the state of nature and that was a state of constant war. Nothing could be worse than that, and so it is definitely worth it to set up a sovereign. It is a much better bet for us to agree to obey him than it is try to make it on our own. The latter way is certain misery, but the former way at least gives us a chance. As Hobbes said, "the state of man can never be without some incommodity or other," and so we should at least try to give ourselves the best chance.

Furthermore, there are reasons to think that the sovereign might not take advantage of his great power over us. Sovereigns too, individuals or groups, are human beings, and so the same forces that work on us also work on them. One of these forces is the desire for a good reputation. The rulers of the past who have been corrupt and exploitative are now looked upon with scorn. Sovereigns know this, and they know that their reputation depends on the health of their subjects. This provides some restraint on them. And then there is also the ubiquitous fear of religion. There is always the unknown future, and the possibility that there is even a greater power that will punish people for their cruelties on the earth. This is also a constraint on sovereigns and is another reason why it would make sense to be obedient subjects.

This argument by Hobbes is an interesting one for a number of reasons. First, it is a practical, one might almost say utilitarian, argument. Hobbes was telling us to look at two situations and pick the one that has the best consequences. The choices are quite stark—either certain chaos or possibly a peaceful situation. If these are the choices, it is quite clear what reasonable people should do. Reasonable people should look at the alternatives, make a cost-benefit analysis, and choose the alternative that has the best consequences for them.

One might think that Hobbes was saying that this is the way that all people actually operate. But it is not necessary to attribute the view to Hobbes that all people are rational egoistic calculators. There is no doubt that many people are of this sort, and it is further undoubtedly true, that all of us have our moments (and plenty of them) when we do calculate in just this way. But whether this is a universal trait of people that they always follow is not a view that has to be attributed to Hobbes, and given his skepticism about other people, it would not be consistent with his main ideas to say that this was his view. Nevertheless, we can admit without much difficulty that arguments of this type will appeal to many, and will appeal to most of us a good deal of the time. For others, who operate under different motives (in particular, religious people), Hobbes provided other arguments.

The other interesting point about the argument is Hobbes' attempt to reassure us that there will probably be some constraints on the sovereign. The constraints though will have to be appeals to the sovereign's self-interest. Again, it is not necessary to think that this is the only motive that people have. Maybe some sovereigns are very altruistic and have no greater desire than to make other people happy, and would gladly shed the burdens of rule except that they worry that no one could do a better job than they can. It is a wonderful thing if this kind of sovereign actually exists. But undoubtedly, there will be others who have coarser desires. Again, we cannot really know which sovereigns will be which, but even if they are of the lower variety, there will be constraints on them too. We have some reason to think that they will not go wild, but even if they do, we are not better off without any sovereign power.

F. A Sovereign Is Not Necessarily a Monarch

Even though Hobbes was a defender of monarchy and he thought that there were no restrictions on what a king could do, he was well aware that there were other possibilities for creating the sovereign power than just giving it to one person. The sovereign is whoever is designated as having the ultimate power, and that can be an individual, a small group, or even a large group—the majority. If the majority is the sovereign, then that is where all power resides. It will be the majority who determines what the laws will be, what punishments will be given to those who break the laws, what wars will be fought, what taxes will be collected, what religions can be practiced and who shall be honored.

As a matter of fact, that is exactly what we occurs in constitutional democracies. The majority, by means of voting, determines all of these things. But, one might object, what about the checks and balances and the other Constitutional limitations on the scope of government? The

Hobbsian answer is that the Constitution is just a document that derives its power from the fact that the majority has given it that power. Even in the Constitution itself, there is a process of amendment that can be used at any time. So if at some point, a big enough majority wants to change the Constitution, it will. If enough people want to scrap the Bill of Rights and institute a national religion, that is what will happen, whether it be Christianity, Islam, Hinduism, or old-time paganism. And even further, if the majority wants to throw out the Constitution completely and write a new document or just give all power to Mighty Joe, then that is what will happen.

That was Hobbes' main point. Once sovereignty has been established, there is no way to keep it in check. Hobbes did talk about some rights that people cannot give up, like the right to self-preservation. A person can never just give up his right to defend his own life, because Hobbes claimed that we only give up our rights to gain something thereby. So if the sovereign goes wild, and begins to kill everyone, people will rebel and fight back. But the sovereign, having so much power, will be very difficult to overthrow. Sovereigns, once established, are very formidable monsters, but hopefully they will be useful ones.

V. FINAL POINTS

The above is the briefest of sketches of Hobbes' argument in *Leviathan*. Many details, arguments, complications have been left out. Many objections could be raised at many points, and in *Leviathan* itself, Hobbes raised many likely criticisms of his own views. One famous one is called "Hobbes' fool." This is the person who asks, why I should keep my agreement with others, if I have an opportunity to cheat for my own benefit? What if I have taken sufficient precaution to avoid detection by the sovereign? Why should I obey the sovereign's laws at that point? Hobbes realized this was an important question for his view, given that he tried to argue that it is in everyone's self-interest to be obedient. He developed an interesting answer, but whether it is convincing is still very debatable.

Another point to be made about the sketch of Hobbes' argument is that it is merely one interpretation of Hobbes' views. My own considered opinion is that it is a favored interpretation, but there are a great number of other people who have read *Leviathan* very carefully and have given a very different account of Hobbes' arguments. This is undoubtedly one of the reasons that Hobbes' work is still read. It is a rich treasure that is not yet exhausted.

In ending this Introduction I will offer a version of the advice Hobbes gave in his own Introduction. He said there "Read yourself" and I say, "Read *Leviathan* yourself." See what you think that Hobbes is saying and decide for yourself whether his arguments are insightful and valuable.

MARSHALL MISSNER

Thomas Hobbes

Leviathan

Author's Introduction

Nature, the art that God made and that governs the world, is imitated by the art of man in that man can make an artificial animal. For seeing that life is but a motion of the limbs that begins in some principal part within, why may we not say that all *automata* (engines that move themselves by springs and wheels, such as watches) have an artificial life? For what is the *heart*, but a *spring*, and the *nerves*, but so many *strings*, and the *joints*, but so many *wheels*, giving motion to the whole body, as was intended by the artificer. *Art* goes yet further, imitating that rational and most excellent work of nature, *man*. For by art is created that great LEVIATHAN, called a COMMONWEALTH or STATE, in Latin, CIVITAS, which is but an artificial man, though of greater stature and strength than the natural man, for whose protection and defense it was intended. In this artificial man *sovereignty* is an artificial *soul*, giving life and motion to the whole body; the *magistrates* and other *officers* of judicature and execution are artificial *joints*; *reward* and *punishment*, by which fastened to the seat of sovereignty every joint and member is moved to perform his duty, are the *nerves* that do the same in the natural body; *the strength, salus populi*[1]; the *people's safety*, its *business; counselors*, who suggest to it all the things that are necessary to know, are the *memory; equity* and *laws*, an artificial *reason* and *will; concord, health; sedition, sickness;* and *civil war, death*. Finally, the *pacts* and *covenants*, by which the parts of this body politic were made, set together and united, resemble that *fiat*, the "Let us make man," pronounced by God in the creation.

To describe the nature of this artificial man, I will consider,

First, its *matter* and its *artificer*, both of which are man.

Second, *how*, and by what *covenants* it is made, what are the *rights* and just *power* and *authority* of a *sovereign*, and what it is that *preserves* and *dissolves* it.

Third, what is a *Christian commonwealth*.

Last, *what is the* kingdom of darkness.

Concerning the first there is a saying that is much usurped of late, that *wisdom* is acquired, not by reading of *books*, but of *men*. Using this say-

I

ing, those persons, that for the most part give no other proof of being wise, take great delight to show what they think they have read in men by uncharitable censures they make of one another behind their backs. But there is another saying that is not lately understood, by which they might truly learn to read one another if they would take the pains. It is *nosce teipsum, read yourself.* This was not meant, as it is now used, to countenance either the barbarous state of men in power towards their inferiors, or to encourage men of low degree to a saucy behavior toward their betters. Rather, it is to teach us that for the similarity of the thoughts and passions of one man to the thoughts and passions of another, whoever looks into himself and considers what he does, when he *thinks, opines, reasons, hopes, fears,* etc, and upon what grounds, he shall thereby read and know what are the thoughts and passions of all other men upon like occasions. I say the similarity of *passions,* which are the same in all men, such as *desire, fear, hope,* etc., not the similarity of the *objects* of the passions, which are the things *desired, feared, hoped,* etc. For these, the individual constitution and particular education vary so, and they are so easy to be kept from our knowledge, that the characters of man's heart, blotted and confounded as they are with dissembling, lying, counterfeiting and erroneous doctrines, are legible only to him that searches hearts. And though by men's actions, we sometimes do discover their designs, to do it without comparing them with our own, and distinguishing all circumstances by which the cases may come to be altered, is to decipher without a key, and be for the most part deceived, by too much trust or by too much diffidence[2], as he that reads is himself a good or evil man.[3]

But let one man read another by his actions ever so perfectly, it only serves him with his acquaintances, which are but few. He that is to govern a whole nation, must read in himself, not this or that particular man, but mankind. Though this be hard to do, harder than to learn any language or science, yet when I have set down my own orderly and perspicuous reading, the pains left to another will be only to consider if he also does not find the same in himself. For this kind of doctrine admits of no other demonstration.[4]

Endnotes

1. Health of the people.
2. The current meaning of 'diffidence' is shyness, but Hobbes' used it to mean suspicion.
3. It is interesting to note that Hobbes in the very Introduction of his work is saying that there are good men. This conflicts with the view that many attribute to Hobbes that everyone is by nature evil, or at least selfish.
4. The method that Hobbes presents for reading other people fits his description of prudence in Chapter 3 that Hobbes says there is a very fallacious method.

PART I: Of Man

CHAPTER I

Of Sense

Sense. Concerning the thoughts of man, I will consider them first, individually, and then in train, or in their dependence upon one another. Individually, every thought is a *representation* or *appearance* of some quality or other accident of a body outside of us, which is commonly called an *object*. These objects work on the eyes, ears, and other parts of a man's body, and by their diverse workings produce a diversity of appearances.

The origin of them all is that which we call SENSE, for there is no conception in a man's mind which has not at first, totally or by parts, been begotten upon the organs of sense. The rest are derived from that origin.[1]

To know the natural cause of sense is not very necessary to the business now in hand, and I have elsewhere written at large on this subject.[2] Nevertheless, to fill each part of my present project, I will briefly here deliver some of the main points.

The cause of sense is the external body or object which presses the organ proper to each sense, either immediately, as in taste and touch, or mediately, as in seeing, hearing and smelling. This pressure, by the mediation of the nerves and other strings and membranes of the body continued inward to the brain and heart, causes a resistance there, or counter-pressure, or endeavor of the heart to deliver itself. This endeavor, because it pushes outward, seems to be some outside object. And this *seeming* or *fancy* is what men call *sense*. It consists of *light* or *a shape of color* to the eye, *sound* to the ear, *odor* to the nostrils, *taste* to the tongue and palate, and *heat, cold, hard-*

3

ness, softness, and such other qualities we discern as *feelings* to the rest of the body. All these qualities which are called *sensible* are in the object that causes them by means of several motions of the matter by which it presses our diverse organs. Sensible qualities in us are just diverse motions, for motion produces nothing but motion. Their appearance to us is merely a fancy,[3] the same in waking as in dreaming. And as pressing, rubbing, or striking the eye makes us fancy a light, and pressing the ear produces a din, so do bodies that we see or hear, produce the same effect by their strong, though unobserved action. For if those colors and sounds were in the bodies or objects that cause them, they could not be separated from them by glasses[4] and in echoes by the reflection of sound, as we experience them to be in cases where we know the thing we see to be in one place, and the appearance in another. And though at some distances, the real and very objects seems to be invested with the fancy it begets in us, yet still the object is one thing, and the image or fancy is another. So sense, in all case, is nothing else but original fancy, caused, as I have said, by the pressure, which is the motion of external things upon our eyes, ears and other such organs.

But the schools of philosophy, through all the universities of Christendom, that are grounded upon certain texts of Aristotle, teach another doctrine.[5] They say that the cause of vision, the thing seen, sends forth on every side a *visible species,* in English a *visible show, apparition,* or *aspect,* or *a being seen,* the reception of which in the eye is *seeing.* And the cause of *hearing,* the thing heard, sends forth an *audible species,* that is an *audible aspect,* or *audible being seen,* which upon entering the ear, makes *hearing.* They even say that the cause of *understanding,* the thing understood, sends forth an *intelligible species,* an *intelligible being seen,* which coming into the understanding makes us understand. I do not say this to criticize the use of universities, but since I will speak later of their role in a commonwealth, I must let you see on all occasions what things should be amended in them, and one among these is the frequency of meaningless speech.

Endnotes

1. In this passage Hobbes presents the standard view of what later came to be called "empiricism". Hobbes is not usually included in the group of philosophers that have been called empiricists.
2. Hobbes is referring to his book *De Corpore* in which he presented his metaphysical view that all that exists is matter in motion.
3. Hobbes himself says that 'fancy' is just another term for 'image'.
4. Hobbes is referring here to mirrors.
5. In this paragraph and in many other places Hobbes took the opportunity to criticize the Scholastic Philosophy developed in the Middle Ages that was based on Aristotle, and that was still being taught at his alma mater, Oxford University.

CHAPTER 2

Of Imagination

Imagination. No man doubts that it is a truth that when a thing lies still, unless somewhat else stirs it, it will lie still forever. But when a thing is in motion, it will eternally be in motion, unless somewhat else stays it. The reason for both is the same, that nothing can change itself, though this is not so easily assented to. For men measure, not only other men, but all other things, by themselves, and since they find themselves subject after undergoing motion to pain and lassitude, think everything else grows weary of motion and seeks repose of its own accord. They little consider whether the desire of rest they find in themselves consists of some other motion. This is the kind of thinking the schools use when they say that heavy bodies fall downwards out of an appetite to rest and conserve their nature in that place which is most proper for them. They absurdly ascribe appetite and knowledge of what is good for their own conservation to inanimate things, which is more knowledge than a man has.

When a body is once in motion, it moves eternally unless something else hinders it, and whatever hinders it, cannot extinguish it in an instant, but can do so in time and by degrees. We see this in the water, when the wind ceases, the waves do not stop rolling over for a long time after. The same thing happens in the motions of the internal parts of a man when he sees or dreams, etc. For after the object is removed, or the eye is shut, we still retain an image of the seen thing, though it is more obscure than when we actually see it. And this is what the Latins call *imagination*, from the image made in seeing, and this applies in the same way, although improperly, to all the other senses. The Greeks call it *fancy* which signifies *appearance* and is as proper to one sense as to another.

IMAGINATION therefore is nothing but *decaying sense* and is found in men and many other living creatures, in sleeping as well as in waking.

The decay of sense in waking men is not the decay of the motion that causes the sense, but is an obscuring of it. In a similar manner the light of the sun obscures the light of the stars, for the stars do no less exercise their virtue by which they are visible in the day as in the night. Because among the many strokes which our eyes, ears and other organs receive from external bodies, only the predominant one is sensible. The light of the sun being predominant, we are not affected by the action of the stars. Any object that is removed from before our eyes, though the impression it made in us remains, is obscured by other objects more present succeeding and working on us. The imagination of the past is obscured and made weak as the voice of a man is by the noise of the day. It follows that the longer the time is after the sight or sense of any object, the weaker is the imagination of it. In time the continual change of man's body destroys the parts that were moved by the sense, so that the distance of time and of place has one and the same effect on us. For as at a great distance of place, what we look at appears dim and without distinction of its smaller parts, and as voices grow weak and inarticulate, so also after a great distance of time, our imagination of the past becomes weak. We lose, for example, many particular streets of cities we have seen and many particular circumstances of actions we performed. This *decaying sense,* when we would refer to the thing itself, I mean *fancy,* we call *imagination,* as I said before. But when we would express the decay and signify that the sense is fading, old and past, it is called *memory.* This means that imagination and memory are one thing, but diverse considerations provide it with different names.

Memory. Much memory, or memory of many things, is called *experience.* Imagination is only of those things which have been earlier perceived, either all at one time or by parts at several times. The former is the imagining of a whole object as it was presented to the sense, is *simple* imagination, as when one imagines a man or a horse that one has seen before. The latter is *compounded,* as when from the sight of a man at one time and of a horse at another, we conceive in our mind a Centaur. So when a man compounds the image of his own person with the image of the actions of another man, as when a man imagines himself a Hercules or an Alexander, which happens often to those that are much taken with reading romances, it is a compound imagination, and is but a fiction of the mind. There are also other imaginations that rise in men while awake from the great impression made in sense. From gazing upon the sun, the impression leaves an image of the sun before our eyes a long time after. From the long and vehement attention to geometrical figures, a man shall while in the dark, though awake, have the images of lines and angles before his eyes. This kind of fancy has no particular name, being a thing that does not commonly fall into men's discourse.

Dreams. The imaginations of those that sleep we call *dreams*. And these like all other imaginations have been before, either totally or by parcels, in the senses. The brains and nerves, the necessary organs of sense, are so benumbed in sleep that they are not easily moved by the action of external objects. So the imaginations in sleep, and thus dreams, proceed from the agitation of the inward parts of a man's body. Those inward parts which are connected with the brain and other organs, keep them in motion when they become distempered. The imagination which is thereby made appears to the man as if he were awake, and since the organs of sense are so benumbed so that there is no new actual object which can master and obscure the imagination with a more vigorous impression, the dream becomes more clear in this silence of sense than our waking thoughts. And that is why it is a hard matter, which many think impossible, to distinguish exactly between sense and dreaming. For my own part, I consider that in dreams I do not often nor constantly think of the same persons, places, objects and actions that I do when awake, nor remember a long train of coherent thoughts when I am dreaming as I do at other times. Also, when I am awake I often observe the absurdity of dreams, but never dream of the absurdity of my waking thoughts. Thus, I am well satisfied, that being awake, I know I do not dream, even though when I dream I think myself awake.

Seeing that dreams are caused by the distemper of some of the inward parts of the body, diverse distempers must necessarily cause different kinds of dreams. And so it is that lying in the cold breeds dreams of fear and raises the thought and image of some fearful object, since the motion to the inner parts and from the inner parts of the brain is reciprocal. As anger causes heat in some part of the body when we are awake, when we sleep, the overheating of the same parts causes anger, and raises up in the brain the imagination of an enemy. In the same manner as natural kindness when we are awake causes desire, and desire makes heat in certain other parts of the body, so also too much heat in those parts, while we sleep, raises in the brain an imagination of some kindness shown. In sum, our dreams are the reverse of our waking imaginations; the motion when we are awake beginning at one end, and when we dream at another.

Apparitions or visions. It is most difficult for us to discern that we are dreaming and not awake, when we do not realize we have fallen asleep, as happens to someone full of fearful thoughts and whose conscience is much troubled, and falls asleep nodding off in a chair without the circumstances of going to bed or putting off his clothes. But for he that takes pains and industriously lays himself to sleep, should any uncouth and exorbitant fancy come to him, he cannot easily think it other than a dream. We read of Marcus Brutus (one that had his life given him by Julius Caesar and was also his favorite, who notwithstanding murdered him) at Philippi, when the night before he entered battle against Augustus Caesar, he saw a fearful apparition. This is commonly related by historians as a vision, but considering the circumstances, one may easily judge it to have been a short dream. For sitting in his tent, pensive and troubled with the horror of his rash act, it was not hard for him, slumbering in the cold to dream of that which most frightened him. This fear, as by degrees it made him awake, so also by degrees it made the apparition vanish. Having no assurance that he slept, he could have no cause to think it a dream or anything else except a vision. And this is not a very rare occurrence, for even those that are perfectly awake who are timorous and superstitious, possessed by fearful tales and alone in the dark, will be subject to similar fancies, and believe they see spirits and dead men's ghosts walking in churchyards. Actually, it is either only their fancy, or else the knavery of such person as make use of such superstitious fear, to pass disguised in the night to places they would not be thought to haunt.

From this ignorance of how to distinguish dreams and other strong fancies from vision and sense, arose the greatest part of the religion of the Gentiles in time past that worshipped satyrs, fawns, nymphs and the like. Nowadays rude people have similar opinions about fairies, ghosts, and goblins, and the power of witches. I do not think that witches have any real power of witchcraft. Still they are justly punished, for the false belief that they have such power to do such mischief, and joined with their aim to do these things if they could, their trade is nearer to a new religion than to a craft or a science. The opinion that there are fairies and walking ghosts, I think, has been purposefully taught and not refuted, to keep in credit the use of exorcism, of crosses, of holy water and other such inventions of ghostly[1] men. Nevertheless, there is no doubt that God can make unnatural apparitions, but it is no point of the Christian faith to believe that he does this any more often than he causes nature to remain or change, as he also has the power to do. But evil men, under the pretext that God can do any thing, are so bold to say any th... serves their turn, though they think it to be untrue. It is the part of a ... man to believe them no farther than right reason makes what they say appear credible. If this superstitious fear of spirits were taken away, and with it, prognostications from dreams, false prophecies and other things which depend on them, by which crafty, ambitious persons abuse simple people, men would be much more fitted than they are for civil obedience.

This ought to be the work of the schools, but rather they nourish such doctrines. Not knowing what imagination or the senses are, what they receive, they teach. Some say that imaginations rise of themselves and have no cause; others say that they rise most commonly from the will and that good thoughts are blown (inspired) into a man by God, and evil thought by the Devil, or that good thought are poured (infused) into a man by God and evil ones by the Devil. Some say the senses receive the species of things and deliver them to the common sense, and the common sense delivers them to the fancy, and the fancy to the memory, and the memory to the judgment, like handing of things from one to another, and with many words they make nothing understood.

Understanding. The imagination that is raised in man, or in any other creature endowed with the faculty of imagining, by words or other voluntary signs is what we generally call *understanding,* and is common to man and beast. For a dog by custom will understand the call or the rating[2] of his master, and so will many other beasts. The understanding which is peculiar to man is not only of his will, but of his conception and thoughts, by forming the sequel and context of the names of things into affirmations, negations and other forms of speech. I shall speak of this kind of understanding later.[3]

Endnotes

1. Religious
2. Scolding
3. The discussion of understanding occurs in chapter 4.

CHAPTER 3

Of the Consequence or
Train of Imaginations

By *Consequence,* or TRAIN of thoughts, I mean that succession of one thought to another which is called *mental discourse* to distinguish it from discourse in words.

When a man thinks on any thing whatsoever, his next thought is not altogether so casual as it seems to be. Not every thought to every thought succeeds indifferently. But just as we have no imagination where we have not formerly had sense, in whole or in parts, so we have no transition from one imagination to another, where we never before had the like in our senses. The reason for this is the following. All fancies are motions within us, relics of those made in the sense. Those motions that immediately succeed one another in the sense, continue also after sense. The original sense takes it place and predominates, and the fancy follows by coherence of the matter that is moved, in the way that water upon a plane table is drawn which way any one part of it is guided by the finger. When we perceive one thing in sense, sometimes it is succeeded by one other thing, and sometimes by another. Later when we imagine something, there is no certainty what we will imagine next. We can only be certain that whatever the succeeding image is that it succeeded the first image at some preceding time or other.

Train of unguided thoughts. The train of thoughts, or mental discourse is of two sorts. The first is *unguided, without design,* and inconstant. This occurs when there is no passionate thought to govern and direct those that follow to itself as the end and scope of some desire or other passion. In this case the thoughts are said to wander and seem impertinent[1] to one another as in a dream. Such are commonly the

10

thoughts of men that are not only without company, but also without care of any thing. Even though their thoughts are as busy as at other times, they are without harmony, as the sound which an out of tune lute would make to any man, or sound in tune, to one that could not play. And still even in this wild ranging of the mind, a man may often perceive the way one thought depends upon another. In a discourse about our present civil war, what could seem more unrelated than to ask, as one did, what was the value of a Roman penny? Yet the coherence was manifest enough to me. For the thought of the war introduced the thought of delivering up the king to his enemies; the thought of that brought in the thought of delivering up of Christ; and that again brought the thought of the thirty pence, which was the price of that treason. Thus, that malicious question easily followed. All of this happened in a moment of time, for thought is quick.

Train of regulated thoughts. The second kind of train of thought is more constant, being *regulated* by some desire and design. For the impression made by such things as we desire or fear is strong and permanent and if they cease for a time, they quickly return. They are so strong that they sometimes hinder or break our sleep. From a desire, the thought arises of some past means we have seen produce what we aim at, and from that thought, the means to that means, and so continually until we come to some beginning within our own power. Because the impression of the goal has such a great effect on our minds, in case our thoughts begin to wander, we are quickly brought back to the consideration of our goal. This was observed by one of the seven wise men who gave the precept, which is now worn out, *Respice finem*. This means in all of your actions consider what you are aiming at as the thing that directs all of your thoughts in the way to attain it.

Remembrance. The train of regulated thoughts is of two kinds. The first is when we seek the causes or means that produce an effect that we imagine. This is common to man and beast. The other is when imagining any thing whatever, we seek all the possible effects that it can produce. That means we imagine what we can do with it when we have it. This second only seems to occur in man, because this kind of curiosity is hardly likely to be part of the nature of any living creature that has only sensual passions, such as hunger, hunger, thirst, lust and anger. In sum, the discourse of the mind when it is governed by design is nothing but *seeking* or the faculty of invention, which the Latins call *sagacitas* and *solertia*. This is the hunting out of the causes of some past or present effect, or of the effects of some present or past cause. Sometimes a man seeks what he lost, and from that place and time where he missed it, his mind runs back from place to place and from time to time to find where and when he had it. He tries to find some certain and limited time and place to begin a method of seeking. From this, his thoughts run over the same places and times to find what action or occasion might have made him lost it. This is what we call *remembrance* or calling to mind. The Latins call it *reminiscentia*, a kind of *re-conning* of our former actions.

Sometimes a man knows a determinate place which is a compass[2] for what he is seeking. When that happens, his thoughts run over all the parts of that area in the same way as one would sweep a room to find a jewel, or as a spaniel ranges over the field until he finds a scent, or as a man would run over the alphabet to start a rhyme.

Prudence. Sometimes a man desires to know the event[3] of an action. He thinks of some similar past action and the effects that followed it, supposing that like effects will follow like actions. He that thinks of what will become of a criminal, reconsiders what he has seen follow a previous similar crime. He then has this order of thoughts: the crime, the officer, the prison, the judge, and the gallows. This train of thoughts is called *foresight*, and *prudence*, or *providence*, and sometimes *wisdom*. Because of the difficulty of observing all of the circumstances, this kind of thinking can be very fallacious. But this is certain: if one man has more experience of past things than another, he is by that proportion more prudent, and his expectations fail him less often. The *present* only has a being in nature. Past things only have a being in memory, but the things *to come* have no being at all. The *future* is but a fiction of the mind, which applies the sequels of past actions to the actions that are present. This is certainly done by those that have the most experience, but they don't thereby achieve certainty. It is called prudence when the event answers our expectation, but in itself, it is only really a presumption. The foresight of things to come, which is providence, belongs only to the him by whose will they are to come. Only from him, supernaturally, comes prophecy. The best prophet is naturally the best guesser, and the best guesser is one that is the most versed and studied in the matters he guesses about, for this person has the most *signs* to guess by.

Signs. A sign is the evidence antecedent to the consequent, and on the other hand, the consequent of the antecedent, when similar consequences have been previously observed. The more often they have been observed, the less uncertain is the sign. And so he that has the most experience in any kind of business, has the most signs to use to guess about the future time. Consequently, he is the most prudent. In fact, he is so much more prudent than someone who is new to a kind of business, that he cannot be equaled even by one who has any advantage of natural and extemporary wit. But perhaps many young men believe the contrary.

Nevertheless, it is not prudence that distinguishes man from beast. There are beasts that at one year old observe more and pursue their own good more prudently than a child can do at ten.

Conjecture of past time. As prudence is a *presumption* of the *future* contracted from the *experience* of *past* time, so there is a presumption of past things taken from other things, not of the future, but also of the past. For example, someone that has seen by what courses and degrees a flourishing state has first come into civil war and then to ruin, when seeing the ruins of any other state will guess that there was a like war the like courses have also been there. But this conjecture has almost the same uncertainty as the conjecture of the future, since both are only grounded upon experience.

The only act of man's mind that is naturally planted in him and needs no other thing for its exercise is the use of his five senses. The other faculties that are unique to man, which I shall speak of by and by, are acquired and increased by study and industry. The most learned attain them by instruction and discipline, and they all proceed from the invention of words and speech. Besides sense, thoughts and the train of thoughts, the mind of man has no other motion. But by the help of speech and method, these faculties may be improved to such a height as to distinguish men from all other living creatures.

Infinite. Whatever we imagine is *finite.* Therefore there is no idea or conception of any thing we can call *infinite.* No man can have in his mind an image of infinite magnitude, nor conceive of infinite swiftness, infinite time, infinite force or infinite power. When we say any thing is infinite, having no conception of the thing because of our own inability, we only mean that we are not able to conceive the ends and the bounds of the thing named. And so the name of God is used so that we may honor him and not to make us conceive him, for he is incomprehensible and his greatness and power are inconceivable. As I said before, what we conceive has been first perceived by sense, either all at once or by parts. So a man can have no thought, representing any thing, that is not subject to sense. To conceive any thing, a man must conceive it is in some place, endowed with some determinate magnitude, which may be divided into parts. Nor can any thing be completely in one place and completely in another place at the same time. Nor can two or more things be in one and the same place at one time. None of these things have ever, nor can be an episode of sense. They are but absurd speeches, taken upon credit, without any meaning at all from the works of deceived philosophers, and deceived, or deceiving, Schoolmen.[4]

Endnotes

1. Unrelated
2. Boundary
3. Effect
4. In this paragraph one might take Hobbes as saying that the traditional conception of God is actually meaningless.

CHAPTER 4

Of Speech

Origin of speech. The invention of *printing*, though ingenious, is of no great matter compared with the invention of *letters*. But it is not known who was the first that found the use of letters. Men say it was Cadmus, the son of Agenor, king of Phoenicia that first brought them into Greece. This was a very profitable invention for continuing the memory of past time, and for conjoining mankind that are dispersed into so many and distant regions of the earth. It was a difficult task to proceed from a watchful observation of the diverse motions of the tongue, palate, lips and other organs of speech, and to make as many differences and characters to remember these motions. But the most noble and profitable invention of all was that of SPEECH, which consists of *names* or *appellations* and their connection. Men use these to register their thoughts, recall them when they are past, and also to declare them to one another for mutual utility and conversation. Without speech among men there would be no more commonwealth, society, contract or peace than there is among lions, bears and *wolves*. The first author of *speech* was God himself, who instructed Adam how to name the creatures as were presented to his sight. The Scripture says no more about this matter. But this was sufficient to direct him to add more names as experience and the use of creatures gave him occasion to do, and to join them in such manner by degrees to make himself understood. By doing this for an amount of time, he derived the language that had found use for, but which was not copious enough for an orator or a philosopher. I do not find anything in Scripture, either directly or by consequence, from which it can be gathered that Adam was taught the names of all of the figures, numbers, measures, colors, sounds, fancies or relations. Neither was he taught the names of words of speech, such as *general, special, affirmative, negative, interrogative, optative,*[1] *and infinitive,* all of which are useful. He also did not learn the names, *entity, intentionality* and *quiddity* and other meaningless words of the school.[2]

But all of this language that was developed and augmented by Adam and his posterity was lost at the Tower of Babel, when every man, because of his rebellion, was stricken by the hand of God with oblivion of his language. This forced men to disperse themselves into several parts of the world, and required them to develop the diversity of tongues as the mother of all inventions taught them. In the course of time, the diversity grew more copious everywhere.

The use of speech. The general us of speech is to transfer our mental discourse into a verbal one, or to transfer the train of our thoughts into a train of words. This has two uses. The first is to register the consequences of our thoughts. They are apt to slip out of our memory, and would require us to labor anew, except that they can be recalled by the words that the original consequences were marked by. This first use of names is to serve as *marks* or *notes* of remembering. The second use is when many use the same words to signify by their connection and order to one another, what they conceive or think of each matter, and what they desire, fear or have any other passion for. In this use, words are called *signs*. The special uses of speech are these: first, to register our thinking about what we find to be the cause of any thing present or past, and also to register what we think present or past things may produce or effect. This, in sum, is the acquisition of the arts. Second, to show others the knowledge we have attained which is used to counsel and teach one another. Third, to make known to others our wills and purposes, so that we may have mutual help from one another. Fourth, to please and delight ourselves and others by innocently playing with our words for pleasure or ornament.

Abuses of speech. Corresponding to these four uses, there are four abuses. First, when by the inconstancy of the signification of their words, men register their thoughts incorrectly. They thus register for their conception something they never actually conceived, and so they deceive themselves. Second, when men use words metaphorically, in some other sense than that for which they were ordained, they thereby deceive others. Third, when they use words which they declare to be their will when it is not. Forth, when they use words to grieve[3] one another. Nature has armed living creatures with teeth, horns, and some with hands to cause grief to an enemy. It is an abuse of speech to grieve someone with tongue, unless it is one that we are obliged to govern, and in that case it is not really causing grief, but we aim to correct and amend.

The manner of how speech serves to the remembrance of the consequences of causes and effects consists in the imposition of *names* and the *connection* of them.

Names, proper and common. Universal. Some names are *proper*, and singular to only one thing, such as *Peter, John, this man,* and *this tree.* Some names are *common* to many things, such as *man, horse,* and *tree.* Every one of these latter names, though is just one name, is nevertheless the name of diverse particular things, in respect of all of them, it is called a *universal.* There is nothing in the world that is universal, but names, for the things named are everyone one of them individual and singular.[4]

A universal name is imposed on many things due to their similarity in some quality or other accident. Whereas a proper name brings only one thing to mind, universals enable us to recall any one of the many things.

Some universal names have greater extent and some have less, the larger comprehending the less large. Some are of equal extent, where each comprehends the other reciprocally. For example, the name *body* is of a larger signification than the word *man,* and comprehends it. The names *man* and *rational* are of equal extent, and mutually comprehend one another. But here we must note that a name should not always be understood, as it is in grammar, to be only one word, but sometimes, by circumlocution[5], a name can be many words together. For all the words, *he that observes the laws of his country in his actions,* form but one name, which is equivalent to this one word, *just.*

By the imposition of names, some having a larger signification and some a narrower, we turn the reckoning of the consequences of things imagined in the mind into a reckoning of the consequences of names. For example, consider a man that has no use of speech at all, and is born and remains perfectly deaf and dumb. If he sees a triangle and then by it sees two right angles that are the two corners of a square, he may, by meditation, compare them and find that the three angles of the triangle are equal to those two right angles that stand near it. But if he is shown another triangle, that is different in shape than the first one, he will not know without exerting some new labor, whether the three angles of this one are also equal to two right angles. But someone who has the use of words, when he observes that the equality was not a result of the length of the sides nor of any other particular thing in this triangle, but it was named a triangle just because the sides of the figure were straight and there were three angles, will boldly conclude universally that the equality of the angles of any triangle is equal to two right angles. This person will register this invention in these general terms, *every triangle has its three*

angles equal to two right angles. So the consequence found in one particular comes to be registered and remembered as a universal rule, and discharges our mental reckoning of time and place and delivers us from
all labor of the mind. This saves us from having to reckon and makes
that which was found to be true *here* and *now,* to be true in *all times*
and *places.*

Nothing provides more evidence of our use of words in registering our
thoughts as in numbering. A natural fool that could never learn by heart
the order of the numerals, *one, two* and *three,* may observe every stroke
of the clock and nod to it, or say *one, one, one,* but would never know
what hour it strikes. It seems there was a time when the names of the
numbers were not in use, and men were fain[6] to apply their fingers of one
or both hands to those things they desired to keep account of. But then it
proceeded that in some nations there are numerals up to ten, and in some
they just go up to five, and then they have to begin again. Even if someone can count to ten, but recites the number out of order, he will get lost
and not know what he has done. Much less will he be able to add, subtract or perform the other operations of arithmetic. Without words there
is no possibility of reckoning of numbers, much less of magnitudes, of
swiftness, of force or the reckoning of other things that are necessary to
the being, or well-being of mankind.

When two names are joined together into a consequence or affirmation, as in *a man is a living creature,* or *if he be a man, he is a living creature,* if the latter name *living creature* signifies all that the former name
man signifies, then the affirmation, or consequence, is *true;* otherwise, it
is *false.* For *true* and *false* are attributes of speech, and not of things.
Where there is no speech, there is neither *truth* nor *falsehood.* There may
be *error* as when we expect that which shall not be or suspect what has
not been. But in neither case can a man be charged with untruth.[7]

Necessity of definitions. Seeing then that the truth consists in the right
ordering of names in our affirmations, a man that seeks precise truth
needs to remember what every name he uses stands for and to place it
accordingly. Otherwise, he will find himself entangled in words, as a bird
in lime twigs, who the more he struggles, the more belimed[8] he becomes.
That is why in geometry, which is the only science that it has pleased
God until now to bestow on mankind, men begin by settling the significations of their words. They call this settling of significations *definitions,*
and place them in the beginning of their reckoning.

This is why it is necessary for any man that aspires to true knowledge
to examine the definitions of former authors, and either to correct them,

where they are negligently set down, or to make the definitions himself. The errors of definitions multiply themselves according as the reckoning proceeds and lead men into absurdities. When men at last see these absurdities, the only way to avoid them is to reckon anew from the beginning where the foundations of their errors lay. Those who trust do the same thing as those that cast up[9] many little sums into a greater without considering whether those little sums were right cast up or not. When at last these people find a visible error, they do not know how to correct it because they failed to mistrust the first grounds. They, thus, spend their time fluttering over their books like birds that enter a chimney, and finding themselves enclosed in a chamber, flutter at the false light of a glass window, for the lack of wit to consider which way they first came in. So the first use of speech lies in the right definition of names and this is the acquisition of science. The first abuse of speech is the wrong or complete lack of definitions, which results in all false and senseless tenets. This is what makes those men who take their instruction from the authority of books, and not from their own meditation, to be as much below the condition of ignorant men as men endowed with true science are above it. Ignorance is in the middle between true science and erroneous doctrines. Natural sense and imagination are not subject to absurdity. Nature itself cannot err, but to the extent that men abound in the copiousness of language, they become more wise or more mad than ordinary. Nor is it possible without language for any man to become either excellently wise or excellently foolish, if his memory be hurt by disease or ill constitution. For words are wise men's counters; they do but reckon with them. But they also are the money of fools that value them by the authority of an Aristotle, a Cicero, a Thomas or any other doctor[10] who is but a man.

Subject to names. *Subject to names* is whatever can enter in or be considered in an account, and be added one to another to make a sum, or subtracted from another to leave a remainder. The Latins called accounts of money *rationes*, and accounting *rationcinatio*. What we call *items* in bills or books of account, the called *nomina*, that is *names*. So they proceeded to extend the word *ratio* to the faculty of reckoning in all other things. The Greeks have but one word [logos] for both *speech* and *reason*. This is not because they thought there was no speech without reason, but rather because they thought there was no reasoning without speech. They called the act of reasoning *syllogism*, which signifies the summing up of the consequences of one saying to another. Because the same thing may enter into account for diverse accidents, their names are diversely applied and diversified to show this diversity. This diversity of names may be reduced to four general heads.

Names. First, a thing may enter into account as *matter* or as *body*. *Living. sensible, rational, hot, cold, moved* or *quiet* are all names which it is understood are names of *matter* or *body*, because all such are names of matter.

Second, a thing may enter into an account, or be considered, because of some accident or quality that we conceive it to be in, such as *being moved, being so long, being hot, etc.* Then by a little change or wresting, we make a name for that accident that we consider, and for *living,* we put *life* into the account, for *moved,* we put *motion,* for *hot, heat,* for *long, length,* and the like. All of these names are the names of accidents and properties by which one matter and body is distinguished from another. These are called *abstract names* because they are severed, not from matter, but from the account of matter.

Third, we bring into the account the properties of our own bodies whereby we make such a distinction. When anything is seen by us, we reckon not the thing itself, but the sight, the color, or the idea of it in the fancy. When anything is heard, we reckon only the hearing or the sound, which is our fancy or conception of it by the ear. Such are the names of fancies.

Use of positive names. Fourth we consider, give names and bring into account names to *names* themselves and to *speeches. General, universal, special* and *equivocal* are names of names. *Affirmation, interrogation, commandment, narration, syllogism, sermon, oration,* and many others are names of speeches. This is all the variety of *positive* names which are used to mark what is in nature or may be feigned by the mind of man. Bodies and their properties that actually are or may be feigned to be can be marked by words and speech.

Negative names, with their uses. There are also other names, called *negative,* which are notes that signify that a word is not the name of the thing in question. Such words are *nothing, no man, infinite, indocible,*[11] *three minus four,* and the like. These names are useful in reckoning, or in the correction of reckoning. They call to mind our past cogitations because they make us refuse to admit the names we did not rightly use, even though they are not themselves the names of any thing.

Insignificant words. All other names are but insignificant sounds and are of two sorts. One is when the names are new and their meaning is not yet explained by a definition. There have been an abundance of these coined by schoolmen and puzzled philosophers.

The other is when men make a name of two names whose meanings are contradictory and inconsistent, as *incorporeal body* or *incorporeal substance*, and a great number more. Whenever any affirmation is false, the two names which compose it, when put together and made one, signify nothing at all. For example, if it is a false affirmation to say *a quadrangle is round*, then the name *round quadrangle* signifies nothing and is a mere sound. Likewise, if it be false to say that virtue can be poured or blown up and down, the names *inpoured virtue* and *inblown virtue* are as absurd and meaningless as a *round quadrangle*. Therefore you shall hardly meet with a senseless and meaningless word that is not made up of some Latin or Greek names. A Frenchman seldom hears our Savior called by the name *parole,* but rather often by the name *verb*. Still the only difference between *verbe* and *parole* is Latin and the other is French.

Understanding. When a man upon hearing some speech has those thoughts which the words of that speech and their connection were ordained and constituted to signify, the he is said to understand it. *Understanding* is nothing else but conception caused by speech. So, if speech is peculiar to man, as far as I know it is, then understanding is also peculiar to him. Even if absurd and false affirmations are universal, there can be no understanding of them, even though many think they understand them when they just repeat the words softly or con[12] them in their minds.

I shall speak below when I discuss the passions of the kinds of speeches that signify the appetites, aversions and passions of man's mind, and of their uses and abuses.

Inconstant names. The names of such things as affects us by pleasing or displeasing us are in the common discourse of men of *inconstant* signification because all men are not alike affected by the same thing, nor the same man similarly affected by the same thing at all times. Since all names are imposed to signify our conceptions, and all of our affections are but conceptions, when we conceive the same things differently, we can hardly avoid the different naming of them. Even though the nature that we all conceive is the same, the diversity of our reception of nature, in respect of different constitutions of the body and prejudices of opinion, gives everything a tincture of our different passions. Therefore, in reasoning a man must take heed of his words. Besides the signification of what we imagine of their nature, words also have a signification of the nature, disposition and interest of the speaker. An example of this is the names of the virtues and vices. What one man calls *wisdom*, another calls *fear*. What one calls *cruelty*, another calls *justice*. *Prodigality* for one is *magnanimity* for another, and *gravity* for one is *stupidity* for another, etc. Therefore such names can never to the true grounds for rationcination. Neither can metaphors and tropes of speech, but these are less dangerous because they profess their inconstancy, which the others do not.

Endnotes

1. This form does not have any role in current English grammar.
2. This last sentence is another Hobbesian gibe at what he considered the useless and confused terminology of Scholastic philosophy.
3. This means to cause each other grief.
4. In this paragraph Hobbes expresses his belief in the theory of nominalism. This view is that names of common terms like 'horse' and 'tree' just stand for collections of individuals, and do not stand for some abstract entity that all of the individuals have in common.
5. In a round about way
6. Obliged
7. In this paragraph Hobbes presents a theory of truth that make all true statements true by definition. This is certainly not the empiricist theory of truth and is one of the reasons that Hobbes is not classified as an empiricist. In this theory his view is much closer to the view of truth of the philosopher, Gottfried Leibniz, who is usually classified as a rationalist.
8. Covered with lime
9. Form
10. Philosopher or theologian
11. Unteachable
12. Consider

CHAPTER 5

Of Reason and Science

R eason, what it is. When a man *reasons*, he does nothing else but conceive a sum total, from the *addition* of parcels, or conceive a remainder from the *subtraction* of one sum from another. If this be done by words, it is a matter of conceiving the consequences of the names from all of the parts to the name of the whole, or from the names of the whole and one part, to the name of another part. In numbers, besides adding and subtracting, men name other operations, such as *multiplying* and *dividing,* yet they are actually the same. Multiplication is just adding equal things together, and division is the subtracting of one thing as often as we can. These operations are not incident[1] to only numbers, but apply to all manner of things that can be added together and taken one out of another. As arithmeticians teach to add and subtract in *numbers,* geometricians teach the same in *lines,* solid and superficial[2] *figures, angles, proportions, times,* degrees of *swiftness, force, power,* and the like. Logicians teach the same in the *consequences of words*—adding together two *names* to make an *affirmation,* and two *affirmations* to make *syllogism,* and *many syllogisms* to make a *demonstration.* From the *sum,* or *conclusion* of a *syllogism,* they subtract one *proposition* to find the other. Writers of politics add together *pactions*[3] to find men's *duties.* Lawyers add *laws* and *facts* to find what is *right* and *wrong* in the actions of private men. In sum, in any matter where there is a place for *addition* and *subtraction,* there is also a place for *reason,* and where these have no place, *reason* there has nothing at all to do.

Reason defined. From all of this we may define, that is to say determine, what is meant by this word *reason* when we reckon it among the faculties of the mind. For REASON is just *reckoning,* which is adding and subtracting the consequences of general names that are agreed upon for the *marking* and *signifying* of our thoughts. I say *marking* when we reckon by ourselves, and *signifying* when we demonstrate or approve our reckonings to other men.

Right reason, where. In arithmetic unpracticed men must, and professors themselves may often err and cast up false results. So also in any other subject of reasoning, the ablest, most attentive and most practiced men may deceive themselves and infer false conclusions. But reason itself is always right reason, as well as arithmetic is a certain and infallible art. But no one man's reason, nor the reason of any number of men, provides certainty, anymore than an account is well cast up because a great many men have unanimously approved it. Therefore when there is a controversy about an account, the parties in order to find right reason, must by their own accord set up the reason of an arbitrator or judge, to whose sentence they will both stand. Otherwise, their controversy must either come to blows or be undecided, for the lack of right reason constituted in us by nature. It is the same in any kind of other debate. When men that think themselves wiser than all others clamor and demand right reason to be the judge, they only seek that things should be determined by no other men's reason but their own. This is as intolerable in the society of men, as it is in a game, when after trump is turned, some people will use for trump on every occasion the suit they have most in their hand. Those who declare right reason to be every passion as it comes to bear sway in them in their own controversies just bewray[4] their lack of right reason by the claim they lay to it.

The use of reason. The use and end of reason is not in finding the sum and truth of one or a few consequences remote from the first definitions and settled significations of names. Rather, it is to begin at these and proceed from one consequence to another. There can be no certainty of the last conclusion without the certainty of all the affirmations and negations on which the last conclusion was grounded and inferred. Consider the master of a family who in making an account of his expenses, casts up the sum of all the bills of expense into one sum, but who does not regard how each bill is summed up by those that give them to him, nor what it is he paid for. He does himself no more advantage than if he allowed the account in gross, trusting each of his accountants' skill and honesty. The same is true in reasoning about all things. He that takes up conclusions on the trust of authors and does not fetch[5] them from the first items in every reckoning which are the significations of names settled by definitions, loses his labor. Such a person does not know anything, but only believes.

Of error and absurdity. Some times men reckon without the use of words, which may be done in particular things. This occurs when upon the sight of any one thing, we conjecture what was likely to have preceded or is likely to follow upon it. If what he thought likely to follow does not follow, or that which he thought likely to have preceded it has not preceded it, it is called *error,* which even the most prudent men are subject to. When we reason in words of general signification and fall upon a general inference which is false, though this be commonly called *error,* is indeed an *absurdity,* or senseless speech. Error is a deception in presuming that something is past or to come which is not actually past or not actually to come, but might possibly be discovered to. But when we make a general assertion, if it is not a true one, the possibility of it is inconceivable. The words whereby we conceive nothing but the sound of them are those we call *absurd, insignificant* and *nonsense.* So if a man should talk to me of a *round quadrangle,* or of *accidents of bread in cheese,* or of *immaterial substances,* or of a *free subject, a free will,* or any use of *free* except being free from being hindered by opposition, I would not say he were in an error, but that his words were without meaning, that is to say, absurd.

I have said before in the second chapter that man does excel all other animals in the faculty that when he conceives anything whatever, he is apt to inquire the consequences of it and what effects he could do with it. Now I add this other degree of the same excellence. Man can reduce the consequences he finds to general rules called *theorems or aphorisms.* Man can reason or reckon not only about number, but about all other things where one may add or subtract one from another.

But this privilege is allayed[6] by another, which is the privilege of absurdity. Only men, of all living creatures are subject to absurdity, and of men, those that are most subject to it are those that profess philosophy. What Cicero says of them somewhere is most true, that there can be nothing so absurd but may be found in the books of philosophers. The reason for this is manifest. There is not one of them that begins his ratiocination from the definitions or explications of the names they are to use. This is a method that has only been used in geometry, whose conclusions have thereby been made indisputable.

Causes of absurdity. I. The first cause of absurd conclusions I ascribe to the lack of method, when men do not begin their ratiocination from definitions, from the settled significations of words. This is like casting an account without knowing the value of the numeral words *one, two,* and *three.*

As I have mentioned in the preceding chapter, all bodies enter into account due to diverse considerations which are diversely named. So diverse absurdities proceed from the confusion and unfit connection of their names into assertions. And therefore,

II. I ascribe the second cause of absurd assertions to the giving of name of *bodies* to *accidents*, or of *accidents* to *bodies*. This happens in cases where people say *faith is infused* or *inspired* when actually nothing can be *poured* or *breathed* into anything but a body. Other examples are *extension* is *body* and that *phantasms* are *spirits*, etc.

III. The third I ascribe to the giving of the names of the *accidents* of *bodies without us* to the *accidents* of our *own bodies*, such as when people say *the color is in the body, the sound is in the air*, etc.

IV. The fourth is the giving of the names of *bodies* to *names* or *speeches*, such as saying that *there be things universal*, that a *living creature is a genus* or a *general thing*, etc.

V. The fifth is the giving of the names of *accidents* to *names* and *speeches*, as they do that say *the nature of a thing is its definition, a man's command is his will*, and the like.

VI. The sixth is the use of metaphors, tropes and other rhetorical figures instead of proper words. Though it is lawful to say, for example, in common speech, *the way goes or leads hither or thither, the proverb says this or that*, where we know that ways cannot go nor proverbs speak, when we are reckoning and seeking truth, such speeches are not to be admitted.

VII. The seventh is names that signify nothing, but are taken up and learned by rote from the schools, such as *hypostatical, transubstantiate, consubstantiate, eternal-now*, and the like canting of schoolmen.

Those that can avoid these things will not fall easily into any absurdity, unless the length of an account may cause someone to forget what went before. All men by nature reason alike and well when they have good principles. Who is so stupid to both make a mistake in geometry and persist in it, when another detects[7] the error to him?

Science. From this it follows that reason is not born with us as is sense and memory, nor is it gotten by experience only, as is prudence. Rather it is attained by industry. It is attained by first aptly imposing names and second, by getting a good and orderly method in proceeding from the elements, names, to assertions made by connecting them together. From this one forms syllogisms, which are the connections of assertions to each other. Finally we come to knowledge of all the consequences of names pertaining to the subject in hand. This is what men call SCIENCE.

Sense and memory are just the knowledge of facts which are past and irrevocable things. *Science* is the knowledge of consequences and the dependence of one fact upon another. This enables us to do something else when we will or the like thing at another time on the basis of what we can presently do. Because when we see how any thing comes about and upon what causes and manner, when the like causes come into our power, we see how to make them produce the like effects.

Children are not endowed with reason at all until they have attained the use of speech. They are called reasonable creatures for the apparent possibility of having the use of reason in the time to come. The majority of men, though they have the use of reasoning a little way, as in number- ing to some degree, it is of little use to them in common life in which they govern themselves. Some use it better, some worse, according to their dif- ferences of experience, quickness of memory and their inclinations to several ends, and especially according to their good or evil fortune, and the errors of one another. But they are very far from having *science*, the certain rules of their actions, and they do not know what it is. They think geometry is but conjuring. Those who have not been taught the begin- nings and some progress in the other sciences and so that they may see how they may be acquired and generated, are in this point like children, who having no idea about generation, are made to believe by women that their brothers and sisters are not born, but are found in the garden.

Still, those who have no *science* are in a better and nobler condition with their natural *prudence* than men who because of misreasoning or trusting those that reason incorrectly, fall upon false and absurd general rules. The ignorance of causes and rules does not set men as far out of the way as does relying on false rules, or taking to be causes what they aspire to, which are actually the causes of the opposite of what they wish for.

To conclude, the light of human minds is perspicuous words that by means of exact definitions are snuffed and purged of ambiguity. *Reason* is the *pace*, increase of *science* is the *way*, and the benefit of mankind is the *end*. On the contrary, metaphors and senseless and ambiguous words are like *ignes fatui*.[8] Reasoning upon them is wandering among innumerable absurdities, and their end is contention and sedition, which amounts to contempt.

The difference between sapience and prudence. As much experience is *prudence*, much science is *sapience*. Even though we usually have one name of wisdom for both of them, the Latins always distinguished between *prudentia* and *sapientia*, ascribing the former to experience and the latter to science. To make the difference appear more clearly, suppose one man is endowed with excellent natural use and dexterity in handling his arms. Suppose another to have added to that dexterity and acquired science that enables him to offend another, or counter the offense of his adversary, in every possible posture or guard. The ability of the former to the ability of the latter would be like prudence to sapience. Both are useful, but sapience is infallible. Those that only trust the authority of books are following the blind blindly. They are like someone who trusting the false rules of a master of fencing, ventures presumptuously upon an adversary, that either kills or disgraces him.

Signs of science. Some of the signs of science are certain and infallible, and some are uncertain. A certain sign is when a person who pretends[9] to have science can teach it to someone. That means the person can demonstrate the truth of the matter perspicuously to another. A sign of science is uncertain when only some particular events answer to the person's pretence[9] but do prove to be as the person says on many occasions. The signs of prudence are all uncertain, because it is impossible to observe by experience and remember all circumstances that may alter the outcome of the case.[10] It is a sign of folly and is generally scorned by the name of pedantry for a man, in any business, that does not have the infallible science to proceed by, and forsakes his own natural judgment to be guided by the general sentences of authors that are subject to many exceptions. Very few of those men that love to show their reading of politics and history in councils of commonwealth, do the same in their domestic affairs where their particular interest is concerned. They have prudence enough for their private affairs, but in public they study[11] more with the reputation of their own wit than the success of another's business.

Endnotes

1. Applicable
2. Plane
3. Agreements
4. Accuse
5. Derive
6. Mitigated
7. Points out
8. The fire of fools
9. Claim
10. Compare this to what Hobbes says about how to read other people in the Author's Introduction.
11. Are concerned

CHAPTER 6

The Passions

Vital and animal motion. Endeavor. There are two sorts of *motions* peculiar to animals. One is called *vital* and continues without interruption through the whole life of the animal. These are the *course* of the *blood,* the *pulse,* the *breathing,* the *concoction,*[1] *nutrition, excretion,* etc. These motions need no help of the imagination. The second is *animal motion,* otherwise called *voluntary motion.* These are to *go,* to *speak,* to *move* any of our limbs in such a manner as is first fancied in our minds. In this second sense the motions of the organs and interior parts of a man's body are caused by the actions of things we see, hear, etc. The fancy that causes the motion are but relics of the same motion, that remains after sense, as has already been discussed in the first and second chapters. Because *going, speaking* and similar voluntary motions always depend upon a preceding thought of *whether, which way,* and *what,* it is evident that the imagination is the first internal beginning of every voluntary motion. Unstudied men do not conceive any motion at all to be there when the thing that is moving is invisible, or because the space it is moved in is so short as to be insensible. Still, that does not hinder the fact that such motions exist. For no matter how little a space is, if it is a part of a greater space, and something is moved over the greater space, it must also be moved over the smaller one. These small beginnings of motion that occur within the body of man before they appear in walking, speaking, striking and other visible actions, are commonly called ENDEAVOR.

Appetite. Desire. Hunger. Thirst. Aversion. Endeavor is called APPETITE or DESIRE when it is toward something that causes it. Desire is the general name and appetite is often restrained[2] to signify the desire of food, namely *hunger* and *thirst.* When the endeavor is away from something, it is generally called AVERSION. We have the words *appetite* and *aversion* from the Latins, and both of them signify motions, one of approaching and the other of retiring. The Greek words *horme* and *aphorme* do the same. Nature itself often presses upon men those truths, which they only stumble at when they look for something beyond nature. The Schools find no actual motion at all in the mere appetite to go or move. Because they must acknowledge some motion, they call it metaphorical motion. This is but absurd speech, because while words may be called metaphorical, bodies and motions can not.

Love. Hate. What men desire, they are also said to LOVE, and to hate those things for which they have aversion. Love and desire are the same thing, except that by desire, we always signify the absence of the object and by love, we most commonly signify the presence of the object. In the same way, by aversion we signify the absence of the object and by hate, its presence.

Contempt. Some appetites and aversions are born with men, such as the appetite of food, and appetite of excretion and exoneration.[3] The latter two may be called aversions as that is somewhat what they feel like in bodies. We have some other appetites, but not many more. The rest which are appetites of particular things, proceed from the experience and trial of the effects of these things on themselves or on other men. Of the things that we do not know, or do not believe to be, we can have no further desire, than to taste and try. But we have aversion for not only the thing which we know have hurt us, but also for those that we do not know whether they will hurt us or not.

Those things which we neither desire nor hate, we are said to *contemn*. CONTEMPT is just the immobility or contumacy[4] of the heart that resists the actions of certain things. This proceeds when there is a lack of experience of these things or the heart is already moved by other more potent objects.

Because the constitution of a man's body is in continual mutation, it is impossible that the same things should always cause the same appetites and aversions in him. Much less can all men consent to the desire of almost any one and the same object.

Good. Evil. A man calls *good* whatever is the object of his appetite or desire. The object of his hate and aversion is call *evil,* and the object of contempt is called *vile* and *inconsiderable.* The words 'good', 'evil' and contemptible are always used in relation to the person that uses them. There is nothing simply and absolutely so, nor is there any common rule of good and evil to be taken from the nature of the objects themselves.

Where there is no commonwealth, these words derive just from the person of the man who uses them. In a commonwealth the use is derived from the person that represents the commonwealth, or from an arbitrator or a judge that people who disagree consent to set up to make his sentence be the rule thereof.[5]

Pulchrum. Turpe. Delightful. Profitable. Unpleasant. Unprofitable. The Latin tongue has two words, *pulchrum* and *turpe*, whose significations approach those of 'good' and 'evil', but are not precisely the same. 'Pulchrum' signifies something that by some apparent signs promises good, and 'turpe' promises evil. But we do not have such general names to express these things in our tongue. For *pulchrum* we sometimes say *full*, in other times we say *beautiful, handsome, gallant, honorable, comely* or *amiable.* For *turpe,* we use *foul, deformed, ugly, base, nauseous,* and the like as the subject requires. All of these words in their proper places just signify the *mien*[6] or countenance that promises good or evil. There are three kinds of good: good in the promise, *pulchrum,* good in effect as the end desired, which is called *jucundum, delightful,* and good as the means, which is called *utile, profitable.* The same applies to evil: *evil* in promise is called *turpe,* evil in effect and end is *molestrum, unpleasant,* or *troublesome,* and evil in the means is *inutile, unprofitable,* or *hurtful.*

As I have said before, in sensing, what is really within us is only motion caused by the action of external objects. This produces the appearance of light and color to sight, sound to the ear, odor to the nostril, etc. When the action of an object is continued from the eyes, ears and other organs to the heart, the real effect there is just motion or endeavor, which consists of appetite or aversion, to or away from the moving object. The appearance, or the sense of that motion is what we either call *delight* or *trouble of mind.*

Pleasure, Offense. The motion which is called appetite, whose appearance is called *delight* or *pleasure* seems to be a corroboration of vital motion and a help to it. Therefore such things that caused delight are properly called *jucunda, a juvando,* from helping or fortifying. The contrary are *molesta, offensive,* from hindering and troubling the vital motion.

Pleasure therefore or *delight* is the appearance or the sense of good, and *molestation* or *displeasure* is the appearance or the sense of evil. Consequently, all appetite, desire and love are accompanied with some delight, more or less. And all hatred and aversion are accompanied with more or less displeasure and offense.

Pleasures of sense. Pleasures of the mind. Joy. Pain. Grief. Some pleasures or delights arise from the sense of a present object, and those may be called *pleasure of sense*. The word *sensual* is used only by those that condemn them, and has no place until there are laws. All onerations[7] and exonerations of the body are of this kind, as also all that is pleasant to the *sight, hearing, smell, taste* or *touch*. Other pleasures arise from the expectation of whether a thing in the sense pleases or displeases that proceeds from the foresight of the end or the consequence of things. These are *pleasures of the mind* of him that draws the consequences, and are generally called JOY. Similarly, displeasures are sometimes in the sense, and are called PAIN. At other times when they are the expectation of consequences, they are called GRIEF.

These simple passions called *appetite, desire, love, aversion, hate, joy* and *grief* gain their names from diverse considerations. First, when they succeed one another, they are called by diverse names because of the differing opinion men have of the likelihood of attaining what they desire. Second, the different names derive from different objects that are loved or hated. A third reason is from the diverse consideration of many of them together. Fourth, is from alteration or succession itself.

Hope. *Appetite* with an opinion of attaining it is called HOPE.

Despair. Appetite but without such an opinion is DESPAIR.

Fear. Aversion combined with the opinion of HURT from that object is FEAR.

Courage. Aversion with the hope of avoiding that hurt by resistance is COURAGE.

Anger. Sudden *courage* is ANGER.

Confidence. Constant *hope* is CONFIDENCE in ourselves.

Diffidence. Constant *despair* is DIFFIDENCE in ourselves.

Indignation. Anger for the great hurt done to someone, when we conceive it to be done by injury, is INDIGNATION.

Benevolence. Good Nature. The *desire* of good to another is BENEVOLENCE, GOOD WILL, CHARITY. The desire for the good of men generally is GOOD NATURE.

Covetousness. The desire for riches is COVETOUSNESS. This name is always used to signify blame, because men who contend for riches are displeased with those who attain them. The desire itself is blamed or allowed according to the means by which the riches are sought.

Ambition. The *desire* of office or precedence is AMBITION. This name is also used in a worse sense for the reason mentioned just above.

Pusillanimity. The *desire* for things that conduce only a little to our ends and the fear of things that are but a little hindrance is PUSILLA-NIMITY.

Magnanimity. *Contempt* of little helps and hindrances is MAGNA-NIMITY.

Valor. *Magnanimity* in danger of death or wounds is VALOR, FORTI-TUDE.

Liberality. *Magnanimity* in the use of riches is LIBERALITY.

Miserableness. *Pusillanimity* in the use of riches is WRETCHED-NESS, MISERABLENESS or PARSIMONY, depending on whether it is liked or disliked.

Kindness. The *love* or persons for society is KINDNESS.

Natural Lust. The *love* of persons only for pleasing the senses is NAT-URAL LUST.

Luxury. The *love* of persons only for pleasing the senses when it is acquired from rumination, that is imagination, of past pleasure is LUXURY.

The passion of love. Jealousy. The *love* of a single person, with the desire to be singularly beloved is THE PASSION OF LOVE. The same but with the fear that the love is not mutual is JEALOUSY.

Revengefulness. The *desire* by doing some hurt to another to make him condemn some fact of his own is REVENGEFULNESS.

Curiosity. The *desire* to know why and how is CURIOSITY. No living creature has it but *man*. Man is thus distinguished from other *animals* not only by his reason, but also by this singular passion for knowing causes. In other animals the appetite for food and other pleasures of sense predominate and take away the care of knowing causes. Curiosity is a lust of the mind and due to the perseverance of delight in the continual and indefatigable generation of knowledge exceeds the short vehemence of any carnal pleasure.

Religion. Superstition. True religion. The *fear* of invisible power, feigned by the mind or imagined from tales publically allowed is RELIGION. When the tales are not allowed, it is SUPERSTITION. When the power imagined is truly such as we imagine, it is TRUE RELIGION.

Panic terror. The *fear*, without the apprehension of why or what, is PANIC TERROR. This is called so from the fables that make Pan the author of the terror. In truth there is always some apprehension of the cause in the person that so fears, even when the rest run away by example. Every one supposes that his fellow knows the cause. Therefore this passion happens only in a throng or multitude of people.

Admiration. The *joy* that occurs from the apprehension of novelty is ADMIRATION. It is proper to man because it excites the appetite of knowing the cause.

Glory. Vain-glory. The *joy* arising from a man's own power and ability is that exultation of the mind is called GLORYING. If it is grounded on the experience of one's own former actions, it is the same as *confidence*. But if it is grounded on the flattery of others, or only supposed by the person himself to delight in the consequences of it, it is called VAIN-GLORY. This name is properly given, because well-grounded *confidence* begets to an attempt to act, whereas the mere supposing of power does not, and is therefore rightly called *vain*.

Dejection. Grief that occurs from a lack of power is called DEJECTION of the mind.

The VAIN-GLORY which consists in the feigning or supposing of abilities in ourselves that we know we do not have is most incident in young men and is nourished by the histories or fictions of gallant persons. It is oftentimes corrected by age and employment.

Sudden glory. Laughter. Sudden glory is the passion which makes those *grimaces* called LAUGHTER. It is caused in people either by some sudden act of their own that pleases them, or when comparing themselves to others, people suddenly applaud themselves because of the apprehension of some deformed thing in the other. It is most often found in those that are conscious of the fewest abilities in themselves, who are forced to keep themselves in their own favor by observing the imperfections of other men. Therefore much laughter at the defects of others is a sign of pusillanimity. One of the proper works of great minds is to help to free others from scorn, and compare themselves only with the most able.

Sudden dejection. Weeping. On the contrary, *sudden dejection* is the passion that causes WEEPING. It is caused by accidents that suddenly take away some vehement hope or some prop of people's power. Those who are most subject to it are women and children who rely principally on external helps. Some weep for the loss of friends, others for their unkindness, and others for the sudden stop to their thoughts of revenge that are caused by reconciliation. But in all cases, both laughter and weeping are sudden motions that custom[8] takes away. No man laughs at old jests or weeps for an old calamity.

Shame. Blushing. Grief at the discovery of some defect of ability is SHAME. This passion discovers itself in BLUSHING, and consists in the apprehension of some dishonorable thing. In young men it is a sign of the love of a good reputation and is commendable. In old men it is a sign of the same thing, but because it comes too late, it is not commendable.

Impudence. The *contempt* of good reputation is called IMPUDENCE.

Pity. Grief for the calamity of another is PITY, and arises when from imagining that a like calamity may befall oneself. It is also called COMPASSION, and in the phrase of this present time, a FELLOW-FEELING. The best men have the least pity for those calamities that result from great wickedness. Those people hate pity who think that they are least obnoxious[9] to this kind of calamity.

Cruelty. Contempt, or little sense of the calamity of others is called CRUELTY. This proceeds from the security of one's own fortune. But I do not conceive it to be possible that a man should take please in some other man's great harms without any connection to his own ends.

Emulation. Envy. Grief at the success of a competitor in wealth, honor or other good is called EMULATION when it is joined with the endeavor to enforce our own abilities to equal or exceed him. When it is joined with an endeavor to supplant or hinder a competitor, it is ENVY.

Deliberation. In the mind of man there arises alternately appetites and aversions, hopes and fears, concerning the same thing. Diverse good and evil consequences of the doing or omitting of a propounded thing come successively into our thoughts. Sometimes we have an appetite for it and sometimes an aversion from it. Sometimes hope to be able to do it, and then sometimes despair or fear to attempt it. This whole sum of desires, aversions, hopes and fears that continue until the thing is either done or thought to be impossible is what we call DELIBERATION.

There is no *deliberation* of past things because it is manifestly impossible for them to be changed. Nor is there deliberation about things that are known to be impossible and are thought to be so, because men know and think that deliberation in such cases is vain. But we may deliberate about impossible things that we think are possible, not knowing it is vain to do so. *Deliberation* is so called because it puts an end to the *liberty* we had of doing something or omitting it, according to our appetite or aversion.

This alternate succession of appetites, aversions, hopes and fears also occurs in other living creatures besides man, and therefore, beasts also deliberate.

Every *deliberation* is then said to *end* when what is deliberated about is either done or thought to be impossible. Until that point we retain the liberty of doing or omitting according to our appetite or aversion.

The Will. In *deliberation* the last appetite or aversion immediately preceding an action or its omission is what we call the WILL. This is the act, not the faculty, of *willing*. Beasts that have the capacity of *delibera-tion*, necessarily must also have *will*. The definition of the *will* commonly given by the Schools, that it is *rational appetite* is not good. If it were, there could be no voluntary act that is against reason. A *voluntary act* is what proceeds from the *will*, and from nothing else. If instead of rational appetite, we just talk of an appetite resulting from a preceding deliberation, then the definition is the same that I have just given. *Will* therefore *is the last appetite in deliberating*. We do say in common discourse that a man at some time had a will to do a thing that he nevertheless forebore to do. But this should more properly be called an inclination that does not lead to a voluntary action. The action that occurs depends not on this inclination, but on the last inclination or appetite. If intervenient[10] appetites make a resulting action voluntary, then by the same reasoning, intervenient aversions would make the same action involuntary. This could result in one and the same action being both voluntary and involuntary.

This is why it is manifest that *voluntary actions* are not only actions that have their beginning from prior appetites such as covetousness, ambition or lust, but are also actions that have their beginning from aversions or fear of those consequences that follow the omission of an action.

Forms of speech, in passion. The forms of speech by which the passions are expressed are partly the same, and partly different, from those by which we express our thoughts. First, generally, all passions may be expressed *indicatively*, as in *I love, I fear, I joy, I deliberate, I will* and *I command*. But some passions have particular expressions, which are not affirmations except when they are used to make other inferences besides the one that the passion is expressing. Deliberation is expressed *subjunctively*, which is the speech used to signify suppositions and their consequences, as in *if this be done, then this will follow*. This does not differ from the language of reasoning, save that reasoning is in terms of general words, and deliberation is for the most part expressed in particulars. The language of desire and aversion is *imperative*, such as *do this* or *forbear that*. When a party is obliged to do or forbear, it is a *command*. Otherwise, it is a *prayer*, or else *counsel*. The language of vain-glory, of indignation, pity and revengefulness is *optative*.[11] There is a peculiar expression for the desire to know that is called *interrogative*, as in *what is it, when shall it, how is it done* and *why so?* I find no other language of the passion, for cursing, swearing, reviling and like do not signify as speech. They are just the actions of an accustomed tongue.

These forms of speech, I say, are expressions or voluntary significations of our passions, but they are not signs that are certain. They may be used arbitrarily, whether those that use them have such passions or not. The best signs of present passions are either in the countenance, motions, body, actions and ends of a person, or by knowing the aims that a person has.

Apparent good and evil. In deliberation the appetites and aversions are raised by the foresight of the good and evil consequences, and the sequels of the actions that we deliberate about. The good and evil effect of deliberation depends then on the foresight of a long chain of consequences, of which very seldom is any man able to see the end. To the extent that a man sees that the good in these consequences is greater than the evil, the whole chain is what writers call *apparent* or *seeming good,* and contrarily, when the evil exceeds the good, the whole is *apparent* or *seeming evil.* The people who deliberate the best for themselves are those who by experience or reason have the surest view of the consequences. Such people, when they will to, also give the best counsel to others.

Felicity. Continual success in obtaining those things which a man from time to time desires, that is to say continual prospering, is what men call FELICITY. I mean felicity of this life for there is no such thing as perpetual tranquillity of mind while we live here. This is so because life itself is just motion, and can never be without desire nor without fear, no more than it can be without sense. As far as the kind of felicity that God has ordained to those that devoutly honor Him, men will soon enjoy or know. These joys are now as incomprehensible to us as are the words of the school-men *beatifical*[12] *vision* is unintelligible to us.

Praise. Magnification. Makarismos. The form of speech that men use to signify their opinion of the goodness of any thing is PRAISE. MAGNIFYING is the way men signify the power and greatness of any thing. *Makarismos* is the Greek term to signify the opinion people have of a person's felicity. We have no such name in our tongue. This is sufficient to say about the PASSIONS for the present purpose.

Endnotes

1. The preparation of food
2. Restricted
3. Discharge, related to excretion
4. Resistance
5. People who disagree have agreed to let a neutral arbitrator decided what is good, evil or contemptible.
6. Character

7. Ingestion
8. Becoming accustomed to
9. Subject to
10. Hobbes is referring here to appetites that occur sometime before the last appetite or aversion that precede an action.
11. A grammatical mood that is not a part of current English that is related to the expression of wishes.
12. Blissful

CHAPTER 7

Of the Ends, or Resolutions of Discourse

For all discourse that is governed by the desire for knowledge, there is at last an *end*, that occurs when knowledge is attained, or the attempt to get it is given up. Whenever a chain of discourse is interrupted, that point of time is the end.

Judgment, or final sentence. Doubt. If the discourse is merely mental it consists of the alternating thoughts that a thing will be or will not be, that it has been or has not been. So wherever you break off the chain of a man's discourse, you leave him in a presumption that *it will be,* or *it will not be,* or *it has been,* or *it has not been.* All of this is *opinion.* In deliberating concerning good and evil, there is an alternation of appetites, and in the enquiry for truth, there are alternating opinions about *past* and *future.* The last appetite in deliberation is called the *will,* and the last opinion in the search for the truth about the past and future is called the JUDGMENT, or the *resolute* or *final sentence* of the one who discourses. The whole chain of appetites that alternate in the question of good or bad is called *deliberation,* and the whole chain of opinions that alternate in the question of true and false is called DOUBT.

No discourse whatever can end in absolute knowledge of fact about the past or what is to come. Knowledge of fact is originally sense, and after that, memory. The knowledge of consequences that I said before is called science, is not absolute, but is conditional. No man can know absolutely by discourse that this or that is, has been or will be. Men can only know that if this is, then that is; if this has been, that has been; and if this shall be, that shall be. This is what it is to know conditionally.

Such knowledge is not the consequence of one thing to another, but is the consequence of one name of a thing to another name of the same thing. *Science. Opinion. Conscious.* When a discourse is put into speech and begins with the definition of words and proceeds by the connection of words into general affirmations, and connecting affirmations into syllogisms, then the end or the last sum is called the conclusion. These thoughts of the mind signify the conditional knowledge, or knowledge of the consequence of words, which is commonly called SCIENCE. But if the first ground of such discourse is not definitions, or if the definitions are not rightly joined together into syllogisms, then the end conclusion is just OPINION. This is the truth of what someone said, though sometimes it is in absurd and senseless words, that has no possibility of being understood. When two or more men know of one and the same fact, they are said to be CONSCIOUS of it together. This is as much as to know it together. Because these men are fittest witnesses of the facts of one another, or of a third person, it was and ever will be reputed to be an evil act for any man to speak against his *conscience*, or to corrupt or force another to do so. The plea of conscience has always been very diligently hearkened to in all times. Afterwards, men made used the same word metaphorically for the knowledge of their own secret facts and secret thoughts. Therefore it is rhetorically said that conscience is a thousand witnesses. Lastly, men gave the reverence name of conscience to the opinions that they vehemently love and which they are obstinately bent to maintain, even when they are absurd. Men would have it seem unlawful to change or speak against these opinions, and so they pretend to know they are true, when they know at most just that they think so.

Belief. Faith. Sometimes a man's discourse does not begin at definitions, but it begins at some other contemplations of his own. In this case, it is still called opinion. Or else the discourse begins with some saying of another whose ability to know the truth and whose honesty in not deceiving is not doubted. In this latter case, the discourse is not so much concerning the thing said, as the person who says it. This resolution is called BELIEF and FAITH: *faith, in* the man, *belief,* both *of* the man and *of* the truth of what he says. So belief involves two opinions: one which concerns the saying of the man, and the other, his virtue. To *have faith in,* or *trust in,* or *believe a man,* signifies the same thing, namely an opinion of the veracity of the man. But to *believe, what is said,* signifies only an opinion of the truth of what was said. We should observe that this phrase, *I believe in,* and in Latin *credo in,* and the Greek, *pisteuo eis,* are only used in the writings of divines. In the place of those phrases, they put in other writings *I believe him, I trust him, I have faith in him, I trust him, I have faith in him* and *I rely on him.* In Latin, they use *credo illi* and *fido ille,* and in Greek, *pisteuo auto.* This singularity of ecclesiastic use of the word has raised many disputes about the right object of the Christian faith.

Believing in, as it is in the creed, means not the trust in the person, but the confession and acknowledgment of the doctrine. For not only Christians, but all manner of men believe in God, and hold everything He says to be the truth whether they understand it or not. This is all the faith and trust that can be had in any person, but still not all people believe the doctrine of the creed.

When we believe anything that is said to be, or to be true, based on arguments taken, not from the thing itself, or from the principles of natural reason, but from the authority and good opinion we have of him that said it, then it is the speaker that we believe and trust. We take his word as the object of our faith and the honor done in believing is done to only him. Consequently, when we believe that the Scriptures are the word of God, since we have no immediate revelation from God himself, our belief, faith and trust is just in the church whose word we take and to which we acquiesce. Those that believe what a prophet relates to them in the name of God, take the word of the prophet and do honor to him. They trust and believe in him, touching[1] the truth of what he relates, whether he is a true or false prophet. It is the same with all other histories. If I should not believe all that is written by historians of the glorious acts of *Alexander* or *Caesar,* I do not offend the ghost of *Alexander* or *Caesar* or anybody else. I just offend the historians. If *Livy* said the Gods once made a cow speak, and we do not believe it, then it is not that we distrust God, but we distrust Livy. So it is evident that whenever we believe something for no other reason than it is drawn only from the authority of men and their writings, then whether they be sent from God or not, we only show faith in men.

Endnotes

1. Accepting

CHAPTER 8

Intellectual Virtues

Intellectual virtue defined. VIRTUE generally, in all sorts of subjects, is something that is valued for eminence and consists in comparison. If all things were equal in all men, nothing would be prized. *Intellectual virtues* are always understood as the abilities of the mind that men praise, value and desire for themselves. They commonly go under the name of *good wit*, though the word *wit* is also used to distinguish one particular ability from others.

Wit, natural or acquired. Natural wit. These *virtues* are of two sorts, *natural* and *acquired.* By 'natural' I do not mean what a man has from birth. That is nothing else but sense, and in this regard men differ so little from each other or from brute beasts, that sense is not reckoned among the virtues. This NATURAL WIT consists principally of two things. The first is *celerity of imagining,* that is the swift succession of one thought to another. The second is *steady direction* to some approved end. The contrary is called DULLNESS and *stupidity* which is defect and the fault of the mind of a slow imagination. This is sometimes called by other names that signify slowness of motion or difficulty to be moved.

Good wit or fancy. Good judgment. Discretion. This difference of quickness is caused by the difference of men's passions that love and dislike, some one thing and some another. Some men's thoughts run one way and some another. They hold and observe differently the things that pass through their imaginations. In this succession of men's thoughts, we can observe that they think of the way things are *like one another,* or in what way they are *unlike,* or *what they serve for,* or *how they serve to such a purpose.* Those that observe similarities in cases where they are rarely observed by others are said to have a *good wit,* which means on this occasion, a *good fancy.* Those that observe differences and dissimilarities between thing and thing that are not easy to discern are said to have *good judgment,* and what they do is called *distinguishing* and *discerning* and *judging*. This virtue is called DISCRETION when in the matter of conversation and business, times, places and persons are discerned. Fancy without the help of judgment is not commended as a virtue, but judgment and discretion without the help of fancy are commended for themselves. Besides the discretion of times, places and persons necessary to a good fancy, there is often an application of this virtue to the thoughts that lead to their end, which is that some use is to be made of these thoughts. He that has this virtue will easily find similarities that will please, not only by illustrations of his discourse and adorning it with new and apt metaphors, but also by the rarity of their invention. But without steadiness and direction to some end, a great fancy is one kind of madness. The ones who have it are snatched from their purpose when entering into any discourse by every thing that comes into their thoughts, which leads to such long digressions and parentheses that they utterly lose themselves. This is a kind of folly that I do not know any particular name for. The cause of it is sometimes a lack of experience when something seems new and rare to a man that does not seem so to others. Sometimes it is caused by a pusillanimity when what seems great to one, other men think to be a trifle. And sometimes the cause is something new and great, that a man thinks is fit to be mentioned, and this withdraws the man by degrees from the intended way of his discourse

In a good poem, whether it is *epic* or *dramatic,* and also in *sonnets, epigrams* and other pieces, both judgment and fancy are required. But the fancy must be more eminent because good poems please by their extravagance, but still ought not to displease by any indiscretion.

In a good history, judgment should be eminent, because its goodness consists in the method, in the truth and in the choice of actions that are most profitable to be known. Fancy has no place here, except for adorning the style.

In orations of praise and in invectives, the fancy is predominant because the aim is not truth, but to honor or dishonor, which is done by noble or vile comparisons. Judgment just suggests what circumstances make an action laudable or culpable.

In hortatives[1] and pleadings to the extent that truth or disguise serves best for the aim at hand, to that extent judgment or fancy are most required.

In demonstration, in counsel, and in all rigorous search of truth, judgment is what does all, except when the understanding has the need to be

opened by some apt similarity, and then there is much use of fancy. But in
this kind of case metaphors are to be utterly excluded. They openly profess
deceit, and so it is manifest folly to admit them into counsel or reasoning.

In any discourse if there is an apparent defect of discretion, no matter
how extravagant the fancy is, the whole discourse will be taken as a sign
of the lack of wit. But this will never be the case when discretion is manifest, and fancy is only ordinary.

The secret thoughts of a man run over all things, holy, profane, clean,
obscene, grave and light without shame or blame. Verbal discourse cannot do this beyond what judgment shall approve of the time, place and
persons. An anatomist or a physician may speak or write of his judgment
of unclean things because it is not their aim to please, but to profit. When
another man, however, writes of his extravagant and pleasant fancies of
the same kind of thing, it is as if a man who has tumbled into the dirt,
comes and presents himself before good company. It is lack of discretion
that makes the difference. A man in the remissness[2] of the mind or in
familiar company may play with the sound and equivocal signification of
words, that lead many times to encounters of extraordinary fancy. But in
sermons, or in public, or before unknown persons whom we ought to
revere, there should be no jingling of words, or else this will be considered folly. The difference is simply in the lack of discretion. Where wit is
lacking, it is not fancy that is lacking, but discretion. Judgment, therefore, without fancy is wit, but fancy without judgment is not wit.

Prudence. Sometimes a the thoughts of man that has an aim in mind,
runs over a multitude of things, and observes how they conduce to that
aim, or what aim they may conduce to. If this man's observations are
such that they are not easy or usual, he has the wit that is called PRU-
DENCE. This depends on much experience and memory of like things
and their prior consequences. There is not as much difference in prudence among men as there is in their fancies and in their judgment. This
is so because there is an equal quantity of experience of men that are
equal in age. The only difference lies in different occasions, as everyone
has his own private designs. To govern a family or a kingdom well, does
not require different degrees of prudence, for they are just different sorts
of business. In the same way, drawing a picture that is smaller than on
object, or the same size or greater are just different degrees of art. A plain
husbandman is more prudent in affairs of his own house than a privy-
counselor is in the affairs of another man.

Craft. If you add the use of unjust or dishonest means to prudence, as
happens to those who are usually prompted by fear or lack of something,

you will have that crooked wisdom which is called CRAFT, that is a sign of pusillanimity. Magnanimity is contempt of unjust or dishonest helps. What the Latins called *versutia*, translated into English as *shifting*, is putting off a present danger of incommodity[3] by engaging a greater danger, as when a man robs one to pay another. This is but a shorter-sighted craft, called *versutia*, from *versura*, that signifies taking money at usury for the present payment of interest.

Acquired wit. By *acquired wit* I mean acquired by method and instruction. The only way to do this is by reason that is grounded on the right use of speech and that produces the sciences. I have already spoken of reason and science in the fifth and sixth chapters.

The causes of the differences of wit is to be found in the passions. The differences of the of passions proceeds partly from the different constitution of bodies and partly from different educations. If the differences proceeded from the temper of the brain and the organs of sense, either exterior or interior, there would be no less difference in men in their sight hearing or other senses than in their fancies and discretions. The differences proceed therefore from the passions, not only because of the difference of men's complexions,[4] but also from the difference of custom and education.

The passions that mainly cause the differences in wit are principally the more or less desire for power, for riches, for knowledge and for honor. All of these may be reduced to the first, the desire for power. Riches, knowledge and honor are just several sorts of power.

Giddiness. Madness. A man who has no great passion for any of these things, who is termed indifferent, though he may be a good man as far as being free from giving offence, yet he cannot possibly have either a great fancy or much judgment. Thoughts are to desires as scouts and spies that range abroad and find the way to the things that are desired. All steadiness and quickness of the mind's motions proceeds from this source. To have no desires is to be dead. To have weak passions is dullness, and to have passions indifferently for every thing is GIDDINESS and *distraction*. To have stronger and more vehement passions for any thing that is ordinarily seen in others is called MADNESS.

There are almost as many kinds of madness as there are passions themselves. Sometimes the extraordinary and extravagant passions proceed from the evil constitution of the organs of the body, or because of the harm done to them. Sometimes the hurt and indisposition of the organs is caused by the vehemence or long continuance of the passion. In both cases the madness has the same nature.

The passions whose violence or continuance makes madness are either great *vain-glory*, which is commonly called *pride* and *self-conceit*, or great *dejection* of the mind.

Rage. Pride subjects a man to anger, whose excess is the madness called RAGE and FURY. Excessive desire for revenge, when it becomes habitual, hurts the organs and becomes rage. Excessive love combined with jealousy also becomes rage. An excessive opinion of oneself for divine inspiration, or for wisdom, learning or form[5] becomes distraction and giddiness, and when these are joined with envy, they become rage. Rage is also the vehement opinion of the truth of anything that is contradicted by others.

Melancholy. Madness. Dejection subjects a man to causeless fears, which is a madness that is commonly called MELANCHOLY. It is apparent in diverse ways, such as the haunting of solitudes[6] and graves, in superstitious behavior, or in fearing someone or some other particular thing. In sum, all passions that produce strange and unusual behavior are called by the general name of madness. He that would take the pains to name the several kinds of madness would enroll a legion. If excesses are madness, there is no doubt but that the passions themselves, when they tend toward evil, are degrees of madness too.

For example, the effect of folly is not always visible in one man by any extravagant action that proceeds from a passion of those possessed of an opinion of being inspired. Yet, when many of these kinds of people conspire together, the rage of the whole multitude is visible enough. For what greater argument of madness can there be than to clamor, strike and throw stones at our best friends? Even this is less than what such a multitude will do. They will clamor, fight against and destroy those who have always protected them and secured them from injury. If this is madness of the multitude, the same occurs in every particular man. Consider that in the midst of the sea, a man perceives no sound of that part of the water that is right next to him, even though it is well assured that part of the water contributes as much to the roaring of the sea as any other part of the quantity. So also, though we perceive no great unquietness in one or two men, we may still be well assured that their singular passions are parts of the seditious roaring of a troubled nation. If there were nothing else that bewrayed[7] their madness, just that arrogating[8] such inspiration to themselves is argument enough. If some man in Bedlam should entertain you with sober discourse, and when you desire to take leave, you ask to know who he is so that you might at another time requite[9] his civility, if he were to tell you he was God the

Father, I think you would need not see any extravagant action on his part to determine his madness.

The opinion of inspiration that is commonly called private spirit, begins very often with some lucky finding of an error generally held by others. The people who find these errors do not know or remember what conduct of reason led them to so singular a truth, even though many times it is an untruth that they light on. They presently admire themselves as being in the special grace of God Almighty, who has revealed all of this to them supernaturally by his Spirit.

That madness is just too much of an appearing passion may be gathered from the effects of wine, which has the same effect as the evil disposition of the organs. The variety of behavior in men that have drunk too much is the same as with madmen. Some of them are raging, others are loving, others are laughing and all are doing these extravagantly according to their several domineering passions. The effect of wine just removes dissimulation and takes away the sight of the deformity of their passions from these men. I believe that the most sober of men, when they walk alone without any care or employment of the mind, would be unwilling to have the vanity and extravagance of their thoughts be publicly seen. This is a confession that the unguided passions are for the most part mere madness.

There have been two opinions concerning the causes of madness both in ancient and later ages. Some say madness derives from the passions, and some say it derives from demons or spirits, either good or bad, that they thought might enter a man, possess him and move his organs in the strange and uncouth ways that madmen do. Those that attribute the former cause call such men madmen, but the latter group sometimes call them *demoniacs*, that is possessed by spirits, and sometimes *energumeni*, which means agitated for moved by spirits. In Italy now they are not only called *pazzi*, madmen, but also *spiritati*, men who are possessed.

There was once a great conflux[10] of people in Abdera, a Greek city, on an extremely hot day at the performance of the tragedy *Andromeda*. A great many of the spectators suffered the accident of falling into fevers brought on by the heat together with the tragedy. These people did nothing but pronounce iambics with the names of Perseus and Andromeda, which together with the fever were cured by the coming on of winter. This madness was thought to have proceeded from the passion imprinted on the people by the tragedy. Likewise a fit of madness reigned in another Grecian city that seized only the young maidens, and caused many of them to hang themselves. This was thought then by most to be an act of the Devil. But someone suspected that this contempt of life proceeded from some passion of the mind, and supposed that these maidens were not also condemning their honor. This person counseled the magistrates to strip those who had hung themselves and let them hang out naked. The story says this cured that madness. But on the other side, the same Grecians often ascribed madness to the operation of Eumenides, or the Furies, and sometimes to Ceres, Phoebus and the other gods. Men attributed so much to phantasms, that they thought them to be aerial[11] living bodies, and generally called them spirits.

The Romans held the same opinion about this as did the Jews. They called madmen prophets or demoniacs according to whether they thought the spirits were good or bad. Some said both prophets and demoniacs were madmen, the same man both prophet and demoniac. It is no wonder that the Gentiles did this, because they named diseases and health, vices and virtues, and some called many natural accidents, as demons and worshipped them as such. A man then understood a demon as well as an ague sometimes to be a devil.

The fact that the Jews had such opinions is somewhat strange. Neither Moses nor Abraham pretended to prophecy from the voice of God or by a vision or a dream and not by the possession of a spirit. Nor is there anything in their law, moral or ceremonial, by which they were taught that there is any such enthusiasm[12] or any possession. When God says (*Numbers, 11.25*) to take from the spirit that was in Moses and give it to the seventy elders, the Spirit of God (taking it for the substance of God) is not divided. In the Scriptures, the Spirit of God in man means a man's spirit that is inclined to godliness. Where it is said (*Exodus, 23.8*) *"Whom I have filled with the spirit of wisdom to make garments for Aaron,"* it does not mean that a spirit that can make garments was put into them, but rather that the wisdom of their own spirits made that kind of work. In a like sense the spirit of a man when it produces unclean actions is ordinarily called an unclean spirit. The same is often said about other spirits when the virtue or vice is extraordinary or eminent. The other prophets of the old Testament did not pretend enthusiasm[12] or that God spoke to them except by voice, vision or dream. The *burthen of the Lord* was not possession, but command. How then could the Jews fall into this opinion of possession? I can imagine no other reason except that which is common to all men. This is the lack of curiosity to search for natural causes, and the placing of felicity in the acquisition of the gross pleasures of the senses, and the things that they most immediately lead to them. Those that see any strange and unusual ability or defect in a man's mind will hardly ever think that it has a natural cause unless they see what from what cause it probably proceeds. If they do not think the cause is natural, they then must think the cause is supernatural, and then what can it be, but that either God or the Devil is in him?

When it came to pass that our Savior (*Mark* 3.21) was compassed about with the multitude, those of the house doubted he was mad and went out to hold him. But the Scribes said he had Beelzebub and that is what he used to cast out devils, as if the greater madman had awed the lesser. Some said (*John* 10.20) *he hath a devil and is mad,* while others holding him for a prophet said, *these are not the words of one that hath a devil.* In the Old Testament the one that came to anoint Jehu (*2 Kings* 9.11) was a prophet, but some of the company asked Jehu, *what came that madman for?* In sum, it is manifest that whoever behaved himself in an extraordinary manner was thought by the Jews to be possessed by either a good or evil spirit. The exception to this is the Sadducees who erred so far on the other hand so as not to believe there were any spirits at all, which is very near to direct atheism. This provoked others even more to call such men demoniacs, rather than madmen.

But why then does our Savior proceed to cure them as if they were possessed and not as if they were mad? I can give the same kind of answer to this question that is given to those who in like manner urge that the Scripture is against the opinion the earth is in motion. The Scripture was written to show men the kingdom of God and to prepare their minds to become His obedient subjects. It leaves the world and the philosophy of it to the disputation of men for the exercise of their natural reason. Our worship of Him does not depend on whether the earth's or sun's motion makes the day and the night, or whether the exorbitant actions of men proceed from passion or from the devil. It is all the same as far as our obedience and subjection to God Almighty, and that is main reason why the Scripture was written. Our Savior speaks to a disease as if it were a person because that is the usual phrase of all those who cure by using only words, as Christ actually did and enchanters pretend to do, whether they speak to a devil or not. For is not Christ also said (*Matthew* 8.26) to have rebuked the winds, and to rebuke a fever (*Luke* 4.39)? This does not show that a fever is a devil. Even though many of the devils are said to have confessed Christ, one can interpret those places as saying that those madmen confessed him. Our Savior (*Matthew* 12.42) does speak of an unclean spirit that having gone out of a man, wanders through dry places seeking rest and finding none, and then returning into the same man with seven other spirits worse than himself. This is manifestly a parable alluding to a man that after a little endeavor to quit his lusts, is vanquished by their strength and becomes seven times worse than he was. So I see nothing at all in the Scriptures that requires a belief that demoniacs were any other thing but madmen.

Insignificant speech. There is yet another fault in the discourse of some men, which may also be numbered among the sorts of madness. It is the abuse of words that goes by the name of absurdity that I have spoken of before in the fifth chapter. This occurs when men speak words that when put together have no signification at all. Some use these words through misunderstanding them when they actually received and then repeat them by rote. Others get these words from others who have the intent to deceive by means of obscurity. This kind of thing is evident in those that converse about questions of incomprehensible matters as do the School-men, or in questions of abstruse philosophy. The common sort of men seldom speak insignificantly and are therefore counted by the above egregious[14] persons to be idiots. To be assured that the words of these people do not correspond to any thing, one would need to consider some examples. One who requires such examples can take a School-man by the hand and see if he can translate any one chapter concerning any difficult point, about the Trinity, the Deity, the nature of Christ, transubstantiation, free will, etc. into any modern tongue to make them intelligible. Or can the School-man translate these points into tolerable Latin, that could be understood by those that lived when the Latin tongue was vulgar.[15] What is the meaning of these words: *The first cause does not necessarily inflow any thing into the second by force of the essential subordination of the second causes, but which it may help it to work?* This is the translation of the title of the sixth chapter of *Suarez'*[16] first book, *Of the concourse, motion and help of God.* When men write whole volumes of such stuff, are they not mad, or intend to make others so? This is particularly the case in the question of transubstantiation,[17] where after certain spoken words, they say the white*ness*, round*ness*, magni*tude*, quali*ty*, and corruptibili*ty*, *all of which are incorporeal, etc. go out of the wafer into the body of our Blessed Savior.* Do they not make those *nesses, tudes* and *ties* to be so many spirits possessing his body? By spirits they always mean things that are incorporeal but are nevertheless moveable from one place to another. This kind of absurdity may rightly be numbered among the many sorts of madness. It is only during lucid intervals when these writers are guided by clear thoughts of their worldly lust and so they forbear from disputing and writing in this absurd way.

This ends the discussion of the intellectual virtues and defects.

Endnotes

1. A kind of writing that encourages an action
2. A condition of slackness, or letting things go
3. Inconvenience.
4. Constitutions
5. Beauty
6. A lonely, unfrequented place
7. Reveal
8. Hobbes is referring to those who claim to be divinely inspired without any warrant.
9. Reciprocate
10. Gathering
11. Airy
12. 'Enthusiasm' originally meant possessed by a god.
13. Distinguished (Hobbes probably is being sarcastic here.)
14. Behold
15. Commonly spoken
16. Francisco Suarez was a Spanish theologian who lived 1549-1617.
17. Transubstantiation is the view that during communion, the wine and the wafer actually change into the substance of Christ's body and blood, even though the tangible properties of the wine and wafer remain the same.

CHAPTER 9

Of the Several Subjects
of Knowledge

*K*nowledge. There are two kinds of KNOWLEDGE. One is *knowledge of fact*, and the other is *knowledge of the consequences of one affirmation to another*. The former is just sense and memory, and is *absolute knowledge*, as when we see a fact as it is occurring, or remember that it was done. This is the knowledge required in a witness. The latter is called *science* and is *conditional*, as when we know that *if the figure shown be a circle, then any straight line through the center shall divide it into two equal parts*. This is the knowledge required in a philosopher, of him that pretends to reasoning.

The register of *knowledge of fact* is *history*, of which there are two sorts. One is called *natural history* which is the history of such facts or effects of nature that have no dependence on man's *will*. These are the histories of *metals, plants, animals, regions* and the like. The other is *civil history* which is the history of voluntary actions of men in commonwealths.

The registers of science are the book that contain the *demonstrations* of consequences of one affirmation to another, and are commonly called *books of philosophy*. The sorts of these books are many due to the diversity of the subject matters. They may be divided in the manner as I have divided them in the following table.

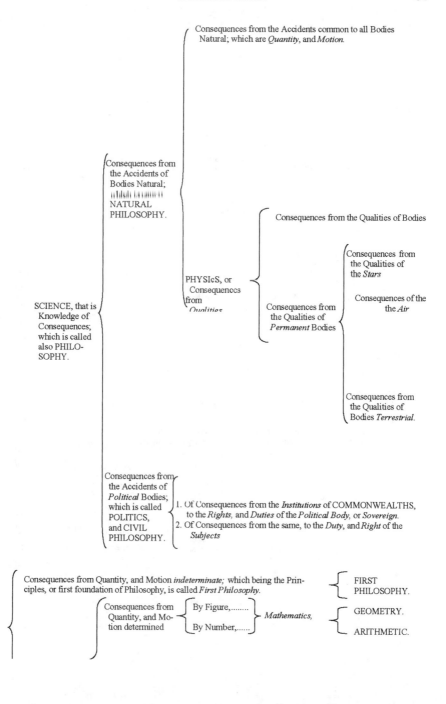

Consequences from the Accidents common to all Bodies Natural; which are *Quantity*, and *Motion*.

Consequences from the Accidents of Bodies Natural; ⊔⊔⊔⊔⊔⊔⊔⊔⊔ NATURAL PHILOSOPHY.

Consequences from the Qualities of Bodies

PHYSIcS, or Consequences from *Qualities*

Consequences from the Qualities of the *Stars*

Consequences of the the *Air*

Consequences from the Qualities of *Permanent* Bodies

SCIENCE, that is Knowledge of Consequences; which is called also PHILO-SOPHY.

Consequences from the Qualities of Bodies *Terrestrial*.

Consequences from the Accidents of *Political* Bodies; which is called POLITICS, and CIVIL PHILOSOPHY.

1. Of Consequences from the *Institutions* of COMMONWEALTHS, to the *Rights*, and *Duties* of the *Political Body*, or *Sovereign*.
2. Of Consequences from the same, to the *Duty*, and *Right* of the *Subjects*

Consequences from Quantity, and Motion *indeterminate*; which being the Principles, or first foundation of Philosophy, is called *First Philosophy*.

FIRST PHILOSOPHY.

Consequences from Quantity, and Motion determined

By Figure,........

By Number,......

Mathematics,

GEOMETRY.

ARITHMETIC.

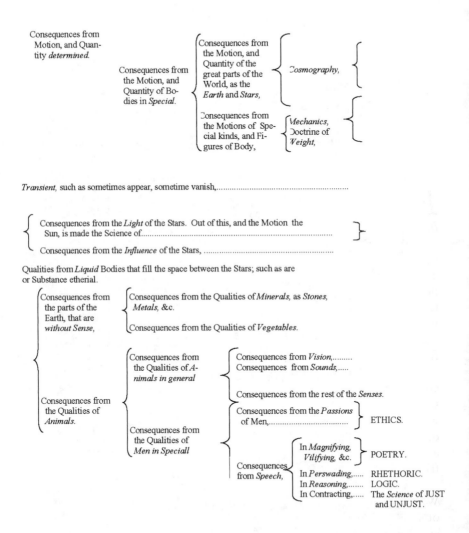

CHAPTER 10

Of Power, Worth, Dignity, Honor and Worthiness

Power. The power *of a man* to take it universally,[1] is his present means to obtain some future apparent good. Power is either *original* or *instrumental.*

Natural power is the eminence of the faculties of the body or mind, such as extraordinary strength, form, prudence, art, eloquence, liberality and nobility. The *instrumental* powers are those acquired by the natural powers or by fortune, that are the means and instruments to acquire more, such as riches, reputation, friends and the secret working of God, which men call good luck. In this point the nature of power is like fame, increasing as it proceeds, or like the motion of heavy bodies, which the further they go, make still more haste.

The greatest of human powers is the power of a commonwealth that is compounded of the powers of most men, united by consent in one person, natural or civil, that has the use of all the powers depending on his will. Another example of this power is the power of a faction or of diverse factions that are leagued together which depends on the wills of each particular party. Therefore, to have servants is power, and to have friends is power, for they both are united strengths.

Riches joined with liberality is power because it procures friends. When riches is without liberality it is not power, because in this case other people will not defend one. Riches, in this case, exposes men to envy, as prey.

The reputation of power is power because it draw with it the adherence of those that need protection.

So, for the same reason, is reputation of love of a man's country, which is called popularity.

Whatever quality, or the reputation of such a quality, that makes a man beloved or feared by many is power because it is a means to have the assistance and service of many.

Good success is power because it makes the reputation of wisdom or good fortune which makes others fear or rely on one.

The affability of men already in power is the increase of power, because it gains love.

The reputation of prudence in the conduct of peace or war is power because we commit the government of ourselves more willingly to prudent men than to others.

Nobility[2] is power, but not in all places. It is only so in those commonwealths where it has privileges, for power consists of such privileges.

Eloquence is power because it is seeming prudence.

Form[3] is power because it is a promise of good and so it recommends men to getting the favor of women and strangers.

The sciences are small power because they are not eminent and therefore, they are not acknowledged in any man. They only exist in a few men, and in those, they just are of a few things. Science has the nature that only those can understand it that have attained it to a good measure.

The arts of public use, such as fortification, the making of engines and other instruments of war that confer to defense and victory, are power. The true mother of all of these is science, and particularly mathematics. Because all of these things are brought into the light by the hand of artificers, they are the ones that are esteemed by the vulgar who take the midwife of the issue to be the mother.

Worth. The *value* or WORTH of a man, is as of all other things, his price. This is how much would be given for the use of his power. This price is not absolute, but is something that is dependant on the need and judgment of others. An able conductor of soldiers has a great price in time or present or imminent war, but not so in peace. A learned and uncorrupt judge is worth much in time of peace, but not so much in war. The price of men, as in other things, is determined by the buyer and not the seller. Even though men rate themselves at the highest value as most men do, but their true value is no more than what it is esteemed by others.

The manifestation of the value we set on one another is what is commonly called honoring and dishonoring. To value a man at a high rate is to *honor* him, and at a low rate is to *dishonor* him. But high and low, in this case, is to be understood by comparison to the rate that each man sets upon himself.

Dignity. The public worth of a man which is the value set on him by the commonwealth is called DIGNITY. This value by the commonwealth is shown by the offices of command, the judicature, public employment and by the names and titles introduced for distinction of such value.

To pray to another for aid of any kind is to HONOR, because it is a sign that we have an opinion that he has the power to help. The more difficult the aid is, the more is the honor.

To honor and dishonor. To obey is to honor because no man obeys those that they think *have no power to help or hurt them.* Consequently, *to disobey is to* dishonor.

To give great gifts to a man is to honor him, because it is buying protection and acknowledging his power. To give little gifts is to dishonor the person, because it is just alms, and signifies the opinion that the person is need of small helps.

To be sedulous[4] in promoting another's good, or to flatter, is to honor. These are signs we seek the person's protection or aid. To neglect is to dishonor.

To give way or place to another in any commodity[5] is to honor, as it is a confession the other has greater power. To arrogate[6] is to dishonor.

To show any sign of love or fear of another is to honor, for both to love and to fear is to value. To contemn,[7] or to love or fear less than one expects is to dishonor, for it is undervaluing.

To praise, magnify or call happy is to honor, because nothing but goodness, power, and felicity are valued. To revile, mock or pity is to dishonor.

To speak to another with consideration or to appear before him with decency and humility is to honor him, as these are signs of being afraid to offend. To speak to him rashly or to do anything before him obscenely, slovenly or impudently is to dishonor him.

To believe, to trust or to rely on another is to honor him, as these are signs that one has an opinion that the person has virtue or power. To distrust or not to believe someone is to dishonor him.

To hearken to a man's counsel or discourse of any kind is to honor him, as these are signs we think him wise, eloquent, or witty. To sleep, go forth or talk while another is talking is to dishonor him.

To do those things to another which he takes for signs of honor or which the law or custom make so, is to honor him, because in approving the honor done by others he acknowledges the power that others acknowledge. To refuse to do so is to dishonor him.

To agree with someone's opinion is to honor him, as it is a sign of approving his judgment and wisdom. To dissent is to dishonor and is to upbraid one for error. If the dissent is of many things, it is to accuse the person of folly.

To imitate is to honor, for it is to vehemently approve. To imitate one's enemy is to dishonor.

To honor those another person honors is to honor him, as it is a sign of approbation of his judgment. To honor his enemies is to dishonor him.

To employ a person in counsel or in difficult actions is to honor him, as it is a sign that one has the opinion the person has wisdom or some other power. To deny employment in these cases to someone who seeks it is to dishonor him.

All of these ways of honoring are natural, and occur within as well as outside of commonwealths. In commonwealths, however, when the one or group that has the supreme authority can make whatever they please stand for signs of honor, there are other kinds of honor.

A sovereign honors a subject with whatever title, office or employment or action that he takes himself to be a sign of his will to honor a person.

The king of Persia honored Mordecai when he appointed that he should be conducted through the streets in the king's garment, upon one of the king's horses, with a crown on his head and a prince before him proclaiming, *thus shall it be done to him that the king will honor.* Another king of Persia, or maybe the same one at another time, gave a person leave to one that demanded to wear one of the king's robes for some great service that he had done. But the king made one addition, which was that this person should wear it as the kings' fool, and then it was a dishonor. When it comes to civil honor, fountain[8] is in the person of the commonwealth, and depends on the will of the sovereign. This kind of honor is therefore temporary and is called *civil honor.* Such honors are magistracy, offices, titles, and in some places coats and painted scutcheons.[9] Men honor those that have these things as having many signs of favor in the commonwealth and this kind of favor is power.

Honorable. Honorable is whatever possession, action or quality is an argument for, or a sign of power.

Dishonorable. To be honored, loved or feared by many is honorable, for these are arguments for power. To be honored by a few or none is *dishonorable.*

Dominion and victory are honorable, because they are acquired by power. Servitude, due to need or fear, is dishonorable.

Good fortune, of lasting, is honorable as it is a sign of the favor of God. Ill fortune and losses are dishonorable. Riches are honorable, for they are power. Poverty is dishonorable. Magnanimity, liberality, hope, courage, confidence are honorable, for they proceed from the conscience[10] of power. Pusillanimity, parsimony, fear and diffidence are dishonorable.

The timely resolution or determination of what a man is to do is honorable, as it shows the contempt for small difficulties and dangers. Irresolution is dishonorable as it is a sign of valuing too much little impediments and little advantages. When a man has weighed things as long as the time permits, and still does not resolve matters, it means there is but little difference between the weights. This means he overvalues little things, which is pusillanimity.

All actions and speeches that proceed, or seem to proceed, from much experience, science, discretion or wit are honorable, for all of these are powers. Actions or words that proceed from error, ignorance or folly are dishonorable.

Gravity, to the extent it seem to proceed from a mind employed on something else, is honorable, because employment is a sign of power. But if gravity seems to proceed from the purpose to appear grave, it is dishonorable. The former gravity is like the steadiness of a ship laden with merchandise, but the latter gravity is like the steadiness of a ship ballasted with sand and other trash.

To be conspicuous, that is to say known for wealth, office great actions or any eminent good is honorable, as they are signs of the power for which the person is conspicuous. On the contrary, obscurity is dishonorable.

To be descended from conspicuous parents is honorable, because they can more easily attain the aids and friends of their ancestors. On the contrary, to be descended from obscure parents is dishonorable.

Actions proceeding from equity[11] joined with loss are honorable as signs of magnanimity, for magnanimity is a sign of power. On the contrary, craft, shifting[12], neglect of equity are dishonorable.

The covetousness of great riches and the ambition for great honors is honorable, as they are signs of the power to obtain them. The covetousness and ambition for little gains or preferments is dishonorable.

It does not alter the case whether an action is honorable, if it is just or unjust, as long as the action is great and difficult and thus displays signs of much power, for honor consists only in the opinion of power. Therefore the ancient heathens did not think they dishonored the Gods, but rather they honored them when they introduced them in their poems committing rapes, thefts, and other great, but unjust and unclean acts. Nothing is as celebrated as Jupiter in his adulteries and Mercury in his frauds and thefts. In the hymn of Homer, Mercury is given the greatest of praises in that being born in the morning, he invented music at noon, and before night, he stole away the cattle of Apollo from his herdsman.

Also until there were constituted great commonwealths, it was thought no dishonor among men to be a pirate or a highway thief. These were considered lawful trades, not only by the Greeks, but also by all other nations, as is manifest by the histories of ancient times. In this time in this part of the world, private duels are and always will be honorable, though unlawful. This will continue until such time as there shall be honor ordained to those who refuse to duel, and ignominy for those that make the challenge. Duels are many times the effects of courage, and the ground of courage is always strength or skill, which are power. But for the most part duels are the effects of rash speaking and of the fear of dishonor in one or both of the combatants, who engaged by rashness are driven into the lists to avoid disgrace.

Coats of arms. Scutcheons and hereditary coats of arms, where they have eminent privileges, are honorable. They are not so if they are not associated with eminent privileges. Their power consists either in such privileges, in riches, or in some such thing as is equally honored in other men. This kind of honor, commonly called gentry, has been derived from the ancient Germans. For this kind of thing is unknown where German customs are unknown. Nor is it now anywhere in use where Germans have not inhabited. The ancient Greek commanders had their shields painted with such devices as they pleased when they went to war. An unpainted buckler[13] was a sign of a common soldier or of poverty. But the Greeks did not transmit these designs by inheritance. The Romans transmitted the marks of their families, but only the images, and not the devices of their ancestors. There was never any such thing among the people of Asia, Africa or America. Only the Germans had this custom, and from them it derived into England, France, Spain and Italy, when in great numbers the Germans either aided the Romans or made their own conquests in these western parts of the world.

Germany, as all other countries, was in its beginning divided among an infinite number of little lords or masters of families who continually had wars with one another. These masters and lords when they were covered with arms, to the end that they might be known by their followers, and partly for ornament, painted their armor, their scutcheons, or their coats with the picture of some beast or other thing. They also put some eminent and visible mark upon the crest of their helmets. This ornament that was on the arms and on the crest descended by inheritance to their children. It was given in its pure form to the eldest and to the rest with some note of diversity, such as the old master, in Dutch, the *Here-alt*, thought fit. But when many such families joined together made a greater monarchy, this duty of the Herealt to distinguish scutcheons, was made a separate private office. The issue of these lords is the great and ancient gentry. For the most part they use marks of living creatures, noted for courage and rapine. Or they use castles, battlements, belts, weapons, bars, palisades and other notes of war, nothing being of honor except military virtue. Afterwards, not only kings, but popular commonwealths, gave diverse manners of scutcheons to those who went forth to war or returned from it, as encouragement or recompense for their services. All of this may be found by an observant reader of the ancient histories, Greek and Latin, that mention the German nation and manners in those times.

Titles of honor. Titles of *honor* such as duke, count, marquis, and baron are honorable. They signify the value set upon them by the sovereign power of the commonwealth. These titles were in old times titles of office and command, some of which come from the Romans, some from the Germans and French. *Dukes*, in Latin *duces*, are generals in war. Count, *comites*, were part of the general company out of friendship and were left to govern and defend conquered and pacified places. Marquises, *marchiones*, were counts that governed the marches or boundaries of the empire. The titles of duke, count, and marquis came into the empire about the time of Constantine the Great from the customs of the German *militia*. But baron seems to have been a title of the Gauls and signifies a great man. These were the king's or prince's men, whom they employed in war about their persons. Baron seems to be derived from *vir* to *ber* and *bar*, that signified the same in the language of the Gauls. So *vir* in Latin became *bero* and *baro*, and such men were called *berones*, and after *barones*, and in Spanish, *varones*. But those that would know more particularly about the origin of titles may find that as I did in Mr. Selden's most excellent treatise on the subject.[14] In the process of time these offices of honor, became the occasion of trouble, and so for reasons of good and peaceable government, were turned into mere titles. They served for the most part to distinguish the precedence, place and order of subjects in the commonwealth. Men were made dukes, counts, marquises and barons of places that they neither possessed nor commanded. Other titles also were devised to the same end.

Worthiness. Fitness. WORTHINESS is something different than the worth, value, merit or desert of a man. It consists in a particular power or ability for which he is said to be worthy. The particular ability is usually named FITNESS or *aptitude.*

The one who is worthiest to be a commander, or a judge or have any other charge is the person that is best fitted with the qualities required to discharge the particular office. The worthiest person for riches is the one that has the qualities most requisite for using them well. If one of these qualities is absent, one may nevertheless be valuable for something else. A man may be worthy of riches, office and employment and nevertheless can plead no right to have it before another. He cannot be said to merit or deserve it. For merit presupposes a right, and that the thing deserved is due by a promise. I shall say more about this later when I shall speak of contracts.15

Endnotes

1. To consider it generally
2. Being a noble, an aristocrat
3. Good manners
4. Diligent
5. Any useful thing
6. Appropriate without a just claim
7. Disdain
8 . The source
9. Shields
10. Realization
11. Fairness
12. Being shifty
13. Shield
14. Hobbes is referring to the book, *Titles of Honor* by John Selden.
15. Hobbers discusses contracts in chapter 14.

CHAPTER 11

Of the Difference of Manners

What is here meant by manners. By MANNERS I do not mean the decency of behavior, such as how one should salute another or how a man should wash his mouth or pick his teeth before company or such other points of *small morals*. What I do mean are those qualities of mankind that concern their living together in peace and unity. To this end we should consider that felicity in this life does not consist in the repose of a satisfied mind. There is no such *finis ultimus,* utmost aim, nor *summum bonum,* greatest good, as is spoken of in the books of the old moral philosophers. A man can no more live when his desires are at an end, than he can when his senses and imagination are at a stand.[1] Felicity is the continual progress of desire from one object to another, where attaining the first object is just the way to the next one. The cause of this is that the object of a man's desire is not to enjoy it only once and for one instant of time, but to assure it forever, as a way to his satisfy future desires. The voluntary actions and inclinations of all men tend not just to the procuring, but also to the assuring of a contented life. The actions and inclinations differ only in diverse men by the way they arise from different passions, and partly from the difference between people in their knowledge or opinion they have of the causes which produce the desired effect.

A restless desire of power in all men. So that in the first place, I put for a general inclination of all mankind, a perpetual and restless desire of power after power that ceases only in death. The cause of this is not always that a man hopes for a more intensive delight than he has already attained, or that he cannot be content with moderate power. Rather, it is because a man cannot assure the power and means to live well, which he might have at present, without the acquisition of more. That is why kings, whose power is the greatest, turn their endeavors to assuring it at home by laws and abroad by wars. When that is done, a new desire arises. In some it is the fame from new conquest. In others it is the desire of ease and sensual pleasure, and in others, it is a desire for admiration or being flattered for excellence in some art or other ability of the mind.

Love of contention from competition. Competition for riches, honor, command and other power inclines people to contention, enmity and war, because the way that one competitor has of attaining his desire is to kill, subdue, supplant or repel the other. In particular, competition for praise inclines people to a reverence for antiquity.[2] Men contend with the living and not with the dead in order to obscure the glory of others and thus will be ascribed more praise than is their due.

Civil obedience from love of ease. From fear of death or wounds. Desire of ease and sensual delight disposes men to obey a common power. Due to these desires, a man abandons the protection that he might hope for from his own industry and labor. Fear of death and wounds disposes men also to obey a common power, and for the same reason. But on the contrary, needy and hardy men and those ambitious of military command who are not contented with their present condition are inclined to stir up the cause of war and to stir up trouble and sedition. There is no military honor but from war, nor do they have any such hope of mending an ill game, but by causing a new shuffle.

And from love of the arts. The desire for knowledge and the arts of peace inclines men to obey a common power. These desires contain a desire for leisure, and consequently, the protection from some other power than their own.

Love of virtue from love of praise. The desire for praise disposes men to do laudable actions that will please those whose judgment they value. But for those men whom we contemn,[3] we also contemn their praise. The desire for fame after death does the same. It may be that after one's death there is no sense[4] of the praise that is being given us on earth as these joys are either swallowed up by the unspeakable joys of Heaven, or are extinguished in the extreme torments of hell. Nevertheless, the desire for such fame is not vain, because men have a present delight from it, from the foresight of it, and from the benefit that may redound from it to their posterity. They may not see this now, yet they can imagine it, and anything that is pleasure to the sense is also a pleasure in the imagination.

Hate, from difficulty of requiting great benefits. To receive from someone that we think is equal to ourselves a greater benefit than we can hope to requite[5] disposes us to counterfeit love which is actually secret hatred. This puts a man into the state of a desperate debtor that in declining to see his creditor tacitly wishes he would be somewhere where he might never see him again. For benefits oblige us, and obligation is thralldom,[6] and unrequitable obligation is perpetual thralldom, and that makes us hate our equal. But to have received benefits from one that we acknowledge to be superior, inclines us to love, because the obligation is not a new depression.[7] The cheerful acceptance which is generally taken for retribution[8] for such an honor done to the obliger[9] is what men call *gratitude*. To receive benefits from an equal or inferior disposes one to love as long as there is hope of requital. In this case in the intention of the receiver there is the obligation of aid and mutual service. When there is an emulation of who shall exceed whom in benefiting, there is the most noble and profitable possible contention. The victor is pleased with his victory and the other is revenged by confessing it.

And from conscience of deserving to be hated. To have done more hurt to a man than he can or is willing to expiate, inclines the doer to hate the sufferer. For the doer must expect revenge or forgiveness, both of which are hateful.

Promptness to hurt, from fear. Fear of oppression disposes a man to anticipate or to seek aid from society. There is no other way by which by which a man can secure his life and liberty.

And from distrust of their own wit. Men that distrust their own subtlety are in times of tumult and sedition better disposed for victory than those that suppose themselves to be wise and crafty. The former love to consult, but the latter strike first, fearing to be circumvented. In sedition men are always in the precincts of battle, and so to hold together and use all the advantages of force is a better strategy than any that proceeds from the subtlety of wit.

Vain undertaking from vain-glory. Vain-glorious men who are not conscious of themselves having great sufficiency, still delight in supposing themselves to be gallant men. They are inclined, though, just to ostentation, but not to attempt anything, because when danger or difficulty appears, they do not look for ways to have their insufficiency discovered.

Vain glorious men are inclined to rash engaging who estimate their sufficiency by the flattery of other men or the fortune of some precedent action without the assured ground of hope from some true knowledge of themselves. When danger or difficulty approach, they retire if they can. When they do not see the way to safety, they would rather hazard their honor which may be salved with an excuse than hazard their lives, for which no salve is sufficient.

Ambition, from opinion of sufficiency. Men that have a strong opinion of their own wisdom in matters of government are disposed to ambition. Without public employment in council or magistracy, the honor of their wisdom is lost. Therefore, eloquent speakers are inclined to ambition, for eloquences seems to be wisdom, both to themselves and others.

Irresolution, from too great valuing of small matters. Pusillanimity disposes men to irresolution, and consequently to lose the occasions and fittest opportunities for action. After men have been deliberating until the time of action approaches, if it is not manifest then what is best to be done, then that is a sign that the differences of motives, this way and that, are not great. To not make a resolution of the issue then is to lose the occasion to act by the weighing of trifles, and this is pusillanimity.

Frugality which is a virtue in poor men, makes a man unapt to achieve such actions that require the strength of many men at once. Frugality weakens men's endeavor which should be nourished and kept in vigor by reward.

Confidence in others, from ignorance of the marks of wisdom and kindness. Eloquence, with flattery, disposes men to confide in those that have it. Eloquence is seeming wisdom and flattery is seeming kindness. If military reputation is added to them, it disposes men to adhere and subject themselves to the men that have these qualities. Eloquence and flattery show people that there is no danger to them from the one who has these qualities. Military reputation shows people that there will not be danger from others.

And from ignorance of natural causes. The lack of science which is the ignorance of causes disposes, or rather constrains, a man to rely on the advice and authority of others. For men who are concerned with the truth, if they do not rely on their own opinion, must rely on the opinion of some other that they think is wiser than themselves and do not see why this person would deceive them.

And from want of understanding. The ignorance of the signification of words which is a lack of understanding disposes men to take on trust, not only what they do not know, but also nonsense and actual errors. Neither errors nor nonsense can be detected without a perfect understanding of words.

It follows from this that men give different names to one and the same thing, because of the difference of their own passions. Those that approve of a private opinion, call it an opinion, but those that do not like it, call it heresy. 'Heresy' signifies nothing more than a private opinion, but it does have a greater tincture of choler.

It also follows that men cannot distinguish, without study and great understanding, between one action of many men and many actions of a multitude. An example of this is the difference between one action of all of the senators of Rome in killing Catiline, and the many actions of a number of senators in killing Caesar. Therefore people are disposed to consider the action of the people what is actually a multitude of actions done by a multitude of men, that were led perhaps by persuasion of one man.

Adherence to custom, from ignorance of the nature of right and wrong. The ignorance of the causes and original constitution of right, equity, law and justices disposes a man to make custom and example the rule of his actions. In this way a man will think that something is unjust which it has only been the custom to punish. A man will also think something to be just when he can produce an example of it being considered with impunity and approbation. Lawyers who only use this false measure of justice barbarously call this kind of thing a precedent. They are like little children that have no other rule of good and evil manners, except the correction they received from their parents and masters. The difference is that children constantly adhere to this rule, whereas adults do not. When people grow old and stubborn, they appeal from custom to reason and from reason to custom as it serves their turn. They recede from custom when their interest requires it, and set themselves against reason as often as reason is against them. This is the cause that the doctrines of what is right and wrong are perpetually disputed, both by the pen and the sword, when this is not the case with the doctrines concerning lines and figures. Men do not really care what is the truth about lines and figures because it does not affect a man's ambition, profit or lust. I do not doubt but if it had been a thing contrary to the interest or right of some man's dominion *that the three angles of a triangle should be equal to the two angles of a square,* then he would have disputed it, and suppressed it by burning all of the books of geometry if he as able to do so.

Adherence to private men, from ignorance of the causes of peace. The ignorance of remote causes disposes men to attribute all events to immediate and instrumental causes, for these are the causes they perceive. That is why in all places men that are grieved by the payments they have to make, discharge their anger upon the publicans,[10] that is to say, on collectors, officers and other farmers of the public revenue. People adhere to those that find fault with public government, and when they have engaged themselves beyond the hope of justification, they fall also upon the supreme authority, out of fear of punishment or shame of receiving pardon.

Credulity, from ignorance of nature. The ignorance of natural causes disposes a man to credulity, so that the man many times believes impossibilities. These men are unable to detect impossibilities, and so as far as they know, the impossibilities may be true. Because men like to be hearkened to in company, credulity disposes men to lying. Ignorance itself is without malice, but it is able to both make a man believe lies and tell them, and sometimes also to invent them.

Curiosity to know, from care of future time. The anxiety for the future time disposes a man to inquire into the causes of things, because the knowledge of them makes men better able to order the present to their best advantage.

Natural religion from the same. Curiosity, or the love of knowledge of causes, draws a man from the consideration of an effect to seek the cause, again, the cause of that cause. Out of necessity then, he must at last come to the thought that there is some cause that has no prior cause, but is eternal. That is what men call God. It is impossible to make any profound inquiry into natural causes without being inclined to believe there is one eternal God, even though people cannot have any idea in their mind that is answerable to His nature. In the same way a man that is born blind, hearing men talk of warming themselves by the fire and being warmed himself by it, may easily conceive and assure himself that there is something there which men call *fire* and that it is the cause of the heat he feels. But this man cannot imagine what it is like nor have any idea in his mind like the people have who see it. So it is that a man may conceive there is a cause of the visible things in the world and of their admirable order, which men call God, and yet not have an idea or image of Him in his mind.

Those that make little or no inquiry into the natural causes of things still have a fear that proceeds from ignorance itself are inclined to feign to themselves several kinds of invisible power that have the power to do them much good or harm. They thus stand in awe of their own imaginations, and in time of distress they invoke these invisible powers. Also, in times of an expected good success, they give them thanks, and thus make gods from the creatures of their own fancy. Because of this, men have created in the world innumerable sorts of gods from the innumerable varieties of their fancies. This fear of invisible things is the natural seed of that which everyone calls religion. When people worship or fear a different power than the one they do, they call it superstition.

This seed of religion has been observed by many. Some of those that have observed it, have been inclined to nourish, dress and form it into laws. They have also added their own invention opinions about the causes of future events by which they thought would aid them to best govern others and to make for themselves the greatest use of their powers.

Endnotes

1. Standstill
2. Hobbes is referring here to those who will come after us, not those who preceded us.
3. Disdain
4. Awareness
5. Reciprocate
6. Slavery
7. Oppression
8. In reciprocity
9. A person who places himself under obligation
10. Tax collectors

CHAPTER 12

Of Religion

Religion in man only. There are no signs nor fruit of *religion* except in man, and thereis no cause to doubt but that the seed of *religion* is also only in man. It consists in some peculiar quality or in some eminent degree of this quality, not to be found in any other living creature.

First, from his desire of knowing causes. First, it is peculiar to the nature of man, some more, some less, to be inquisitive into the causes of the events they see. All men, however, are curious to search for the causes of their own good or evil fortune.

From the consideration of the beginning of things. Second, when men see that something had a beginning, they think also that it had a cause which determined the thing to begin when it did, rather than sooner or later.

From his observation of the sequel of things. Third, there is no felicity in beasts except the enjoying of their quotidian food, ease and lusts, as they have little or no foresight of the time to come. They lack observation and memory of the order, consequence and dependence of the things that they see. But men observe how one event has been produced by another and they remember their antecedents and consequences. When men cannot assure themselves of the true causes of things (for the causes of good and evil fortune for the most part are invisible), they suppose causes for them. These causes derive from the suggestions of their own fancies, or from their trust in the authority of other men they think are their friends or are wiser than themselves.

The natural cause of religion, the anxiety of the time to come. The above first two points cause anxiety. People are assured that there are causes of all things that have arrived so far or shall arrive hereafter. It is impossible for a man not to be in perpetual solicitude of the time to come when they continually endeavor to secure for themselves against the evil they fear, and procure the good they desire. So every man, and especially those that are over provident[1] are in a state like that of Prometheus. Prometheus, who has been interpreted as *the prudent man,* was bound to the hill Caucasus, a place of large prospect, where an eagle fed on his liver and devoured in the day as much as was repaired in the night. In the same way a man who looks too far before him in the care of future time, has his heart gnawed on by the fear of death all day long, and has no repose nor pause from anxiety, except in sleep.

Which makes them fear the power of invisible things. The perpetual fear that always accompanies mankind in their ignorance of causes as if they were always in the dark, must have something as an object to be afraid of. When there is nothing to be seen, then there is nothing to accuse of being the cause of either good or evil fortune, except some *power* or *invisible* agent. In this sense perhaps some of the old poets said that the gods were at first created by human fear. When this is spoken of the gods, or of the many gods, of the Gentiles, it is very true. However, the acknowledgment of one God, that is eternal, infinite and omnipotent more simply derives from the desire that men have to know the causes of natural bodies and their several virtues and operations than from the fear of what was to befall men in the time to come. Anyone that from an effect that he sees, reasons to its immediate cause, and then to the cause of that cause, will at last come to conclude that there must be one first mover, as even the heathen philosophers confessed. That is, there must be a first and an eternal cause of all things, which is that which men mean by the name of God. This kind of reasoning does not derive from thoughts about men's fortunes. When people are solicitous of their fortune, it both inclines them to fear and hinders them from the search of the causes of other things. This provides the occasion of the feigning as many gods as there are men that feign them.

And suppose them incorporeal. As far as fancying the matter or substance of the invisible agents, by natural cogitation, men just fell upon the conceit, that the substance must be the same as the soul of man. The soul of man was the same substance that appeared in a dream to one who slept, or appeared in a looking-glass to one that is awake. When men do not know that such apparitions are just creatures of the fancy, they think them to be real and external substances that they call ghosts. The Latins called them *imagines* and *umbra,* and thought them to be spirits, which were thin, aerial bodies. The invisible agents, which they feared, they thought to be like these apparitions, except that the spirits appear and vanish when they please. The opinion that such spirits were incorporeal or immaterial could never enter into the mind of any man by nature. Even though men may put together words of contradictory signification, such as *spirit* and *incorporeal,* they could not imagine any thing answering to these words. Therefore, the men who upon their own meditation arrived at the acknowledgement of one infinite, omnipotent and eternal God, chose to confess that He is incomprehensible and above their understanding. They did this rather than define His nature as a *spirit incorporeal,* and then confess that this definition is unintelligible. If they did give Him such a title, it was not *dogmatically,* with the intention of making the divine nature something that can be understood. The rather gave this title *piously,* to honor Him with the attributes of significations as remote as they can be from the grossness of visible bodies.

But know not the way how they effect any thing. Men did not know how these invisible agents wrought their effects. They did not know what immediate causes they used in bringing things to pass, which is called *causing.* Almost all men have no other rule to guess what will happen except by observing and remembering what they have seen to precede the like effect at some other time or prior times. They do not see any dependence or connection between the antecedent and the consequent events.[2] That is why people expect from the similarity of past things, similar things will occur. Men superstitiously hope for good or evil luck from things that have no part at all in the actual causing of some event. For example, the Athenians demanded another Phormio for their war at Lepanto, and the Pompeian faction wanted another Scipio for their war in Africa. Others have done the same thing in diverse occasions ever since. In a like manner, people attribute their fortune to a bystander, to a lucky or unlucky place, to spoken words, especially if the name of God is among them. They believe that the liturgy of witches, by charming and conjuring, has the power to turn a stone into bread, bread into a man, or any thing into any thing.

But honor them as they honor men. Third, the way that people naturally worship the invisible powers are provided by the same expressions of reverence that they would use towards other men. They use gifts, petitions, thanks, submission of the body, considerate addresses, sober behavior, premeditated words and swearing which is assuring one another of their promises by invoking the other men. Reason suggests nothing beyond these expressions, or else people rely on those they believe wiser than themselves to provide further ceremonies.

And attribute to them all extraordinary events. The last point is to consider how these invisible powers declare to men the things that shall come to pass, especially concerning their good or evil fortune in general, or good or ill success in some particular undertaking. Men are at a stand[3] on this issue. The only thing they can do is conjecture of the time to come based on past time. They also take casual things, after one or two encounters, as prognosticators for similar encounters ever after. They also believe similar prognostications from other men about whom they once conceived a good opinion.

Four things, natural seeds of religion. *The natural seeds of* religion *consists of these four things: the opinions about ghosts, the ignorance of* *second causes, devotion towards what men fear and considering casual things to be prognostics. Because of the different fancies, judgments and passions of men, these seeds have grown into ceremonies that are so different, that those which are used by one man are for the most part ridiculous to another.*

Made different by culture. These seeds have been cultured by two sorts of men. One sort of men have nourished and ordered them according to their own invention. The other kind have done it by God's commandment and direction. Both sorts of men, however, have done it with the purpose to make those that relied on them more apt to obedience, laws, peace, charity and civil society. The religion of the former sort is a part of human politics and teaches part of the duty which earthly kings require of their subjects. The religion of the latter sort is divine politics that contains precepts to those that have yielded themselves as subjects in the kingdom of God. Of the former sort were all the founders of commonwealths and law-givers of the Gentiles. Of the latter sort were Abraham, Moses and our blessed Savior, who have given us the laws of the kingdom of God.

The absurd opinion of Gentilism. For that part of religion that consists of opinions concerning the nature of invisible powers, there is almost nothing that has a name that has not been esteemed by the Gentiles to be a god or a devil in one place or another. Their poets have also feigned these things to be animated, inhabited or possessed by some spirit or other.

The unformed matter of the world was a god that had the name Chaos.

They considered the heaven, the ocean, the planets, fire, the earth and the winds to be so many gods.

Men, women, a bird, a crocodile, a calf, a dog, a snake, an onion, and a leek were deified. Besides they fill almost all places with spirits they called *demons*. The filled the plains with Pan, Panises or Satyrs, the woods with Fawns and Nymphs, and the sea with Tritons and other Nymphs. They filled every river and fountain with a ghost of its name and also with Nymphs. They filled every house with its *Lares* or familiars, every man with his *Genius,* hell with ghosts and spiritual officers such as Charon, Cerberus and the Furies. In the night time they filled all places with *larvoe, lumures,* the ghosts of deceased men and also a whole kingdom of fairies and bugbears. They have also ascribed divinity and built temples to mere accidents or qualities, such as time, night, day, peace, concord, love, contention, virtue, honor, health, rust, fever, and the like. They prayed for and against these things as if they were ghosts of those names that were hanging over their heads, who would let fall or withhold the good or evil for which they prayed. They invoked their own wit by the name of the Muses, their own ignorance by the name of Fortune, their own lusts by the name of Cupid, their own rage by the name of the Furies, and their own privy members by the name of Priapus. They attributed their own pollutions to Incubi and Succubae. There was nothing which a poet might introduce as a person in his poem which they did not make either a *god* or a *devil*.

The same authors of the religions of the Gentiles also used the second ground for religion, which is men's ignorance of causes. The aptness of people to attribute their fortune to causes for which there was no dependence that was apparent, gave the poets an opportunity to obtrude[4] on people's ignorance a kind of second and ministerial god instead of a second cause. Thus, they ascribed the cause of fecundity to Venus, the cause of arts to Apollo, of subtlety and craft to Mercury, of tempest and storms to Aeolus, and other effects to other gods. Among the heathens there was almost as great a variety of gods as there were different kinds of business.

The same legislators of the Gentiles added images, both in picture and sculpture, to the worship that men naturally conceived to be used to towards their gods in the forms of oblations,[5] prayers, thanks and the rest. The more ignorant sort of people, that is the most part or generality of men, think that the gods whose representations they made were really included in them and were housed within them, and they stood that much more in fear of them. They endowed the representations with lands, houses and officers and revenues that were set apart from all human uses. They consecrated and made holy to their idols caverns, groves, woods, mountains and whole islands. They attributed to these idols not only the shapes of men, but also of beasts and monsters. They gave them the faculties and passions of men and beasts, such as sense, speech, sex, lust, and generation. They not only had the gods mixing with one another to propagate kinds of gods, but they also had them mixing with men and women to beget mongrel gods, as did the inmates of heaven, Bacchus, Hercules and others. Besides having the passions of living creatures such as anger, revenge, and other passions, they also said the gods performed the actions following such passions, such as fraud, theft, adultery, sodomy and any vice that may be taken as an effect of power, or a cause of pleasure. All of these vices are considered among men to be against the law, rather than against honor.

Last, the same authors of the religion of the Gentiles used the prognostics of time to come. These are naturally just conjectures based upon experiences of past time and in supernatural cases, experiences of divine revelation. But these authors, partly by pretended experiences and partly on pretended revelation, added innumerable other superstitious ways of divination. They made men believe they could find their fortunes sometimes in the ambiguous and senseless answers of the priests at Delphi, Delos, Ammon and other famous oracles. Their answers were made ambiguous by design to own[6] the event both ways. Sometimes their words were absurd because of the intoxicating vapor or the place, which frequently occurs in sulphurous caverns. Sometimes the absurd words were caused by leaves, as in the case of the Sybils, whose prophecies were in books of some reputation in the time of Roman republic. This is like those perhaps of Nostradamus as the fragments now extant of their books seem to be the invention of later times. Sometimes the prophecies or theomancy were based on the insignificant[7] speeches of madmen who were supposed to be possessed with a divine spirit, which is called enthusiasm, and were supposed to foretell events. Sometimes the signs of future events were taken to be the aspect of the stars at the time of their nativity, which was called horoscopy and was esteemed as a part of judiciary astrology. Sometimes the signs were their own hopes and fears which is called thumomancy, or presage. Sometimes the prognostics were the prediction of witches that pretended to have conferences with the dead. This is called necromancy, conjury and witchcraft and if but juggling and confederate knavery. Sometimes the signs are the casual flight or feeding of birds called augury. Sometimes it is in the entrails of a sacrificed beast which was called *aruspicina*. Sometimes the signs were in dreams, and sometimes in the croaking of ravens or the chattering of birds. Sometimes the signs were the lineaments of the face, which was called metoposcopy, or by the lines of the hands, called palmistry, or in casual words called, *omina*. Sometimes the signs were monsters or unusual accidents, such as eclipses, comets, rare meteors, earthquakes, inundations, uncouth birds and the like. They called these *portenta* and *ostenta*, because they thought them to portend or foreshow some great calamity to come. Sometimes the signs were a mere lottery, as cross and pile, counting holes in a sieve, dipping into the verses in Homer and Virgil, and innumerable other such vain conceits. It is so easy for men to be drawn to believe anything from the men that that have gained some credit with them and who can with gentleness and dexterity take hold of their fear and ignorance.

The designs of the authors of the religion of the heathen. The first founders and legislators of commonwealths among the Gentiles had the ends of keeping the people in obedience and peace and so have in all places taken care to do a number of things. First, to imprint in peoples' minds the belief that the precepts that the founders gave concerning religion should not be thought to proceed from their own devices, but are the dictates of some god or spirit. Sometimes the founders claimed that they themselves were of a higher nature than mere mortals, so that their laws might be more easily received. Thus, Numa Pomipilius pretended that the ceremonies he instituted among the Romans were received from the nymph, Egeria. The first king and founder of the kingdom of Peru pretended that he and his wife were the children of the Sun. When Mahomet set up his new religion, he pretended to have conferences with the Holy Ghost, in the form of a dove. Second, the founders took care to make it believed that the same things that were displeasing to the gods were forbidden by the laws. Third, they prescribed ceremonies, supplications, sacrifices and festivals which people were to believe might appease the anger of the gods. They made the people believe that ill success in war, great contagions of sickness, earthquakes and each man's private misery came from the anger of the gods. This anger resulted from the neglect of their worship, or the forgetting or mistaking of some point of the required ceremonies. Among the ancient Romans men were not forbidden to deny what the poets had written about the pains and pleasures of the afterlife. Even though diverse people of great authority and gravity in Rome openly derided these beliefs in their harangues; still, those beliefs were more cherished than the contrary.

By these and other institutions, the founders of commonwealths obtained to accomplish their end, which was the peace of the commonwealth. The common people were less apt to mutiny against their governors when they were encouraged to lay the fault of their misfortunes on the neglect or error in their ceremonies, or in their own disobedience to the laws. The people were entertained with the pomp and pastime of festivals and public games made in honor of the gods. They then needed nothing else but bread to keep them from discontent, murmuring and commotion against the state. The Romans who had conquered the greatest part of the then known world, only tolerated any religion in the city of Rome itself that had something in it that was consistent with their own civil government. The only religion that was forbidden in Rome was that of the Jews. They thought it was unlawful to acknowledge subjection to any moral king or state as they thought they were a peculiar[8] part of the Kingdom of God. From this you can see how the religion of the Gentiles was part of their policy.

The true religion and the laws of God's kingdom the same. Where God Himself, by supernatural revelation, planted religion, He also made to Himself a peculiar kingdom. He gave laws, not only for behavior to Himself, but also towards one another. Therefore, in the kingdom of God, policy and civil laws are a part of religion. The distinction between temporal and spiritual domination has no place there. It is true that God is king of all the earth. Still, He may be the king of a peculiar and chosen nation. There is no more incongruity in this than when a general has command of an entire army, should also have a peculiar regiment or company of his own. God is the king of all the earth by His power, but He is king of his chosen people by covenant. I have assigned another place in the following discourse to speak more about the kingdom of God, both by nature and covenant.[9]

The causes of change in religion. From the propagation of religion, it is not hard to understand the causes of religion's resolutions into its first seeds or principles. They are just an opinion about a deity and invisible and supernatural powers. Religion can never be abolished out of human nature. An attempt to abolish religion would just lead to new religions springing out of the old ones, by the culture of such men that would use it for purposes of reputation.

All formed religion is founded at first upon the faith which a multitude has in some one person. They believe this person not only to be a wise man who labors to procure their happiness, but also to be a holy man to whom God Himself vouchsafes to supernaturally declare His will. It follows then that in a case where religion is used to establish a government, and when the wisdom, sincerity and love of those who

established it becomes suspected and the founders are unable to show
any probable token of divine revelation, then the religion they desire to
uphold will also be suspected. If there is no fear of the civil sword, the
religion will be contradicted and rejected.

Enjoining[10] *belief of impossibilities.* Whatever takes away the reputation of the one that formed a religion, or adds to when it is already
formed, is the enjoining of a belief of contradictories. Both parts of a
contradiction cannot possibly be true, and therefore to enjoin a belief in
them is an argument from ignorance. This will serve to detect that such
an offer who recommends this is to be discredited in all the other things
he shall propound as deriving from supernatural revelation. A man may
indeed have revelation of many things above, but not of anything that is
against natural reason.

Doing contrary to the religion they establish. What takes away the
reputation of sincerity is the doing or saying such things that appear to
be signs that what some people require other men to believe is not
believed by themselves. All of these doings and saying are therefore
called scandalous, because they are stumbling blocks that make men fall
as regards to religion. The same is true for injustice, cruelty, profaneness,
avarice and luxury. Who can believe that those who do actions that proceed from any of these roots, believes that there are invisible powers to
be feared, even when they try to frighten other men for lesser faults, by
referring to the same invisible powers?

What takes away the reputation of love is being detected of having
private ends. This occurs when the belief that the founders require of
others conduces, or seems to conduce, the acquisition of dominion,
riches, dignity, or secure pleasure to only or especially themselves. That
which men use to reap benefit to themselves, they are thought to do so
for their own sakes, and not for the love of others.

Want of the testimony of miracles. The testimony that men can render for divine calling can only be the operation of miracles, or of true
prophecy, which is also a miracle, or extraordinary felicity. Some points
of religion have been received from those that did such miracles. When
others try to add to these points, but do not have the basis of other miracles, these others obtain no greater belief than what the customs and
laws of the places in which they have been educated have brought
them. In natural things, men of judgment require natural signs and
arguments. But in supernatural things, they require supernatural signs,
which are miracles, before they will consent inwardly and from their
hearts.

The causes of weakening of men's faith manifestly appear in the following examples. First is the example of the children of Israel. When Moses was absent for but forty days, even though they had approved his calling to them by miracles and by their happy conduct of out of Egypt, they revolted from the worship of the true God recommended to them by Moses. They set up (*Exodus*, 23.1,2) a golden calf for their god, and relapsed into the idolatry of the Egyptians from whom they had been so lately delivered. Again, after Moses, Aaron, Joshua and that generation which had seen the great works of God in Israel were dead (*Judges*, 2.11), another generation arose that served Baal. So when miracles failed, faith also failed.

Again, when the sons of Samuel (1 *Samuel*, 8.3) who were constituted by their fathers to be judges in Bersabee received bribes and judged unjustly, the people of Israel refused any more to have God be their king in any other manner than he was a king to other people. They therefore cried out to Samuel to choose a king for them after the manner of other nations. So when justice failed, faith also failed, to the extent they deposed God from reigning over them.

But in the planting of the Christian religion, the oracles ceased in all parts of the Roman empire, and the number of Christians increased wonderfully every day and in every place by the preaching of the Apostles and Evangelists. A great part of that success may be reasonably attributed to the contempt that the priests of the Gentiles of that time had brought upon themselves by their uncleanness, avarice and juggling between princes. Also, the religion of the church of Rome was partly, for the same cause, abolished in England in many other parts of Christendom. This was partly the failing of virtue in the pastors that made faith fail in the people. Another part of this was due to bringing the philosophy and doctrine of Aristotle into religion by the Schoolmen. This introduction of Aristotle brought so many contradictions and absurdities, that it brought the reputation of ignorance and fraudulent intention to the clergy. This inclined the people to revolt against them, either against the will of their own princes, as in France and Holland, or with their will, as in England.

Lastly, there were so many of the points declared by the church of Rome that were declared necessary for salvation that were manifestly to the advantage of the Pope and of his spiritual subjects, residing in the territories of other Christian princes. Were it not for the mutual emulation of these princes, they might have without war or trouble, have excluded all foreign authority, as easily as it has been excluded in England. For who does not see to whose benefit it conduces to have it believed that a king has no authority from Christ, unless a bishop crown him? Or that king, if he is a priest, cannot marry? That whether a prince be born in a lawful marriage or not, must be judged by authority from Rome? That subjects may be freed from their allegiance if the king is judged a heretic by the court of Rome? That a king, for example Chilperic of France, may be deposed by a pope, for example Pope Zachary, for no cause and his kingdom be given to one of his subjects? That the clergy and regulars[11] in any country shall be exempt from the jurisdiction of their king in criminal cases? Or who does not see to whose profit redounds the fees of private masses and the vales of purgatory? These and other signs of private interest would be enough to mortify the most lively faith, if as I said, the civil magistrates and customs did not sustain them more than did the sanctity, wisdom and probity of the religion's supposed teachers. I attribute all the changes in the religions in the world to one and the same cause, and that is to unpleasing priests. This occurs not only among Catholics, but even in that church that has most presumed to be reformed.[12]

Endnotes

1. People who are concerned to provide for the future.
2. This sentence anticipates David Hume's later critique of the concept of causation.
3. Not being swayed by any particular view.
4. Put forth
5. Offerings
6. Predict
7. Meaningless
8. Special
9. Chapter 35
10. Prescribing
11. Laity
12. There are many possible Protestant religions that may be the target of this particular Hobbesian gibe. Hobbes did not overlook many occasions for criticizing official religions.

CHAPTER 13

Of the Natural Condition of Mankind as Concerning Their Felicity and Misery

Men by nature equal. Nature has made men quite equal in the faculties of body and mind. Though some man may be found to be manifestly stronger of body or quicker of mind than another, yet when all is reckoned together, the difference between man and man is not so considerable that one man can claim to himself a benefit to which another many not pretend[1] as well. Considering strength of body, the weakest has strength enough to kill the strongest, either by secret machination, or by means of confederacy with others that are in the same danger.

In considering the faculties of the mind, we can set aside the arts grounded up on words and especially the skill of proceeding upon general and infallible rules called science. Very few men have this and for very few things, as science is not a native faculty born with us. But I find a greater equality among men in prudence, which is attained while we look after something else, than in strength. Prudence is but experience that equal time equally bestows on all men in those things they apply themselves equally to. What makes this kind of equality incredible is the vain conceit concerning one's own wisdom. Almost all men think they have wisdom in a greater degree than do the vulgar. They have this opinion of themselves compared to all men. The only exceptions are a few others who they approve of for being famous or concurring with themselves. It is the nature of men that even though they may acknowledge that many others are more witty, or more eloquent or more learned, they will hardly believe these others are as wise as themselves. The reason is *all men are the same* [handwritten annotation]

that they see their own wit at hand, and other men's at a distance. This proves that men are in this point equal, rather than unequal. There is ordinarily no greater sign of the equal distribution of any thing but that every man is contented with his share.

From equality proceeds diffidence.[2] From the equality of ability arises the equality of hope in attaining our ends. If any two men desire the same thing, which nevertheless they cannot both enjoy, they become enemies. In trying to attain their end, which is principally their own conservation, but sometimes it is only their delectation, men will endeavor to destroy or subdue one another. So when an invader has no more to fear than the other man's single power, if this single man has planted, sown, built or possessed some convenient seat,[3] others probably may be expected to come prepared with united forces to dispossess and deprive him, not only of the fruit of his labor, but also of his life and liberty. The invaders then will be in like danger of other invaders.

From diffidence to war. From this diffidence of one another, the most reasonable way for a man to secure himself is by anticipation. That means to use force or wiles to master the persons of all other men that can, as long and as until he sees no other power great enough to endanger himself. This is no more than his own conservation requires, and this is generally allowed. Also, there are some people that take pleasure in contemplating their own power in acts of conquest, which they pursue farther than their security requires. Others who would be glad to be at ease within modest bounds, if they would not be able to increase their power by invasion, they would not be able to subsist very long just by only standing still for their defense. As a result, the augmentation of dominion over other men is necessary to a man's conservation, and so it ought to be allowed to him.

Also, men have no pleasure, but to the contrary have a great deal of grief, in keeping company when there is no power able to over-awe them all. Every man looks that his companions should value him at the same rate he sets upon himself. So upon any sign of contempt or undervaluing by others, men will naturally endeavor, as far as they may dare, to extort a greater value from their contemners by damage, and from others, by this example. Among those that have no common power to keep everyone quiet, this is enough to make people destroy each other.

So, in the nature of man, we find three principal causes of quarrel. First, competition, second, diffidence, and third, glory.

The first makes men invade for gain, the second, for safety and the third, for reputation. The first uses violence to make people masters of other men's person, wives, children and cattle. The second uses violence to defend these things. The third uses violence for trifles, such as a word or a smile, or a different opinion or any other sign of being undervalued, either direct or indirect in their person, or by reflection in their kin, their friends, their nation, their profession, or their name.

Out of civil states, there is always war of every one against every one. So it is manifest that during the time that men live without a common power to keep them all in awe, they are in that condition which is called war. This war is every man against every other man. WAR consists not only in battle or the act of fighting, but also in the tract of time when it is sufficiently known that there is the will to contend in battle. The notion of *time* is to be considered in the nature of war as it is in the nature of weather.

The nature of foul weather does not lie in a shower or two of rain, but in the inclination of rain for many days together. In the same way the nature of war consists not in actual fighting, but in the known disposition to fight, during all the time there is no assurance of the contrary. All other time is PEACE.

The incommodities of such a war. Whatever is the case in a time of war, where every man is an enemy to every man, the same is true when men live without any other security besides what can be gained by their own strength and invention. In such a condition there is no industry, because its fruit would be uncertain. There is no culture of the earth, no navigation, nor use of the commodities that may be imported by sea. There is no commodious building, no instruments of moving and removing those things that require much force. There is no knowledge of the face of the earth, no account of time, no arts, no letters and no society. Worst of all there is continual fear and danger of violent death, and the life of man is solitary, poor, nasty, brutish and short.

It may seem strange to a man that has not weighed these things well, that nature should thus dissociate[4] and render men apt to invade and destroy one another. This man may not trust this inference made from the passions and would desire to have the same conclusion confirmed by experience. Let this man consider that when he takes a journey, he arms himself and seeks to go well accompanied. When he goes to sleep, he locks the doors and even in his own house, he locks his chests. He does this even when he knows there are laws and public officers who are armed to revenge all the injuries that might be done to him. What opinion does he have of his fellow-subjects when he rides armed, of his fellow citizens when he locks his doors, and of his children and servants when he locks his chests? Does he not thereby accuse mankind as much by his actions, as I do by my words? But neither of us is accusing man's nature. The desire and other passions of man are in themselves no sin. Nor are the actions that proceed from those passions, until people know that a law forbids them. There cannot be laws that are known or made until men have agreed about the person that shall make them.

It may be thought there was never such a time, nor a condition of war such as this. I believe it was never generally so all over the worlds, but there are many places that people live like this now. The savage people in many places of America live at this day in the brutish manner I described above, except for the government of small families where the concord depends on natural lust. No matter what manner of life there might have been, where there is no common power to fear, the manner of life in which men formerly lived under a peaceful government degenerates into civil war.

There may never have been any time where particular men were in a condition of war against one another. Yet in all times, kings and persons of sovereign authority because of their independence, are in continual jealousy, and are in the state and posture of gladiators, having their weapons pointing and their eyes fixed on one another. They have forts, garrison and guns on the frontiers of their kingdoms and are continually spying on their neighbors. This is a posture of war. But because they uphold by this the industry of their subjects, the misery which accompanies the liberty of particular men does not occur in the kingdoms.

In such a war nothing is unjust. It follows that in this war of every man against every man, nothing can be unjust. The notions of right and wrong, justice and injustice have no place there. Where there is no common power, there is no law, and where there is no law, there is no injustice. Force and fraud are the two cardinal virtues in war. Justice and injustice are neither faculties of the body or the mind. If they were, they would be in a man that is alone in the world, as are his senses and passions. Justice and injustice are qualities that related to men in society, not in solitude. It also follows that in this same condition, there is no propriety, no dominion, and no distinct *mine* or *thine*. All that is a man's is what he can get, and as long as he can keep it. This is the ill condition in which nature has actually placed man. But there is the possibility he can come out of it, partly by his passions, and partly by his reason.

The passions that incline men to peace are fear of death, the desire of such thing as are necessary for commodious living, and the hope to obtain them by their industry. Reason suggests convenient articles of peace, by which men may be drawn to agreement. These articles are called the Laws of Nature, and I shall speak more particularly about them in the following two chapters.

Endnotes

1. Claim
2. Suspicion
3. Office or status
4. Separate

CHAPTER 14

Of the First and Second Natural Laws and of Contracts

Right of nature, what. THE RIGHT OF NATURE, which writers commonly call *jus naturale,* is the liberty each man has to use his own power as he wills himself, for the preservation of his own nature, that is to say, his life. Consequently, it is the right to do any thing which in his own judgment and reason, he conceives to be the aptest means to accomplish this.

Liberty, what. LIBERTY is understood, according to the proper signification of the word, to be the absence of external impediments. These impediments may often take away part of a man's power to do what he would, but they cannot hinder him from using the power left him according as his judgment and reason shall dictate to him.

A law of nature what. Difference of right and law. A LAW OF NATURE, *lex naturalis,* is a precept or general rule, found out by reason, by which a man is forbidden to do what is destructive to his life, or takes away the means of preserving it, or to omit that by which he thinks his life may be best preserved. Those that speak of this subject confound *jus* and *lex,* and *right* and *law,* but they ought to be distinguished. RIGHT consists in the liberty to do or to forbear; whereas LAW determines and binds people to do or to forbear. Law and right differ as much as do obligation and liberty, which are inconsistent when applied to the same thing.

Naturally every man has right to every thing. The fundamental law of nature.

The condition of man is what has been declared in the preceding chapter. It is a condition of war of every one against every one, where every-

86

one is governed by his own reason, and he can make use of anything that may be a help to him in preserving his life against his enemies. It follows that in such a condition, every man has a right to every thing, even to one another's body. Therefore, as long as this natural right of every man to every thing endures, there can be no security to any man of living out the time which nature ordinarily allows men to live, no matter how strong or wise the man might be. Consequently it is a precept or general rule of reason, *that every man, ought to endeavor for peace as far as he has hope of obtaining it, and when he cannot obtain it, he may seek and use all helps and advantages of war.* The first branch of this rule contains the first and fundamental law of nature, which is *to seek peace and follow it.* The second branch is the sum of the rights of nature, which are, *by all means we can, to defend ourselves.*

The second law of nature. The second law is derived from this fundamental law of nature by which man are commanded to endeavor peace. It is, *that a man be willing as he shall think necessary to lay down the right to all things when others are too, as far as they are, for peace and the defense of himself, and be contented with as much liberty against other men as he would allow other men against himself.* As long as every man holds this right of doing anything he likes, so long are all men in the condition of war.

But if other men will not lay down their right as well as he, then there is no reason for any one to divest himself of his right. To do so would be to expose himself to be preyed upon rather than to dispose himself to peace, which no man is bound to do. This is the same law as the Gospel's, *whatsoever you require that others should do to you, that do you to them.* It is the same as that law of all men, *quiod tibe fieri non vis, alteri ne feceris.*[1]

What it is to lay down a right. To *lay down* a man's *right* to anything is to *divest* himself of the *liberty* of hindering another of the benefit of his own right to the thing. He that renounces or passes away his right does not give to any other man a right that he did not have before, because every man has a right to everything by nature. To lay down a right means to just stand out of the other person's way, that the other person may enjoy his original right without hindrance from oneself, but not without hindrance from some other person. The effect that redounds to one man by another's defecting from his right, is just a diminution of impediments to the use of his own original right.

Renouncing a right, what it is. Transferring right what. Obligation. Duty. Injustice. A right is laid aside, either by simply renouncing it or by transferring it to another. It is *simply* RENOUNCING when the person does not care to whom the benefit redounds from laying aside the right. It is TRANSFERRING, when the person that is laying aside the right intends the benefit of doing so to go to some certain person or persons. When a man has in either manner abandoned or granted away his right, then he is said to be OBLIGED or BOUND not to hinder those from the benefit of it to whom this right is granted or abandoned. The person laying aside the right *ought,* and it is his DUTY, not to make void that voluntary act of his own. Such a hindrance is INJUSTICE and INJURY, as being *sine jure*[2] as the right was earlier renounced or transferred. *Injury* and *injustice* in the controversies of the world are somewhat like what is called *absurdity* in the disputations of scholars. With scholars, it is called an absurdity when one contradicts what one maintained in the beginning. In the same way in the world, it is called injustice and injury to voluntarily undo that which from the beginning one had voluntarily done. The ways a man either simply renounces or transfers his right are a declaration or signification by some voluntary and sufficient sign or signs, that he does (or has) so renounce or transfer his right to the one that accepted it. These signs are either just words or just actions, or as it happens most often, both words and actions. These words and actions are the BONDS by which men are bound and obliged. These bonds have their strength, not from their own nature, for nothing is more easily broken than a man's word. They rather get their strength from the fear of some evil consequence that will occur upon their rupture.

Not all rights are alienable. Whenever a man transfers his right or renounces it, it is either in consideration of some right reciprocally transferred to himself or for some other good he hopes to gain. These actions are voluntary acts, and the object of the voluntary acts of every man is some *good to himself.* Thus, there are some rights that no man can be understood by any words or other signs to have abandoned or transferred. First, a man cannot lay down the right of resisting those that assault him by force to take away his life, because he could not be understood to aim thereby at any good to himself. The same may be said of wounds and chains and imprisonment. There is no benefit that results from such patience[3] as there is to the patience of suffering another to be wounded or imprisoned. Also, because a man cannot tell when he sees men proceed against him by violence, whether they intend his death or not. Lastly, the motive and end for which the renunciation and transference of right is introduced is just to increase the security of a man's person in his life, and in the means of preserving his life, so as not to become weary of it. Therefore, if a man by words or signs seems to to despoil himself of the end for which those signs were intended, he is not to be understood as if he meant it or that it was his will. Rather, he should be understood as being ignorant of how such words and actions were to be interpreted.

Contract, what. The mutual transferring of rights is that which men call a CONTRACT.

There is a difference between transferring the right to a thing, and transferring, or tradition,[4] the delivery of the thing itself. For the thing may be delivered together with the translation[5] of the right, as in buying and selling with ready-money, or as in the exchange of goods or lands, the thing may be delivered at some time after.

Covenant, what. One of the contractors may deliver the thing contracted for on his part and leave the other to perform his part at some determinate time after. In the meantime the second person is trusted to do his part. In this case the contract on the part of the one who is trusted is called a PACT or a COVENANT. Both parties may contract now to perform later. In these cases, the one who is to perform his part in the time to come is being trusted, and his performance is called the *keeping of a promise*, or faith. The failure of performance, if it is voluntary, is a *violation of faith.*

Free-gift. *Sometimes the transferring of right is not mutual, but one of the parties transfers in the hope of gain. Such gains are friendship, or service from another or from his friends, or in the hope to gain the reputation of charity or magnanimity, or to deliver one's mind from the pain of compassion, or in the hope of a reward in heaven. These cases are not contract, but are GIFTS, FREE-GIFTS, or GRACE. All of these words signify the same thing.*

Signs of contract express. Promise. The signs of a contract are either *express* or *by inference.* It is express when there are words spoken with understanding of what they signify. Such words are either of the *present* or *past* time, such as *I give, I grant, I have given, I have granted, I will that this be yours.* When the words pertain to the future, they are such as, *I will give,* or *I will grant.* When the words pertain to the future, they are called PROMISES.

Signs of contract by inference. The signs of contract by inference are sometimes the consequences of words, sometimes the consequences of silence, sometimes the consequences of actions, and sometimes the consequences of forebearing an action. Generally a sign of contract by inference is whatever sufficiently argues the will of the contractor.

Free gift passes by words of the present or past. Just words, if they are of the time to come, and contain a bare promise, are an insufficient sign of a free-gift and therefore, are not obligatory. For if they are about the time to come, as *tomorrow I will give,* they are a sign I have not given yet, and consequently that my right has not been transferred, but it remains until I transfer it by some other act. But if the words are about the present or past time, as *I have given* or *do give to be delivered tomorrow,* then my tomorrow's right is given away today. This has been done by virtue of my words, even if there were no other argument of my will. There is a great difference between the signification of these words: *volo hoc tuum esse cras,* and *cras debo,* that is between *I will that this be thine tomorrow,* and *I will give it to thee tomorrow.* For the words *I will* in the former expression of speech signify an act of the present will, but these words in the latter expression signify a promise of an act of will to come. That is why the former expression, being about the present, transfers a future right, and the latter expression, being about the future, transfers nothing. If there are other signs, besides words, of the will to transfer a right, then though the gift be free, the right may still be understood to pass by words about the future. It is like when a man propounds that a prize will given to the one that comes first to the end of a race, the gift then is free. Even though the words are about the future, the right still passes, for if the person who said this did not want his words to be so understood, he should not have let them run the race.

Signs of contract are words both of the past, present and future. In contracts the right passes, not only where the words are about the present or past time, but also where they are about the future. This is so because all contracts are mutual translation, or change of rights. He that makes a promise only because he has already received the benefit for which he promised, is to be understood as if he intended that his right should pass. Unless this person had been content to have his words so understood, the other would not have performed his part first. That is why in buying and selling and other acts of contract, a promise is equivalent to a covenant, and is therefore, obligatory.

Merit what. The one who performs first in the case of a contract is said to MERIT what he is to receive by the performance of the other, and the first one has it as *due.* Also, when a prize is propounded to many that is to be given only to the one who wins, or when money is thrown among many to be enjoyed by those that catch it, though these are free gifts, yet to win the prize or to catch the money is to *merit,* and to have it as DUE. The right is transferred in the propounding of the prize or in throwing down the money, even though it is not determined who shall get them except by the event of the contention. But there is a difference between these two sorts of merit. In the case of contract I merit by virtue of my own power and the contractor's need. In the case of free gift, I am enabled to merit only by the benignity of the giver. In a contract I merit at the contractor's hand that he should depart from his right. In a case of a gift, I do not merit that the giver should part with his right, but that when he has parted with it, it should be mine rather than another's. This I think is the meaning of the distinction of the Schools between *meritum congrui*[6] and *meritum condigni*.[7] God Almighty promised Paradise to those men that can walk through this world according to the precepts and limits prescribed by Him, even though they may be hood-winked by carnal desires. Those that can walk in the world in this way shall merit Paradise *ex congruo*. But because no man can demand a right to Paradise by his own righteousness or any power in himself, and can only achieve it by the free grace of God, the School-men say that no man can merit Paradise *ex condigno*. This I say is what I think is the meaning of that distinction, but because the disputers do not agree upon the signification of their own terms of art any longer than it serves their turn, I will not affirm any thing about their meaning. I will only say that when a gift is given indefinitely, as a prize to be contended for, then the one who wins, merits it and may claim the prize as his due.

Covenant of mutual trust, when invalid. A covenant is void if it is made in the condition of mere nature which is a condition of war of every man against every man upon any reasonable suspicion., and the covenant involves neither party performing in the present and they are both relying on trust of one another. But the covenant is not void if there is a common power set over them both that has the right and force sufficient to compel performance. When there is no such power, the one that performs first has no assurance the other will perform after. This is so because the bonds of words are too weak to bridle men's ambition, avarice, anger and other passions without the fear of some coercive power. But in the condition of mere nature, where all men are equal and judges of the justness of their own fears, the first person cannot possibly suppose the other will perform his part. The one who performs first in this condition just betrays himself to his enemy. This is contrary to the right he can never abandon to defend his life and the means of living.

However, in a civil state, where there is a power set up to constrain those that would otherwise violate their faith, the fear of non-compliance by the other is no longer reasonable. For that reason, the one who according to the covenant is to perform first is obliged to do so.

The cause of fear that makes a covenant invalid must always be something arising after the covenant was made. Unless there is some new fact or other sign of the will not to perform, there is nothing to make the covenant void. If something does not hinder a man from promising, it ought not to be admitted as a hindrance to performing.

Right to the end contains right to the means. The one who transfers any right, transfers the mean of enjoying it, to the extent that the means lies in his power. So that one who sells land is understood to transfer the herbage and whatever else grows upon it. Nor can one sell a mill and turn away the stream that drives it. Further, those that give a man the right of government in sovereignty, are understood to give him the right of levying money to maintain soldiers, and of appointing magistrates for the administration of justice.

No covenants with beasts. It is impossible to make covenants with brute beasts. Because they have no understanding of our speech, they do not understand, nor can they accept any translation of rights. Nor can they translate any right to another, and without mutual acceptance, there is no covenant.

Nor with God without special revelation. It is impossible to make a covenant with God, except through the mediation of someone that God has spoken to, either by supernatural revelation, or by this person's lieutenants or those that govern under his name. Without a mediator we do not know if our covenants are accepted or not. So that those who vow anything contrary to any law of nature, vow in vain, as it is unjust to pay such a vow. If it is a thing that is commanded by the law of nature, it is not the vow, but the law that is binding on them.

No covenant but of possible and future. The matter or subject of a covenant is something that falls under deliberation. To covenant is an act of the will. Such an act is the last act of deliberation, and is therefore always to be understood as something to come, that is judged to be possible to perform by the person making the covenant.

Therefore it is not a covenant to promise something that is known to be impossible. If a person promised something he thought was possible that proves afterwards to be impossible, the covenant is valid and binds to the value of the thing promised, though not to the thing itself. If the value turns out also to be impossible, then the person is obliged, as much as he can, to the unfeigned endeavor to perform as much as is possible. A man can be obliged to do no more than this.

Covenants how made void. Men are freed from their covenants by two ways: by performing or by being forgiven. Performance is the natural end of obligation and forgiveness is the restitution of liberty, as it is a retransference of that right in which the obligation consisted.

Covenants extorted by fear are valid. Covenants entered into by fear in the condition of mere nature are obligatory. For example, if I covenant to pay a ransom or service to an enemy in exchange for my life, I am bound by it. It is a contract where one party receives the benefit of life, and the other receives for the life, money or service. When no other law, as in the condition of mere nature, forbids the performance of the actions, the covenant is valid. When prisoners of war are trusted to pay their ransom, they are obliged to pay it. If a weaker prince makes a disadvantageous peace with a stronger prince out of fear, he is bound to keep it, unless as has been said before, some new and just cause of fear arises to renew the war. Even in a commonwealth, if I am forced to redeem myself from a thief by promising him money, I am bound to pay it, until the civil law discharges me from the obligation. Whatever I may lawfully do without obligation, I may lawfully covenant to do the same through fear, and what I lawfully covenant, I cannot lawfully break.

The former covenant to one, makes void the later to another. A former covenant makes a later one void. A man that has passed away his right to one man today, does not have it to pass to another tomorrow. Therefore, the later promise passes no right, and is null.

A man's covenant not to defend himself is void. A covenant not to defend myself from force by force is always void. As I have shown before, no man can transfer or lay down his right to save himself from death, wounds and imprisonment. The only end of laying down any right is to avoid these things. Therefore, the promise to not resist force does not transfer a right in any covenant, nor does it create an obligation. A man may make the following covenant: *unless I do so and so, kill me.* But he cannot make this covenant: *unless I do so and so, I will not resist you, when you come to kill me.* Men by nature choose the lesser evil. When there is the danger of death, the lesser evil is resisting, and the greater evil is certain and present death by not resisting. This is granted to be true by all men, as when those that lead criminals to execution and prison do so with armed men, even when the criminals have consented to the law by which they are condemned.

No man obliged to accuse himself. A covenant to accuse oneself without the assurance of pardon is likewise invalid. In the condition of nature where every man is a judge, there is no place for accusation. In a civil state, an accusation is followed by punishment, which is force and so there is no obligation to not resist. The same is also true of the accusation of those whose condemnation would cause a man to fall into misery, such as the accusation of father, wife or benefactor. The testimony of this kind of accuser, if not willingly given, is presumed to be corrupted by nature, and is therefore not to be credited. Where a man's testimony is not to be credited, he is not bound to give it. Also accusations that result from torture are not to be reputed as testimonies. Torture is used as a means to achieve conjecture and light in the further examination and search for the truth. However, what is confessed from torture tends just to the ease of the one that is tortured, and not to the informing of the torturers. Therefore such confessions ought not to have the credit of sufficient testimony, for whether the tortured person delivers a true or false accusation, he just does it by the right of preserving his own life.

The end of an oath. The form of an oath. The force of words, as I have formerly noted, are too weak to hold men to the performance of their covenants. But there are in man's nature two imaginable helps to strengthen it. They are the fear of the consequence of breaking their word, or the glory or pride in appearing not to need to break it. This latter help is a generosity too rarely found to be presumed on, especially in the pursuers of wealth, command, or sensual pleasure which are the greatest part of mankind. The passion to be reckoned on is fear of two very general objects. One is the power of invisible spirits, and the other is the power of the men they might offend. Of these two, though the former is the greater power, yet the fear of the latter is commonly the greater fear. The fear of invisible spirits is in every man in his religion, and this has a place in the nature of man before there is civil society. The second object of fear is not part of man's nature, at least not enough to keep men to their promises, because in the condition of mere nature, the inequality of power is not discerned except by the event of Letbattle. So, before the time of civil society, or in its interruption by war, there is nothing that can strengthen a covenant of peace that is agreed on against the temptations of avarice, ambition, lust or other strong desire, but the fear of invisible power, which everyone worships as God and fears as a revenger of their perfidy. All that can be done between two men who are not subject to civil power is to make each other swear by the God each one fears. This *swearing* or OATH is a *form of speech, added to a promise by which he that promises signifies that unless he performs, he renounces the mercy of his God, or calls to him for vengeance on himself.* This was the heathen form, *Let* Jupiter *kill me as I kill this beast.* So if our form, *I shall do thus and thus, so help me God.* This is what people use with the rites and ceremonies which everyone uses in his own religion, to increase the fear of breaking one's faith.

No oath but by God. An oath taken according to a form or rite that is not according to the religion of a person, is not an oath and is swearing in vain. There is no swearing by any thing that the swearer does not think to be God. When men sometimes swear by their kings for fear or flattery, they would have it understood that they are attributing divine honor to the kings. Swearing unnecessarily by God is just profaning his name. Swearing by other things, as men do in common discourse, is not swearing, but is an impious custom, resulting from too much vehemence in talking.

An oath adds nothing to the obligation. It appears also, that an oath adds nothing to an obligation. A lawful covenant binds in the sight of God without the oath as much as with it. If it is unlawful, it does not bind at all, even though it be confirmed with an oath.

Endnotes

1. Another version of the Golden Rule—what you would not have done to yourself, do not do unto others.
2. Not right
3. Allowing something to happen
4. Handing over
5. Exchange
6. Merit by comparison
7. Merit that is given because of love

CHAPTER 15

Of Other Laws of Nature

The third law of nature, justice. A third law of nature follows from the law of nature that obliges us to transfer to another the rights that hinder the peace of mankind when they are retained. This third law is, *that men perform the covenants they make.* Without this, covenants are in vain and are but empty words. The right of all men to all things would still remain, and we would still be in the condition of war.

Justice and injustice, what. In this law of nature, consists the fountain[1] and origin of JUSTICE. Where no covenant has preceded, no right has been transferred, and every man has a right to every thing, and consequently, no action can be unjust. But when a covenant is made, then to break it is *unjust.* The definition of INJUSTICE is the *not performance of a covenant.* Whatever is not unjust is just.

Justice and propriety begin with the constitution of a commonwealth. As has been said the previous chapter, covenants of mutual trust where there is a fear that neither will perform are invalid. Even though the origin of justice is the making of covenants, until the fear of the other not performing is taken away, there can be no injustice. But while men are in the natural condition of war, taking away this fear cannot be done. Before the names of 'just' and 'unjust' can have a place, there must be some coercive power to equally compel men to the performance of their covenants. This can be done by the terror of some punishment greater than the benefit they expect by the breach of their covenant. This will make good the propriety that men acquire by mutual contract in recompense for the universal right they abandon. There is no such power before the erection of a commonwealth. This can also be gathered out of the ordinary definition of justice that is provided by the Schools. They say that *justice is the constant will of giving to every man his own*. But where there is no *own*, that is not propriety, there is no injustice. Where there is no coercive power erected, that is where there is no common-wealth, there is no propriety, as all men have a right to all things. There-fore where there is no commonwealth, nothing is unjust. The nature of justice consists in keeping valid covenants, and the validity of covenants only begins with the constitution of a civil power sufficient to compel men to keep them. That is also the origin of propriety.

Justice not contrary to reason. The fool has said in his heart, and sometimes also with his tongue, that there is no such thing as justice. The fool seriously alleges that since every man's conservation and content-ment are committed to his own care, there can be no reason why every man should not do what he thinks leads to these aims. Therefore to make or not make, to keep or not keep one's covenants is not against reason, when it conduces to one's benefit. He does not deny that there are covenants, and that they are sometimes broken and sometimes kept, and that breaching covenants is called injustice and observing them is called justice. What he does question is whether injustice may not sometimes stand with reason which dictates to every man his own good, especially when the fear of God is taken away. (Actually, the same fool says in his heart that there is no God.) The fool has this view particularly when something conduces to his benefit when he is in a situation that he can neglect the dispraise and revilings, and also the power of other men. He asks, the kingdom of God is gotten by violence, but what if it could be gotten by unjust violence? Would it be against reason to get it this way, when it is impossible to be hurt by doing so? He reasons, that if it is not against reason, it is not against justice, or else justice is not to be approved as being good. From reasoning such as this, successful wicked-ness has obtained the name of virtue. Some that have disallowed the vio-lation of faith in all other things, have allowed it when it is for getting a kingdom. The heathen that believed that Saturn was deposed by his son Jupiter, believed that nevertheless that Jupiter was an avenger of injus-tice. This is like a piece of law in Coke's *Commentaries on Littleton*, where he says that if the right heir of the crown be attainted[2] with trea-son, the crown may still descend to him, and that *eo instante*[3] the attain-der[4] is void. From these instances someone might be prone to infer that when the heir apparent of a kingdom shall kill the one who is in posses-sion of the kingdom, even though it is his father, you may call it injustice or whatever name you will, but it can never be against reason. This is so because all voluntary actions of men tend to the benefit of themselves and those actions that are the most reasonable are those that conduce the most to their ends. However, this specious reasoning is nevertheless false.

The question is not about mutual promises where there is no security of performance on either side. This occurs when there is no civil power erected over the parties that are promising, for such promises are not covenants. The question is whether it is against reason, that is against the benefit of someone to perform or not, when either one of the parties has performed already, or where there is a power to make him perform. I say it is not against reason. To make this manifest, we should consider the following. First, when a man does something, notwithstanding anything that can be foreseen or reckoned on, that tends to his own destruction, it is not reasonably or wisely done, if some accident which he could not have expected, arrives to turn the event to his benefit. Second, in the condition of war where every man is an enemy to every man because of a lack of a common power to keep them all in awe, there is no man who can hope by his own strength or wit to defend himself without the help of confederates. Everyone in this condition will expect the same defense by a confederation that anyone else does. So, the one who declares[5] that he thinks it is according to reason to deceive those that help him, can according to reason expect no other means of safety than what he can have from his own single power. Therefore, one who breaks his covenant and then declares that he thinks he may with reason do so, cannot be received into any society that unite themselves for peace and defense. They will only receive him into their society by error. Nor will he be retained in the society unless they do not see the danger of their error. A man cannot reasonably reckon that these errors will continue to be the means of his security. If he is left out of society or cast out, he will perish. But if he lives in society, it is because of the errors of other men, which he could not foresee or reckon upon. Therefore, his preservation is against reason, and so the other men that do not destroy him, only forbear him out of ignorance of what is good for themselves.

It would be frivolous to think that the fool could gain the secure and perpetual felicity of heaven by his way. There is but one way imaginable to gain this felicity, and that is by keeping, and not breaking a covenant.

As for other instances of gaining sovereignty by rebellion, it is manifest that this cannot reasonably be expected. Rather, the contrary is more likely, because by gaining sovereignty in this way, others are taught to gain it also in the same manner, and that is why the initial attempt is against reason. Justice therefore, that is to say, the keeping of covenants is a rule of reason by which we are forbidden to do any thing that is destructive of our lives, and consequently, this is a law of nature.

There are some that would proceed even further. They think the laws of nature are not those rules which conduce to the preservation of a man's life on earth. They look on the laws of nature as rules which will enable one to attain felicity after death. They think that a breach of covenants may conduce to this end, and so they think it is just and reasonable and a work of merit to kill or depose or rebel against the sovereign power constituted over them by their own consent. But there is no natural knowledge of man's estate after death, much less of the reward that is given then to those that breach their faith. One can only have a belief on these matters that is grounded upon the sayings of other men that know it supernaturally, or that know others, that know those that knew those that knew it supernaturally. Therefore, breach of faith cannot be called a precept of reason, or of nature.

Covenants are not discharged by the vice of the person to whom they are made. Some who allow that it is a law of nature to keep one's faith, nevertheless make an exception when the covenant is made with certain persons. These persons are heretics, and others who are not used to keeping their covenants with others. But this is also against reason. For if there is any fault of a man that is sufficient of discharge us from a covenant already made, the same fault ought in reason to have been sufficient to have hindered the making of the covenant in the first place.

Justice of men and justice of actions, what. The names of just and unjust signify one thing when they are attributed to men, and signify another thing when they are attributed to actions. When they are attributed to men, they signify the conformity or nonconformity of a man's manners to reason. But when they are attributed to actions, they signify the conformity or nonconformity of particular actions to reason, and not manners or manners of life. A just man is one that takes all the care that he can that all of his actions will be just. An unjust man neglects this. These kinds of men are more often in our language styled by the names 'righteous' and 'unrighteous' than 'just' and 'unjust', even though the meanings of these terms are the same. A righteous man does not lose his title by one, or a few, unjust actions that proceed from a sudden passion or a mistake about things or persons. Nor does an unrighteous man lose his character because of the actions that he does, or forbears to do, from fear. This is so because his will is not framed by justice of what he does, but by its apparent benefit. What give human actions the relish of justice is a certain nobleness or gallantness of courage. It is rarely found, that a man will scorn to have a life of contentment if it is by means of fraud or breach of promise. This justice of the manners is what is meant when justice is called a virtue and injustice a vice.

The justice of actions not only signifies men to be just, but also *guiltless*. The same is the case for injustice, which is also called injury, and gives those that have it, the name of *guilty*.

Justice of manners and justice of actions. The injustice of manners is the disposition or aptitude to do injury. There is injustice even before one proceeds to act, and even without supposing any individual person is injured. But the injustice of an action, that is to say an injury, does suppose that some individual person is injured, namely the one to whom the covenant was made. Many times the injury is received by one man, when the damage redounds to another. For example, when a master commands his servant to give money to a stranger, if this is not done, the injury is done to the master whom the servant had before covenanted to obey. The damage, however, redounds to the stranger, to whom the servant had no obligation and therefore could not injure. The same is the case in commonwealths. Private men may remit[6] to one another their debts, but not robberies or damages whereby they are endamaged.[7] The detaining of a debt is an injury to themselves, but robbery and violence are injures to the person of the commonwealth.

Nothing done to a man by his own consent can be injury. Whatever is done to a man is not injury to him, if it is conformable to his own will and was signified such to the doer. If the person who allows this to happen has not passed away his original right by some antecedent covenant to do what he pleases, then there is no breach of a covenant, and so no injury done to him. And if this person did pass away his original right, then his will to have something done to him was signified, is a release of that covenant, and so again there is no injury done to him.

Justice commutative and distributive. Writers divide the justice of actions into two kinds: *commutative* and *distributive*. Commutative consists in arithmetical proportions and distributive consists in geometrical proportions. Commutative justice concerns the equality of value of the things contracted for, and distributive justice concerns the distribution of equal benefit to men of equal merit. In this latter case it would be an injustice to sell dearer than we buy, or to give more to a man than he merits. The value of all things that are contracted for is measured by the appetite of the contractors, and therefore the just value is that which they are contented to give. Merit is not due to justice, but is rewarded only by grace, except where it is by covenant, where the performance on one person's part merits performance on the other's part and thus falls under commutative justice and not distributive. Therefore this distinction is not right in the way its use is expounded. To speak properly, commutative justice is the justice of a contractor, which are the acts of the performance of a covenant in buying and selling, hiring and letting to hire, lending and borrowing, exchanging, bartering and other acts of contract.

Distributive justice is the justice of an arbitrator which is the act of defining what is just. If the parties that made him an arbitrator trust him, if he performs his trust, he is said to distribute to every man his own, and this is indeed a just distribution. It may improperly be called distributive justice, but it would more properly called equity, which is also a law of nature as will be shown in its due place.[8]

The fourth law of nature, gratitude. As justice depends on an antecedent covenant, so does GRATITUDE depend on antecedent grace, which is an antecedent free gift. This is the fourth law of nature which can be conceived in this form: *that a man who receives a benefit from another because of mere grace, should endeavor that the person who gave it should have no reasonable cause to repent of his free will.* No man gives except with the intention of some good to himself, because gifts are voluntary, and the object of all voluntary acts is to every man his own good. If men see that this object will be frustrated, there will be no beginning of benevolence or trust, nor consequently of mutual help, nor or the reconciliation of one man to another. Which is contrary to the first and fundamental law of nature, commands men to *seek peace.* The breach of this law is called *ingratitude,* and has the same relation to grace that injustice has to obligation by covenant.

The fifth, mutual accommodation, or complaisance. A fifth law of nature is COMPLAISANCE, that is to say, *that every man should strive to accommodate himself to the rest.* To understand this we may consider that there is a diversity of nature in men's aptness to society, rising from their diversity of affections. This is not unlike what we see in stones brought together for building an edifice. Some stones, because of their asperity[9] and irregularity of figure, take more room from others than they fill themselves. When their hardness cannot easily be made plain, and so they hinder the building, they are cast away by the builders as unprofitable and troublesome. In the same way some men have an asperity by nature and strive to retain those things which are superfluous to themselves, but are necessary to others. If the stubbornness of their passions cannot be corrected, they will be left out or cast out of society as being too cumbersome. Every man is supposed to endeavor all he can to obtain that which is necessary for his conservation, not only by right, but also by the necessity of nature. Those that oppose themselves against this for superfluous things are guilty of the war that will follow thereupon. Therefore, they do what is contrary to the fundamental law of nature, which commands us *to seek peace*. The observers of this law may be called SOCIABLE. The Latins call them *commodi*. The contrary of the sociable are called *stubborn, insociable, forward* and *intactable*.

The sixth, facility to pardon. A sixth law of nature is this: *that for caution of future time, a man ought to pardon those that desire to repent for past offenses.* PARDON is just the granting of peace. If pardon is granted to those that persevere in their hostility, this is not peace, but fear. If it is not granted to those who do show caution for the future, it is a sign to an aversion to peace, and therefore is contrary to the law of nature.

The seventh, that in revenges, men respect only the future good. The seventh is, *that in cases of revenge*, that is retribution of evil for evil, *men should not look at the greatness of the past evil, but of the greatness of the good to follow*. We are thus forbidden from inflicting punishment with any other design but for the correction of the offender or the direction of others. This law is consequent on the previous one that commands pardon for the security of future time. Revenge without respect to the example it is making or profit to come is just a triumph or glorying in the hurt of another, tending to no end. The end is always something to come, and glorying to no end is vain-glory and contrary to reason. To hurt someone without reason tends to the introduction of war, which is against the law of nature and is commonly styled by the name of *cruelty*.

The eighth, against contumely.[10] *All signs of hatred or contempt provoke fighting, as most men choose rather to hazard their life then not to be revenged. So, in the eighth place for a law of nature, set down this precept:* that no man by deed, word, countenance or gesture declare hatred or contempt of another. *The breach of this law is commonly called* contumely.

The ninth, against pride. *The question who is the better man has no place in the condition of mere nature, where as has been shown before, all men are equal. The inequality that exists now has been introduced by the civil laws. I know that Aristotle in the first book of his* Politics, *makes it a foundation of his doctrine that by nature some men are more worthy to command. He means the wiser sort, such as he thought himself to be because of his philosophy. Others were to serve, by which he meant that they had strong bodies, but were not philosophers as he was. He thought that master and servant were not introduced by consent of men, but by the difference in wit, which is not only against reason, but also against experience. There are very few men who are so foolish that they would rather be governed by others than govern themselves.* Nor is it the case that those who are wise in their own conceit contend by force always, or often or almost any time, get the victory when they contend with those who distrust their supposed wisdom. If nature therefore has made men equal, that equality is to be acknowledged. And if nature has made men unequal, because men think themselves equal and will not enter into conditions of peace except on equal terms, then such equality must be admitted. Therefore, for the ninth law of nature, I put the following: *that every man acknowledge another for his equal by nature.* The breach of this precept is pride.

The tenth, against arrogance. On this law depends another: *that at the entrance into conditions of peace, no man should require to reserve to himself any right which he is not content should be reserved to every one of the rest.* It is necessary for all men that seek peace to lay down certain rights of nature, which means not to have the liberty to do all they might list.[11] It is also necessary for a man's life to retain some rights, as the right to govern their own bodies, enjoy air, water, motion, ways to go from place to place and all other things that without them a man cannot live, or live well. If at the making of peace, men require for themselves something which they would not grant to others, they do something contrary to the preceding law that commands the acknowledgment of natural equality. Therefore, they also do something against the law of nature. The observers of this law are those we call *modest,* and the breakers are *arrogant* men. The Greeks call the violation of this law *pleonexia,* that is a desire for more than their share.

The eleventh, equity. It is a precept of the law of nature, *that if a man be trusted to judge between man and man, that he deal equally between them.* For without that, the controversies of men can just be determined by war. One who is partial in judgment does what deters men from the use of judges and arbitrators, and consequently does what is against the law of nature, and this is a cause of war.

The observance of this law is called EQUITY from the equal distribution to each man of what reason says belongs to him. As I said before, it is called distributive justice, and the violation of it is the *acception*[12] *of persons,* which is in Greek, *prosopolepsia.*

The twelfth, equal use of common things. From the eleventh law there follows another law: *that such things that cannot be divided, be enjoyed in common, if that can be, and if the equality of the thing permits; other-*

wise, it is to be enjoyed proportionally by the number of those that have the right. Otherwise the distribution is unequal and contrary to equity.

The thirteenth, of lot. But there are some things that can neither be divided, nor enjoyed in common. In those cases the law of nature that prescribes equity requires, *that the entire right, or else the alternative making the use by the first possession, be determined by lot.* For equal distribution is the law of nature, and other means of equal distribution cannot be imagined.

The fourteenth of primogeniture and first seizing. There are two sorts of *lots, arbitrary* and *natural.* The arbitrary kind is what is agreed upon by the competitors. The natural kind is either *primogeniture,* which the Greeks called *kleronomia,* which signifies, *given by lot,* or *first seizure.*

Therefore, those things which cannot be enjoyed in common nor divided, ought to be adjudged to belong to the first possessor as acquired by lot and in some cases to the first born.

The fifteenth, of mediators. It is also a law of nature, *that all men that mediate peace be allowed safe conduct.* The law that commands peace as the *end,* commands intercession as the *means,* and for intercession, the means is safe conduct.

The sixteenth, of submission to arbitration. Even when men are willing to observe these laws, there will nevertheless arise questions concerning a man's actions. These questions are first, whether an act was done or not done, a question of *fact,* and second, whether an act is or is not against the law, a question of *right.* Unless the parties to these questions mutually covenant to accept the sentence of some other person, they are as far from peace as ever. This other person whose sentence they submit to is called an ARBITRATOR. Therefore, it is a law of nature, *that they that have a controversy, submit their right of judgment to an arbitrator.*

The seventeenth, no man is his own judge. Since every man is presumed to do all things in order to increase his own benefit, no man is a fit arbitrator in his own cause. If no one is so fit, then if equity allows each party equal benefit, if one person is admitted to be the judge, the other is to be also admitted. In this case the cause of the controversy, which is the cause of war, will remain, and is against the law of nature.

The eighteenth, no man to be judge, that has in him a natural cause of partiality. For the same reason as the one above, no man in any cause should be an arbitrator, to whom greater profit, honor or pleasure will apparently arise out of the victory of one party rather than of the other. Anyone who has taken an unavoidable bribe, has still taken a bribe, and no man can be obliged to trust such a person. In this case the controversy and the condition of war remains, contrary to the law of nature.

The nineteenth, of witnesses. In controversies about question of *fact,* the judge should give no more credit to one witness than to another. If there are no more arguments on either side, then the credit must be given to a third or fourth witness. Otherwise, the question is undecided and is left to force to settle, and this is contrary to the law of nature.

These are the laws of nature, dictating peace as a means for the conservation of men in multitudes, and only concern the doctrine of a civil society. There are other things that tend to the destruction of particular men, such as drunkenness and other kinds of intemperance. These are other things with may also be reckoned among those things which the law of nature has forbidden, but they are not necessary to be mentioned, nor are they pertinent enough to this place.

A rule, by which the laws of nature may easily be examined. All of the above may be too subtle a deduction from the laws of nature to be taken notice by all men, who for the most part are too busy getting food, and the rest are too negligent to understand. Still, there is no excuse, even for those with the meanest capacity from following one summary and intelligible law: *Do not do to another which you would not have done to yourself.* This shows those what to do to learn the laws of nature, which is that when weighing the actions of other men against one's own, if one's own actions seem too heavy, to put them into the other part of the balance and the other's into their own place. It means that one's own passions and self-love add nothing to the weight of one's own actions, and then all of these laws of nature will appear to be very reasonable.

The laws of nature oblige in conscience always, but in effect, only when there is security. The laws of nature oblige in *foro interno,*[14] which means they bind to a desire that they should take place. But in *foro externo,*[15] which means putting them into action, they do not always oblige. Someone who is modest and tractable and performs all that he promises to do in a time and place where no else does likewise, just makes himself a prey to others and procures his own certain ruin. This is contrary to the ground of all laws of nature which tend to the preservation of nature. Also, one seeks peace and not war when one does not observe these laws oneself but has sufficient security that others will observe the same laws toward oneself. The result will be the destruction of this person by violence.

Whatever laws bind in *foro interno,* would be broken not only by a fact contrary to the law, but also by a fact that is in accord with the law, but which a man thinks is contrary. In this latter case, although a man's action is according to the law, his purpose was against the law, and so in the case of obligation *foro interno,* the action is a breach.

The laws of nature are eternal. The laws of nature are immutable and eternal. Injustice, ingratitude, arrogance, pride, iniquity, acception[16] of persons and the rest, can never be lawful. It can never be that war will preserve life and peace will destroy it.

And yet, easy. The same laws are easy to observe because they only oblige desire, and endeavor—an unfeigned and constant endeavor. They actually require nothing but endeavor, for he that endeavors their performance, fulfills them, and he that fulfills the Law, is just.

The Science of these Laws is the true Moral Philosophy. The science of them is the true and only moral philosophy. Moral Philosophy is nothing else but the science of what is good and evil in the conversation and society of mankind. 'Good' and 'evil' are names that signify our appetites and aversions, which are different in people who have different tempers, customs and doctrines. Diverse men differ not only in their judgments of what is pleasant and unpleasant to taste, smell, hearing, touch and sight, but also about what is conforming or in disagreement with reason in the actions of common life. The same person even can differ from himself in different times, and will at one time praise something calling it good, and at another time dispraising it, calling it evil. These differences are the source of disputes, controversies, and finally, war. So as long as men are in the condition of mere Nature, where private appetite is the measure of good and evil, there will be a condition of war. Since all men agree that peace is good, they therefore also agree the means of peace are good, which I have shown to be Justice, Gratitude, Modesty, Equity, Mercy and the rest of the Laws of Nature. These are the moral virtues and their contraries are evil—the vices. The science of virtue and vice is moral philosophy, and therefore the true doctrine of the Laws of Nature is true moral philosophy. But those who write about moral philosophy, even though they acknowledge the same virtues and vices, do not see what their goodness consists in. Nor do they see that the virtues come to be praised because they are the means of peaceful, sociable and comfortable living. These writers consider virtues to be mediocre[17] passions, thinking that the degree of daring makes the virtue of fortitude, and not what the cause of it is. Similarly, they do not understand what the cause is of the virtue liberality, but only consider the quantity of the gift.

While men call these dictates of reason "laws", this is actually improper, for they are more conclusions or theorems, concerning what conduces to the conservation and defense of men. 'Law' is more properly a word that applies to the person who has the right to command others. But if we consider these same theorems to be delivered in the word of God that commands all things, then they can properly be called "laws".

Endnotes

1. Source
2. Accused
3. That instant
4. Accusation
5. One would really have to be a fool to declare this to one's confederates
6. Forgive
7. Damaged
8. Hobbes is referring to the eleventh law of nature that he describes later on in this chapter.
9. Roughness of surface, unevenness
10. Humiliating insult
11. Desire
12. Being partial to, giving some a special advantage
13. Another example of Hobbes' view that science can only be understood by a few.
14. Internal forum
15. External forum
16. Corruption
17. Indifferent

CHAPTER 16

Of Persons, Authors, and Things Personated

What is a person. A person is one whose words or actions are considered either as his own, as representing the words or actions of some other man, or of any other thing to whom they are attributed, whether the thing is real or just a fiction.

Person natural, and artificial. When the words or actions are considered as one's own, then the person is called "natural." When the words or actions are considered as representing the words or actions of some other, then the person is called "feigned" or "artificial".

The derivation of the word, 'person'. The word 'person' is Latin, whereas the Greeks use the word *prosopon,* which signifies the face. The Latin word *'persona'* means disguise or outward appearance of a man who is playing a role on the stage. Sometimes the word refers to some more particular part of an actor's appearance, such as what disguises the face-a mask or a visard.[1] From its use on the stage, the term has been translated to mean any representer of speech or action, not only in theaters, but also in tribunals. So 'person' is used the same way 'actor' is on the stage and in common conversation. It means to personate, which means to act or represent oneself or some other. When one acts as another, one is said to bear that person or act in his name. (This is the sense that Cicero uses it when he says, *Unus sustineo tres Personas; Mei, Adversarii and Judicis,* which means, I bear three persons: myself, my adversaries, and the judges.) On diverse occasions the person who is represented is called a representer or representative, a lieutenant, a vicar, an attorney, a deputy, a procurator[2], an actor, etc.

Actor, Author, Authority. Some artificial persons have their words and actions owned by those whom they represent. In these cases the person is the actor and the one that owns the words and actions is the author. In these cases the actor acts by someone else's authority. When speaking of good and possessions, the author is called an owner, (in Latin, *dominus*, and in Greek, *kurios*). The one who owns an action is called the author. As the right of possession is called dominion, the right of doing any action is called authority. It is understood that one who is an authority has the right of doing any act, and when an act is done by authority, it is done by the commission, or license, of the one who whose right it is.

Covenants by authority bind the author. From this it follows that when an actor makes a covenant by authority, the actor thereby binds the author as much as if the author made the covenant himself, and the author is subject to all of the consequences of the covenant. So everything that was said before (chapter 14) about the nature of covenants between man and man in their natural capacity, is true also when they are made by their actors, representers, or procurators, to the extent that they have been given commission by the authority, but no further.

Therefore, one that makes a covenant with an actor or representer, who does not know the authority of these people, does so at one's own peril. For no man is obliged to keep a covenant, when he is not the author of it, nor to keep a covenant made against the authority he gave.

But not the actor. Suppose an actor is obliged by a prior covenant to obey an author and the author commands the actor to do something against a Law of Nature. In that case the author, and not the actor, breaks the Law of Nature. Still the actor cannot refuse to do this, as it is against the Law of Nature which forbids anyone from breaching a covenant.

The authority is to be shown. Suppose one makes a covenant with an actor, not knowing what authority the actor has, but only taking the actor's word for it. If the actual authority is not made manifest to the person when demanding to know it, the person is not obliged to keep the covenant. For a covenant made with an author is not valid, unless there is a counter-assurance. But if the person making this covenant knew beforehand that he was to expect no more assurance than the actor's word, then the covenant is valid, because in this case the actor has become the author. Therefore, when the authority is evident, the covenant does oblige the author, but not the actor. But when the authority is feigned, the covenant only obliges the actor because there is no author besides the actor.

Things personated, inanimate. Many things are capable of being represented by a fiction. Inanimate things such as a church, a hospital, or a bridge, may be represented respectively by a rector, a master or an overseer. But inanimate things cannot be authors nor give authority to actors. Nevertheless, actors may have the authority to maintain these inanimate things, if it is given to them by those that are the owners or governors of those things. Therefore such things cannot be personated, or represented, before there is a state of civil government.

Irrational. Children, fools and mad-men that have no use of reason may be represented by guardians or curators. Until such people recover the use of reason and are able to judge actions to be reasonable, they cannot be authors of any action done by them. During the time of their folly or madness, the one who has the right of governing over them may give authority to a guardian. But this again has no place except in a civil state, because before a civil state is in place, there is no dominion of persons.

False gods. An idol or a mere figment of the brain may be personated or represented. This occurred with the gods of the heathens, which were personated by officers that the state appointed. These officers held possessions and other goods and rights, which from time to time were dedicated and consecrated to them. But idols cannot be authors, for an idol is nothing. The authority came from the state and therefore, before the introduction of civil government, the gods of the heathens could not be personated.

The true God. The true God may be personated. He was first by Moses who governed the Israelites that were not his people, but were God's. He did not do this in his own name by saying *hoc dicit Moses*[3], but in God's name, by saying *hoc dicit Dominus*.[4] Secondly, he was personated by the son of man, his own son, our blessed savior, Jesus Christ. He came to reduce[5] the Jews and induce all nations into the kingdom of His father, not of Himself, but as sent from His father. Thirdly, he was personated by the Holy Ghost, or Comforter, the speaker who worked in the Apostles. The Holy Ghost was a comforter that came not as himself, but was sent and proceeded from both God and His son.

A multitude of men, how they may be one person. A multitude of men are made into one person when they are represented by one man or one person, who has the consent of every one of that multitude. It is the unity of the representer and not the unity of the represented that makes the person one. And it is the representer that bears the person and is but one person, as a unity of a multitude cannot be otherwise understood.

Every one is author. Since a multitude is naturally not a "one" but a "many", they cannot be considered to be a "one". They are many authors of every thing that their representative says or does in their name. Every individual man gives the common representative the authority from himself in particular, and owns all of the actions that the representer does, when they give him authority without stint.[6] If the individuals limit what the authority does and how far he can represent them, then the individuals only own what they gave him commission to do.

An actor may be many men made one by plurality of voices. If the representative consists of many men, the voice of the greater number must be considered as the voice of them all. For if there is a lesser number that proclaims an affirmative (for example), and a greater number proclaims the negative, then there will be more than enough negatives to destroy the affirmatives, and so the excess of negatives, standing uncontradicted, are the only voice the representative has.

Representatives, when the number is even is unprofitable. When there is an even number of representatives, especially when the number is not great, the contradictory voices are often equal and are therefore mute and incapable of action. Yet, in some cases equal contradictory voices may determine a question. Consider a case of absolving or condemning. If there is an equality of votes, then they do not condemn, but do absolve. The contrary—since they do not absolve, they thereby condemn—does not hold. For when a cause is heard, to not condemn is to absolve, but the contrary, to say that not absolving is condemning, is not true. The same holds for a deliberation about whether to execute an action or defer it until another time. When the voices are equal, not decreeing the execution of an act is a decree of dilation.[7]

Negative voice. When the number of voices is odd but small in individuals and assemblies, such as three or more, even if all of voices are negative, there is not the authority to take away all of the affirmative voices of the rest of the people. The odd, but small number, is not representative, because the diversity of opinions and interests of men makes the representative a mute and unapt[8] person (representative). This is especially the case in matters of the greatest consequence, such as in time of war, where the government of a multitude is ineffective.

There are two sorts of authors. The first is simply called an author, and I have defined it before to be the one that simply owns an action.

The second is one that owns an action or the covenant of another conditionally. That means he undertakes to do it, if the other does not do it or before a certain time. Conditional authors are generally called sureties. In Latin these are called *fidejussores* and *sponsores*. When talking about debts, they are called *praedes*, and when talking about appearances before a judge or magistrate, *vades*.

Endnotes

1. Visor
2. Agent
3. Thus says Moses
4. Thus says God
5. Save
6. Limit
7. Deferment
8. Incapable

PART 2: Of Commonwealth

CHAPTER 17

Of the Causes, Generation and Definition of a Commonwealth

The end of commonwealth, in particular, security. Men, who naturally love liberty and dominion over others introduce a restraint upon themselves when they live in commonwealths. They have the foresight to pursue the final cause or design of their own preservation and thus to live a more contented life. They get themselves out from the miserable condition of war, which is a necessary consequence (as has been shown in chapter 13) of the natural passions of men when there is no visible power to keep them in awe and tie them by fear of punishment to the performance of their covenants and the observation of the Laws of Nature that are set down in chapters 14 and 15.

Security is not provided by the Laws of Nature. Men would not observe the Laws of Nature, such as justice, equity, modesty, mercy, in sum, doing to others as we would be done to, without the terror of some power. Without this power, our natural passions carry us to partiality, pride, revenge and the like. Covenants not supported by the sword, are but words and have no strength to secure a man at all. Even if everyone has a will to keep and follow the Laws of Nature when one can do so safely, if there is no power that is erected that is great enough for our security, then every man will, and may, lawfully rely on his own strength and art as a precaution against all other men. In all places where men have lived in small families, their trade has been to rob and spoil[1] one another. This has not been considered to be against the Law of Nature; on the contrary, the greater the spoil gained, the greater was a family's honor. In these conditions men observed no other laws but the Laws of Honor, which said to abstain from cruelty and to leave victims their lives and the instruments of husbandry. As small families acted then, so now do cities and kingdoms, which are just greater families. For their own security, cities and kingdoms enlarge their dominions on any pretence[2] of danger and fear of invasion or assistance that may be given to invaders. They endeavor as much as they can to subdue or weaken their neighbors by open force and secret arts, and are proper to do so, and are remembered for it in after ages with honor.

Security is not provided by the conjunction of a few men or families. The joining together of a small number of men does not provide them with security. In small numbers the addition on one side or the other might be sufficient to provide victory, but it therefore also encourages others to do the same and to mount an invasion. The multitude sufficient to provide for our security is not determined by any certain number, but rather by comparison with the enemy we fear. Security is provided when an enemy is not looking for a visible and conspicuous moment for war and is not even moved to attempt one.

Security is not provided by a great multitude, unless directed by one judgment: Even if there is a great multitude, if their actions are directed according to their individual judgments and individual appetites, they can expect no defense nor protection against a common enemy or against the injuries of one another. They will be distracted in their opinions concerning the best use and application of their strength, and so they will not help, but rather hinder one another. They will reduce their strength by mutual opposition to nothing, and so they will easily be subdued, not only by a few that agree together, but also when there is no common enemy, they will make war upon each other for their individual interest. If we could suppose that a great multitude of men would consent in the observation of justice and other Laws of Nature without a common power to keep them in awe, we might as well suppose that all mankind could do the same. In that case there would be no need for a civil government or commonwealth at all, because there would be peace without subjection.

The direction by one judgment must be continual. It is not enough for the security that all men desire should last all the time of their life, that they be governed and directed by one judgment for a limited time, as in one battle in a war. They may obtain one victory by their unanimous endeavor against a foreign enemy, but afterwards when the requirements of their differences dissolve, they will fall again into a war against themselves when they have no common enemy or when one of the multitude is considered by one to be an enemy and by another to be a friend.

Why certain creatures without reason or speech, do nevertheless live in society, without any coercive power. It is true that certain living creatures, bees and ants, live sociably with one another, which are numbered by Aristotle among the political creatures. They are able to do this with no direction besides their particular judgments and appetites. Neither do they have speech whereby one of them can signify to another what he thinks is expedient for the common benefit. Some may perhaps to desire to know why mankind cannot do the same. To this question, I answer:

First, men are continually in competition for honor and dignity, which these creatures are not. Consequently, on this basis, envy, hatred and finally war arises among men, but this does not happen for these creatures.

Secondly, among these creatures the common good does not differ from the private good, and so being inclined by nature to the private good, they thereby procure the common benefit. But for men, their joy consists in comparing themselves with other men and they can relish nothing except where they are eminent.

Thirdly, since these creatures do not have the use of reason, they do not see, nor think they see any fault in the administration of their common business. But among men there are very many that think themselves wiser and abler than the rest to govern the public. Such men strive to reform and innovate, one this way, another that way, and thereby bring the public to distraction and to civil war

Fourthly, these creatures, through the use of their voices, are able to make known to one another their desires and affections. But they lack the art of words, by which some men can represent to others that which is good in the likeness of evil, and evil in the likeness of good. Men are also able to augment or diminish the apparent greatness of good and evil, by which they can at their pleasure discontent other men and trouble their peace.

Fifthly, irrational creatures cannot distinguish between injury and damage; therefore, as long as they are at ease, they are not offended by their fellows. But men are most troublesome when they are at their ease. At that time men love to show their wisdom and control the actions of those that govern the commonwealth.

Lastly, the agreement of creatures is natural, but the agreement of men is only by covenant, which is thus, artificial. Therefore it is no wonder that there is something else required besides covenants to make men's agreements constant and lasting. This is the common power that keeps them in awe, and directs their actions to the common benefit.

The generation of a commonwealth. The definition of a common-wealth. There is only one way to erect such a common power that will be able to defend men from the invasion of foreigners, and from the injuries of one another which will secure them so that by their own industry, they may nourish themselves from the fruit of the earth and live contentedly. This way is to confer all of their power and strength upon one man, or upon assembly of men, that will reduce all of their wills, from a plurality of voices into one will. This means to appoint one man, or assembly of men, to bear their person. It also means that that everyone will own and acknowledge himself to be the author of whatever the one who bears their person shall do, or cause to be done, for the things that concern the common peace and safety. Everyone thereby submits their wills to his will, and their judgments to his judgments. This is more than consent or concord; it is a real unity of them all into one and the same person, made by covenant of every man with every man. In this manner it is as if every man should say to every man, "I authorize and give up my right of governing myself, to this man, or to this assembly of men, on the condition that you give up your right to him, and authorize all of his actions in a like manner." When this is done, the multitude is united in one person that is called a commonwealth—in Latin, *civitas*. This is the generation of that great Leviathan, or rather, to speak more reverently, of that mortal god, to which we owe our peace and defense under the immortal God. By the authority given him by every particular man in the common-wealth, he has the terror derived from so much power and strength conferred on him, that he is enabled to perform the wills of all of them concerning peace at home and mutual aid against their enemies abroad. The essence of the commonwealth consists in this: By mutual covenant with one another, a multitude have made by their individual authority one person who can act for the ends of using his strength and any means he thinks is expedient for the multitude's peace and common defense.

Sovereign and subject. The one who carries this person is called the sovereign, and is said to have sovereign power. Everyone else is his subject.

There are two ways to attain sovereign power. One is by natural force. This occurs when a man makes his children and their children to submit themselves to his government, since he is able to destroy them if they refuse.[3] Another instance of natural force occurs when by war, a person subdues his enemies to his will, giving them their lives on that condition. The other way to attain sovereign power is when men agree among themselves to voluntarily submit to some man, or assembly of men, being confident that he will protect them against all others. This latter can be a called a political commonwealth, or a commonwealth by institution. The former is a commonwealth by acquisition. First, I shall speak of a commonwealth by institution.

Endnotes

1. Take by plunder or force
2. Pretext
3. Hobbes means here that parents can force their children to submit to their parental authority, not to the authority of the political or governmental leaders.

CHAPTER 18

Of the Rights of Sovereigns
by Institution

What is the act of instituting a commonwealth. A commonwealth is said to be instituted when a multitude of men agree and covenant, every one with every one, that a man, or assembly of men, that is selected by the majority of the multitude will have the right to present the person of them all—that means to be their representative. Every one, those who voted for it as well as those who voted against it, authorizes all of the actions and judgments of the man or assembly of men as if they were their own. The end of this is to live peaceably among themselves and be protected against other men.

The consequences of such an institution: All the rights and faculties of him, or them, on whom the sovereign power is conferred by the consent of the people assembled in their institution of a commonwealth.

1. The subjects cannot change the form of government. First, when people make a covenant, it is understood that they are not obliged by any former covenant to do anything that is repugnant to the latter one. Consequently, when people have already instituted a commonwealth, they are thereby bound by covenant to the actions and judgments of the sovereign. They therefore, cannot lawfully make a new covenant among themselves to be obedient to any other in any thing whatever, without the sovereign's permission. If they are subjects to a monarch, they cannot without his leave cast off the monarchy and return to the confusion of a disunited multitude. They cannot transfer from the person who bears their person to another man, or to an assembly of men. They are bound, every man to every man, to own and accept the authority of all that the one who is already their sovereign shall do and judge fit to be done. It is an injustice for any one man to dissent and claim that all should break their covenant made to him. It is also an injustice if once every man has given sovereignty to one that will bear their person, to then depose him and take away from him that which is his own. Besides, if one that attempts to depose his sovereign be killed or punished for the attempt, this person is the author of his own punishment, since by institution he is the author of all that his sovereign shall do. Because it is an injustice for a man to do any thing for which he will be punished by his own authority, a person trying to depose his sovereign is unjust. It is also unjust for some men to pretend[1] their disobedience is due to a new covenant supposedly made with God and not with other men. There is no covenant that can be made with God except through the mediation of some body that represents God's person, and which only God's lieutenants have, since they have sovereignty under God. But this pretence of a covenant with God is so evidently a lie, even in the pretenders of their consciences, that it is not only an act of injustice, but also the act of a vile and unmanly disposition.

2. *Sovereign power cannot be forfeited.* The right of bearing the person of all the multitude is given to the one made sovereign by the people making a covenant with each other and not to the one who is the sovereign. Therefore, there can be no breach of covenant on the part of sovereign, and consequently, none of his subjects can be freed from his subjection by any pretence of forfeiture. It is manifest that the one who is made sovereign has not beforehand made any covenant with his subjects. If he were to do so, he must have either made it with the whole multitude as one party to the covenant, or he must have made an individual covenant with every man. It is impossible for him to make a covenant to the whole as one party, because they are not yet one person. The other alternative is that he makes as many individual covenants as there are individual people. In that case those covenants would be void after he has sovereignty. This is so because then anyone can claim that any act of the sovereign is a breach of the covenant, because the act would be done by the sovereign supposedly for all the rest of the people and not for anyone in particular. Besides, if any one or more people pretend that there is a breach of the covenant made by the sovereign at institution, and others, or the sovereign claim there is no such breach, there is in this case no judge to decide the controversy. The situation then returns to the sword again[2] and every man recovers the right of protecting himself by his own

strength, which is contrary to the design they have when they formed the institution of the sovereign. It is therefore vain to grant sovereignty by way of precedent covenant.[3] The opinion that any monarch receives his power by covenant, that is to say on some condition, proceeds from lack of understanding of an easy truth. This is that covenants are but words and breath, and have no force to oblige, contain, constrain or protect any man, except when it is supported by the public sword. The public sword is the untied hands of that man, or an assembly of men, that has the sovereignty, and whose actions and strength result from the united affirmation of all. When an assembly of men is made sovereign, no one can imagine that there has been a covenant of institution in the past. No one is so dull to say, for example, that the people of Rome, made a covenant with the Romans, to hold sovereignty on such or such conditions, and if these conditions were not performed, the Romans might lawfully depose the Roman people. The reason that people do not see the similar nonsense in the case of a monarchy is due to the ambition of some, that are more inclined to government by assembly, where they hope to participate, since they despair to enjoy the same position in a monarchy.

3. *No man can without injustice protest against the institution of the sovereign declared by the major part.* When a major part of the people has by consenting voices declared a sovereign, one that dissents must now consent with the rest. That means that the dissenter consents to avow[4] with all the actions the sovereign will do, or else can be justly destroyed by the majority. If the dissenter voluntarily entered into the congregation of those that were assembled, he thereby sufficiently declares his will, and so tacitly covenants to stand by what the majority should ordain. Therefore, if he refuses to stand by the majority's decision or protests against any of their decrees, he does so contrary to his covenant and is therefore unjust. And whether he is a part of the congregation or not, or whether his consent is asked for or not, he must either submit to the congregation's decrees or be left in the condition of war he was in before. In that condition he can be destroyed by any man whatsoever without injustice.

4. *The sovereign's actions cannot be justly accused by the subject.* Fourthly, since every subject is the author of the institution of the sovereign and of all the sovereign's actions and judgments, it follows what whatever the sovereign does cannot be an injury to any of the subject, nor ought he be accused by any of them of committing an injustice. One who does anything by authority of another cannot thereby injure the one

by whose authority he acts. By the institution of a commonwealth, every particular man is the author of all that the sovereign does. Consequently, one who complains of an injury from his sovereign complains of something he himself is the author of. Such a person ought not to accuse anyone except himself and thus accuse himself of injuring himself, but to do injury to oneself is impossible. It is true that those who have sovereign power can commit iniquity, but not injustice or injury in their proper meaning.

5. *Whatsoever the sovereign does is unpunishable by the subject.* Fifthly, by what was just said, no one that has sovereign power can justly be put to death or be justly punished in any manner by his subjects. As every subject is the author of the actions of his sovereign, when a subject punishes the sovereign, he is punishing him for actions committed by himself.

6. *The sovereign is judge of what is necessary for the peace and defense of his subjects.* The end of the institution of sovereignty is the peace and defense of all, and whoever has the right to the end has the right to the means. So a man, or assembly, that is sovereign has the right to be the judge of both the means of peace and defense, and also of their hindrances and disturbances. This means that the sovereign has the right to do whatever he shall think necessary to be done beforehand for the preserving of peace and security by prevention of discord at home and hostility from abroad. When peace and security are lost, he has the right to do what is necessary to recover them.

And judge what doctrines are fit to be taught. Sixthly, the sovereign has the right to judge what opinions and doctrines conduce or are averse to peace. Consequently he can judge on what occasions, how far, and what men are to be trusted to speak to multitudes of people, and who shall examine the doctrines of all books before they are published. The actions of men proceed from their opinions, and the well governing of men's actions consists in the well governing of their opinions to produce peace and concord.⁵ In matters of doctrine the only thing that should be regarded is truth. But the same result will occur when regulating doctrines to produce peace, for a doctrine repugnant to peace can no more be true than peace and concord can be against the Law of Nature. It is the case that in a commonwealth false doctrines can be generally accepted because of the negligence and lack of skill of governors and teachers, and the contrary truths may be considered to be generally offensive. Yet the most sudden and rough bustling in of a new truth, whatever it might be, never does break the peace, but only sometimes leads to war. For those men that are so remissely[6] governed that they would take up arms to defend or introduce an opinion, are still in a state of war and their condition is not peace. They only observe a cessation of arms for fear of one another. They live as it were continually in the precincts of battle. Therefore the sovereign has the power to be judge, or to constitute all judges, of opinions and doctrines, for this is necessary for peace and to prevent discord and civil war.

7. *The right of making rules, whereby the subjects may know what is his own, so that no other subject can take it from him without justice.* Seventhly, the sovereign has the right to prescribe the rules whereby every man may know what goods he may enjoy and what actions he may do without being molested by any of his fellow subjects. This is what men call propriety.[7] As has been already shown, before the constitution of sovereign power, all men have the right to all things. This necessarily causes war, and therefore this propriety is necessary for peace, and depends on the sovereign power to enact it in order to maintain the public peace. These rules of propriety (or *meum* and *tuum*)[8] and of good, evil, lawful and unlawful in the actions of subjects are the civil laws, which are the laws of each commonwealth. The term 'civil law' is now just used for the ancient civil laws of the city of Rome, which was the head of a great part of the world, and so in those parts her laws at that time were the civil law.

8. *To him also belongs the right of judicature and decision of controversy.* Eighthly, the sovereign has the right of judicature, which involves hearing and deciding all controversies that may arise concerning law, either civil or natural, or concerning fact.

Without the ability to decide controversies, there is no protection of one subject against the injuries of another. The laws concerning *meum* and *tuum* would be in vain, and every man would retain the right of protecting himself by means of his private strength in order to maintain his natural and necessary appetites. This is the condition of war, and is contrary to the end for which every commonwealth is instituted.

9. *And of making war and peace as he shall think best.* Ninthly, the sovereign has the right of making war and peace with other nations and commonwealths. This involves judging when war is for the public good, and how great the forces are to be assembled, armed and paid for that end, and to levy money from the subjects to defray the expenses. The power by which the people are to be defended consists in their armies, and the strength of an army consists in the union of their strength under one command. The instituted sovereign has this command, because the

command of the militia,[9] without any other institution, makes the one that has it sovereign. Therefore, whoever is made the general of an army is the one that has sovereign power and is always the generalissimo.

10. *And of choosing all counselors and ministers, both of peace and war.* Tenthly, the sovereign has the right to choose all counselors, ministers, magistrates, and officers, both for peace and war. Since the sovereign is charged with the end, which is the common peace and defense, he is understood to have the power to use such means as he shall think most fit to discharge these purposes.

11. *And of rewarding and punishing and being arbitrary where there is no relevant law.* Eleventhly, the sovereign has the right to reward with riches or honor, and to punish by corporal or pecuniary means, or with ignominy, every subject according to the laws he has made. If there is no law, he can judge what to do according to what will conduce and encourage men to serve the commonwealth or deter them from doing disservice to it.

12. *And of honor and order.* Lastly, men are naturally apt to set a certain value upon themselves, to look for respect from others, and to little value other men. This leads to a continual eruption among them of emulation, quarrels, factions and at last war, and this destruction of one another leads to the diminution of their strength against a common enemy. To avoid this, it is necessary that there be laws of honor and a public rate of the worth of men as they deserve, or in terms of how well they serve the Commonwealth. There must be some force to execute these laws. It has already been shown that not only the whole militia, or forces of the commonwealth, but also the judgment of all controversies is part of the power of the sovereign. Therefore the sovereign also have the right to give titles of honor, and to appoint the order of place and dignity that each man shall hold, and what signs of respect they shall give to one another in public or private meetings.

These rights are indivisible. These are the rights which are the essence of sovereignty, and are the marks that will enable one to discern in what man, or assembly of men, sovereign power resides and is placed. These rights are incommunicable[10] and inseparable. The power to coin money, to dispose of the estate and persons of infant heirs, to have pre-emption in markets, and all other statute prerogatives may be transferred by the sovereign, and yet, the power to protect his subjects will be retained. But if he transfers his power over the militia, he will retain the judicature in vain, for he will be unable to execute the laws. If he gives away the power to raise money, his control over the militia will be in vain. If he gives away the government of doctrines, men will be frightened into rebellion due to the fear of spirits. If one takes away any one of the rights of the sovereign, we shall presently see that holding all of the rest will not allow the sovereign to conserve peace and justice, which are the ends for which all commonwealths are instituted. This is the division that is referred to when it is said, "A kingdom divided in itself cannot stand." When there is such a division, division into opposite armies happens. If there had not first been the received opinion in the greatest part of England that these powers were divided between the King, the Lords, and the House of Commons, the people would never have been divided and would not have fallen into this civil war. This occurred when first disagreement arose about politics, and after between dissenters about the liberty of religion. The results have instructed men on the point of sovereign rights, so that there are now few in England that do not see that these rights are inseparable. This will be generally acknowledged at the next return of peace, and will continue until the miseries of the civil war are forgotten. At that time, the point about the inseparability of sovereign rights will be forgotten too, unless the vulgar are better taught then they have been hitherto.[11]

The sovereign cannot pass away these rights without the direct renunciation of the sovereign power. These are essential and inseparable rights of sovereign power. It follows necessarily, that even if there are some words that indicate that some of the rights have been granted away, the grant is void. If the sovereign power itself is not renounced in direct terms, then those who have received the rights can no longer use the name of sovereign to refer to the one who granted the rights. Even if the sovereign granted away all that he can, if we grant back the sovereignty, all is restored as inseparably as it had been previously.

The power and honor of subjects vanishes in the presence of the sovereign power.

This great authority is indivisible and is inseparably annexed to the sovereign. There is little ground for the opinion that says that sovereign kings, though they be *singulis majores,* which means of greater power than every one of their subjects, are still *universis minores,* that is, of less power than all of them together. But if by "all together" they mean not the collective body as one person, then 'all together' and 'every one' means the same thing, and the statement is absurd. But if by "all together" they understand that to mean as one person, which the sovereign bears, then the power of all together is the same as the sovereign's power, and so again the statement is absurd. This absurdity is easily seen when the sovereignty is in an assembly of people. But people do not see this in a monarchy, even though the power of sovereignty is the same in whomever it is placed.

As the power of the sovereign is greater than any, or all of the subjects, so is the honor of the sovereign. For the sovereign is the fountain[12] of honor. The titles of Lord, Earl, Duke and Prince are his creations. Just as in the presence of the master, the servants are equal and without any honor at all, so it is with subjects in the presence of the sovereign. Though some might shine more and some less when they are out of his sight, in his presence they shine no more than the stars do in the presence of the sun.

Sovereign power not as hurtful as the lack of it, and the hurt proceeds for the greatest part from not submitting readily to a lesser part. Someone might here object that the condition of subjects is very miserable, as being liable to the lusts and other irregular passions of him, or them, that have such an unlimited power in their hands. Those that live in a monarchy, think the fault lies with the monarch, and those that live under the government of a democracy or other sovereign assembly attribute all of their inconveniences to that form of commonwealth. But the power in all its forms, if it is good enough to protect people, is the same. The estate of man can never be without some incommodity or another, and the greatest of them that can possibly happen to the people in general in any form of government, is a civil war, where the miseries and horrible calamities that accompany it are scarcely sensible. Or consider the dissolute condition of masterless men without being subject to laws, when they have no coercive power to tie their hands from rapine and revenge. Consider that the greatest pressure on sovereign governors does not proceed from any delight or profit they can gain from the damage or the weakening of their subjects. Their own strength and glory consists in their subjects' vigor. The pressure on sovereign governors comes from the restiveness[13] of themselves and their unwillingness to draw contributions from their subjects in time of peace for their own defense, so that the governors may have the means on any emergent occasion, or sudden need, to resist or take advantage of their enemies. All men are provided with notable multiplying glasses,[14] which are their passions and self-love, and make every little payment appear to be a great grievance. But people are lacking those prospective glasses,[15] namely moral and civil science, which would enable them to see far-off miseries that hang over them, and cannot be avoided without making such payments.

Endnotes

1. Claim
2. That is, the state of nature
3. Hobbes means here that there is no covenant between the sovereign and the people. Rather, the people covenant with each other to form a sovereign. The sovereign is not a party to the covenant.
4. Agree
5. Hobbes himself was prevented from publishing any political works in England after the Fire of London in 1666.
6. Poorly
7. Property
8. Mine and yours
9. Military
10. Unchangeable
11. Hobbes gave his view of the history of English Revolution in *Behemoth*, 1679.
12. Source
13. Refusal
14. Magnifying lenses
15. Telescopes

CHAPTER 19

Of the Several Kinds of Commonwealth by Institution and the Secession to the Sovereign Power

The different forms of commonwealth are but three. The differences of commonwealths consists in the difference of the sovereign, or the person that is representative of all and every one of the multitude. The sovereignty is either in one man or in an assembly of more than one man. If the latter, every man has a right to be in it, or if not, only certain men who are distinguished from the rest. It is thus manifest that there can be but three kinds of commonwealths. For the sovereign must be either one man or more, and if it is more, than it is the assembly of all, or a part of the all. When the representative is one men, then the commonwealth is a monarchy. When the assembly is of all that come together, it is a democracy, or popular commonwealth. When the assembly is only a part of the whole group, it is called an aristocracy. There can be no other kinds of commonwealths, for either one or more or all must have the entire sovereign power, which I have shown to be indivisible.

Tyranny and oligarchy are but different names of monarchy and aristocracy. There are other names of kinds of government such as tyranny and oligarchy in histories and books about policy. But these are not names of other forms of government, but are just are names of forms that are not liked. Those that are discontented with monarchy, call it tyranny, and those displeased with aristocracy, call it oligarchy. In the same way, those who find themselves with grievances under a democracy, call it anarchy, which signifies a lack of government. Yet I think that no man believes that the lack of government is a new kind of government. Nor for the same reason should they believe that the government is of one kind when they like it, and of another when they do not like it, or are oppressed by the governors.

Subordinate representatives are dangerous. It is manifest that men who are in absolute liberty may, if they please, give authority to one man to represent every one of them as well as give such authority to an assembly of men. Consequently, these men may subject themselves if they think it is good to a monarch as absolutely to any other kind of representative. Where there is already an established sovereign, there can be no other representative of the same people, except for certain particular ends that are limited by the sovereign. Otherwise, there would be two sovereigns, and every man would have his person represented by two actors that may oppose each other. This would divide that power which is indivisible if men are to live in peace. This would reduce the multitude to the condition of war, contrary to the end for which all sovereignty is instituted. Therefore it is absurd to think that a sovereign assembly would invite people of their dominion to send up their deputies to give advice and make known their desires, and the assembly would consider the deputies, rather than themselves, to be the absolute representatives of the people. Such a thing would be just as absurd in a monarchy. I do not know how so obvious a truth should lately be so little observed. Consider a monarchy in which the sovereignty had an ancestry of 600 years[1] where the king was alone called sovereign and had the title of "Majesty" from every one of his subjects and was unquestionably taken by them for their king, and was nevertheless, not considered as their representative. The title of representative was given to those men at his command who were sent up by the people to carry their petitions to him and give him their advice if he permitted it. This may serve as an admonition for those that are the true and absolute representatives of a people to instruct men in the nature of the office of representation, and take heed how they admit general representation on any occasion if they are to discharge the trust committed to them.

Comparison of monarchy with sovereign assemblies. The difference between these three kinds of commonwealth does not consist in the difference in power. Rather, the difference is a matter of convenience, or the aptitude to produce the peace and security of the people, which is the end for which commonwealths were instituted. To compare monarchies with the other two forms we may observe the following. First, whoever bears the person of the people, or is on of that assembly that bears it, also bears his own natural person. And though he may be careful in his political person to procure the common interest, yet he is also more, and not less careful to procure the private good of himself, his family and kin, and his friends. For the most part if the public interest chances to conflict with the private, he will prefer the private, for the passions of men are commonly more potent than their reason. It thus follows that when the public and private interest are most closely united, the public's interest will be the most advanced. In a monarchy the private interest is the same as the public. The riches, power and honor of a monarch arise only from the riches, strength and reputation of his subjects. For no king can be rich, nor glorious, nor secure, whose subjects are either poor or contemptible or too weak through want or dissension to maintain a war against their enemies. But in a democracy or an aristocracy, public prosperity does not coincide so much with the private fortune of one that is corrupt or ambitious. Many times it is in the interest of such people to offer perfidious advice, perform treacherous actions or even foment civil war.

Secondly, a monarch can receive the counsel of anyone, when and where he pleases. He can hear the opinion of men versed in the matter about which he deliberates. They can be of any rank or quality, and can hear them long before the time of action, and with as much secrecy as he wills. But when a sovereign assembly has the need of counsel, none are admitted but those that have a right to be there from the beginning. For the most part these are people who have been more versed in the acquisition of wealth than of knowledge. They usually give their advice in the form of long discourses, which may, and commonly do excite men to action, but do not govern them in it. The understanding is dazzled by the flame of the passions, but is never enlightened by them. Nor is there any place or time where an assembly can receive counsel in secrecy because of their own multitude.

Thirdly, the resolutions of a monarch are subject to no other inconstancy besides that of human nature. But in assemblies, besides the matter of human nature, there is the inconstancy that is a result of numbers. The absence of a few might make a resolution once made, continue to be firmly held, and this can happen by security, negligence or private impediments. But the appearance of a few that have a contrary opinion, can undo today, all that was concluded yesterday.

Fourthly, a monarch cannot disagree with himself out of envy or interest. But an assembly may and to such an extent that it may produce a civil war.

Fifthly, in monarchies there is the inconvenience, which I confess can be great and inevitable, that any subject may be deprived of all he possesses by the power of one man in order to enrich a favorite or a flatterer. But the same may happen where the sovereign power is an assembly, where the power of the members is the same, and they are as subject to evil counsel and to be seduced by orators as monarchs by flatterers. Members of an assembly can also become one another's flatterers, and serve each other's covetousness and ambition by turns. Whereas the favorites of monarchs are few, and the monarchs have no one else to advance besides their own kin, the favorites of an assembly are many, and their kin are much more numerous than of any monarch. Besides, there is no favorite of a monarch who cannot as well succor his friends as hurt his enemies. But orators, who are the favorites of sovereign assemblies, though they have great power to hurt, have little to save. This is so because such is man's nature that to accuse requires less eloquence than to excuse, and condemnation, rather than absolution, resembles justice more.

Sixthly, there is the inconvenience in monarchy that sovereignty may descend upon an infant, or on one that cannot discern the difference between good and evil. In those cases the use of his power must be in the hand of another man, or an assembly of men who are to govern by his right and in his name as curators, and protectors of his person, and as the authority. But saying that there is an inconvenience in putting the use of the sovereign power into the hands of a man, or an assembly of men, implies that all government is more inconvenient than confusion and civil war. All the danger that can be pretended[2] arises from the contention of those who are competing for an office of such great honor and profit. But this inconvenience does not proceed just from the form of government that is called monarchy. For consider that the preceding monarch could have appointed someone who shall have tuition[3] of his infant successor. He might do this expressly by testament, or tacitly, by not changing the custom in this particular case. Then, if the inconvenience does occur, it should not be attributed to monarchy as a form of government, but to the ambition and injustice of the subjects, which occurs in all kinds of governments where the people are not well instructed in their duty and the rights of sovereignty. But suppose the preceding monarch did not provide for the tuition of his successor. In that case the Laws of Nature provide a sufficient rule. That is that the tuition of the successor shall be given to the one who has by nature the most interest in the preservation of the authority of the infant, and to whom the least benefit can accrue by the infant's death or diminution. Since every man by nature seeks his own benefit and promotion, to put an infant into the power of those that can promote themselves by his destruction or damage is not tuition, but treachery. If sufficient provision is taken to prevent a quarrel about the government under a child, then any contention that arises that leads to the disturbance of the public peace should not be attributed to the form of monarchy, but to the ambition of the subjects and to their ignorance of their duty. On the other hand, in any commonwealth where the sovereignty is a great assembly, the consultations concerning peace, war and the making of laws are in the same condition as if the government resided in a child. Just as child lacks the judgment to dissent from the counsel given him, and is thus necessitated to take the advice of him, or them, to whom he is committed, an assembly also lacks the liberty to dissent from the counsel of the majority, be it good or bad. Just as a child needs a tutor or protector to preserve his person and authority, so a sovereign assembly in great commonwealths, needs to have *custodes libertatis*[4] in times of great danger and troubles. These are dictators[5] or protectors of their authority, who are in effect, temporary monarchs to whom for time the assembly commits the entire exercise of their power. These temporary monarchs have more often deprived the assembly of their sovereignty than infant kings have been deposed by their protectors, regents, or any other tutors.

As I have shown there are but three kinds of sovereignty. They are monarchy, where one man has it, democracy where the general assembly of subjects has it, and aristocracy, where the assembly is just some nominated certain persons or others somehow distinguished from the rest. But some people that consider the actual commonwealths have been and are in the world, will perhaps think that all the forms cannot be reduced to just three, and that there are other forms derived by mingling the three forms together. One example is elective kingdoms, where kings have the sovereign power put into their hands for a time. Another example is kingdoms where kings have limited power, which most writers still call monarchies. Also, if a popular or aristocratic commonwealth subdues an enemy country, and governs it by a president, procurator, or other magistrate, this may appear at first sight to be an example of a democratic or aristocratic government. But it is not so. Elective kings are not sovereigns, but are ministers of the sovereign, nor are limited kings sovereigns, but are ministers of those that have the sovereign power. Nor are the provinces that are subjected by democracies or aristocracies of another commonwealth, democratically or aristocratically governed. Rather, they are governed monarchically.

First, consider elective kings whose power is limited to their life, as occurs in many places in Christendom to this day, or to certain years and months, as occurred with the dictators' power among the Romans. If the king or dictator has the right to appoint his successor, he is no longer an elective monarch, but a hereditary one. If he has no power to elect his successor, then there is some other man, or assembly, which after his death may elect someone new. Otherwise, the commonwealth will die and dissolve with him and will return to the condition of war. If it is known who has the power to give the sovereignty after the king or dictator's death, it is also known that the sovereignty resided in them before the death. For no one has the right to give something that they do not have the right to possess, or to keep it for themselves if they think doing so is good. But if there is no one that can give the sovereignty to anyone after the death of a king who was elected, then the king has the power. In fact, he is obliged by the Law of Nature to provide a successor, to keep those that had trusted him with the government from relapsing into the miserable condition of civil war. In that case, when he was elected, he became an absolute sovereign.

Secondly, the king whose power is limited is not superior to him, or them, that have the power to limit it. He that is not superior is not supreme, which mean he is not sovereign. The sovereignty therefore was always in the assembly that had the right to limit him. As a result the government is not a monarchy, but is either a democracy or an aristocracy. An example of this was in ancient times in Sparta, where the kings had the privilege to lead the armies, but the sovereignty was in the Ephori.

Thirdly, consider the example of the Roman people that governed the land of Judea by means of a president. This did not make Judea a democracy. They were not governed by an assembly in which any of them had a right to enter. Nor were they governed by an aristocracy, because they were not governed by an elected assembly. Rather, they were governed by one person, and while this person was appointed by the people of Rome by their democratic assembly, as far as the people of Judea were concerned, since they had no right to participate in the government, this one appointed person was a monarch. Where the people are governed by an assembly chosen by themselves out of their own number, the government is called a democracy or aristocracy. But when a people is governed by an assembly not of their own choosing, it is a monarchy—not of one man over another man, but of one people over another people.

Of the right of succession. All forms of government are mortal, as not only monarchs, but assemblies also die. As it is necessary for the conservation of the peace of men to construct an artificial man, it is also necessary for the artificial man to have an eternity of life. Without this, men that are governed by an assembly would return into the condition of war in every age, as would those who are governed by one man as soon as this man dies. This artificial eternity is what is called the right of succession.

There is no perfect form of government where the disposing[6] of the succession is not in the hands of the present sovereign. If the right is in any particular one's hand, either one man or in a private assembly, it is in a person, and may be assumed by the sovereign at his pleasure, and so the sovereign has the right in himself. If the right does not exist in any particular person, but is left to a new choice, then the commonwealth is dissolved, and the right belongs to anyone that can get it. This is contrary to the intention of those that instituted the commonwealth, for they did so for their perpetual, and not temporary, security.

In a democracy the whole assembly cannot fail unless the multitude fails that are to be governed. And therefore questions of the right of succession in that form of government have no place at all.

In an aristocracy, when any member of the assembly dies, the election of another to replace him belongs to the assembly, as it is the sovereign that has the power to choose all counselors and officers. For what the representative does in the role of actor, every one of the subjects do in the role of the author. Even though a sovereign assembly may give power to others to elect new men to supply their court, yet the election is done by the authority of the assembly. In the same way the election may be recalled when the public requires it.

The present monarch has the right to dispose of the succession. The greatest difficulty about the right of succession occurs in monarchies. The difficulty arises from this—at first sight, it is not manifest who is to appoint the successor, nor many times, who it is that he has appointed. In both of these cases, there is the requirement for more exact ratiocination[7] than every man is accustomed to use.

Consider the question of who shall appoint the successor of a monarch. This is the question of who has the sovereign power to determine the right of inheritance, as elective kings and princes do not own this right, but only can use it. If the king does not have the right to dispose the succession, then the right belongs to the dissolved multitude. If a monarch who owns the right of succession dies, that leaves the multitude without any sovereign at all. They are without any representative in whom they can be united and thus are incapable of unified action. Therefore this multitude would be incapable of electing a new monarch. Every individual man would have an equal right to do whatever he thought best to protect himself. If he thinks he can protect himself best with his own sword, this will be a return to confusion and to the condition of war of every man against every man. This is contrary to the end for which monarchy was first instituted. Therefore, it is manifest that by the institution of monarchy, the disposing of the successor is always left to the judgment and will of the present possessor of sovereignty.

As for the question, which sometimes may arise, of whom the monarch has designated to be his successor and inherit his *power, it is to be determined by his express words and testament, or by other tacit signs that are sufficient for this purpose.*

Succession passes by express words. The first emperors of Rome declared who should be their heirs by express words, or testament, when they declared, *viva voce,*[8] during their lifetime, or else by writing. The word 'heir' does not by itself designate one's children or nearest kin, but rather whomever a man shall in any way declare should succeed him in his estate. If a monarch declares expressly by word or writing that a particular man shall be his heir, then that man is invested with the right of being the monarch immediately after the decease of his predecessor.

Or, by not controlling a custom: If testament and express words are absent, other natural signs of the will are to be followed. One of them is custom. Where the custom is that the next of kin absolutely is the successor, then the next of kin has the right to the succession. If the will of the one who owned the right to appoint a successor had wished otherwise, he could have easily declared so during his life. Likewise, where the custom is that the next male kin is the successor, then the right of succession is owned by the next male kin. The same follows if the custom is that the next female kin is the one that is advanced. For whatever the custom is, if the monarch may control it by a word and does not, that is a natural sign he would have that custom stand.

Or by presumption of natural affection. But suppose neither custom nor testament is in place. Then the following is to be understood: First, that the monarch's will is that the government remain monarchical. Secondly, that his own child, either male or female, is to be preferred before any other, because men are presumed to be more inclined by nature to advance their own children than the children of other men. And of their own children, they are more inclined to their sons rather than their daughters, because men are naturally more fit than women for actions of labor and danger. Thirdly, if a monarch has no children, then he would prefer a brother to a stranger, and someone nearer by blood to him than more remote, because it is always presumed that the nearer of kin is the nearer in affection. It is also evident that a man receives the most reflected honor from the greatness of his nearest kin.

To dispose the succession to a king of another nation is not unlawful. If it is lawful for a monarch to dispose of the succession by words of contract or testament, some may perhaps object that this raises a great inconvenience. The monarch may sell or give his right of governing to a stranger. Strangers are those that live under a different government and speak a different language. Strangers commonly undervalue one another, and so they may turn to the oppression of the subjects, and this is indeed a great inconvenience. However, this inconvenience does not proceed necessarily from subjection to the government of a stranger, but from the lack of skill of governors who are ignorant of the true rules of politics. The Romans who subdued many nations, in order to make their government digestible, were accustomed to take away this particular grievance as much as they thought necessary, by giving the name of Romans and Roman privileges sometimes to whole nations and sometimes to the principal men of every nation they conquered. They took many of the men of these nations into the Senate, and gave them offices in charge, even in Rome itself. This is also what our most wise king, King James, aimed to do by endeavoring to form a union of his two realms of England and Scotland. If he would have been successful, it would have in likelihood prevented the civil wars which currently make both of these kingdoms miserable. It is therefore not an injury to the people for a monarch to dispose of the succession by his will. Rather, the inconvenience that is sometimes found in this is the fault of many princes. It is in any case clearly lawful for a monarch to give his kingdom to a stranger. Whatever inconvenience this might produce can also occur by a monarch marrying a stranger, as the right of succession may descend upon the spouse. Yet everyone considers this to be lawful.

Endnotes

1. Hobbes is referring to the English monarchy.
2. Claimed
3. Teacher or instructor
4. Guardians of liberty
5. In ancient Rome a person constitutionally invested with great authority during a crisis.
6. Arranging
7. Calculation
8. By actual utterance

CHAPTER 20

Of Paternal and Despotic Dominion

Commonwealth by acquisition. Commonwealth by acquisition occurs where the sovereign power is acquired by force. It is acquired by force when men singly, or many together, by a plurality of voices, from fear of death or bonds, authorize all the actions of the man, or an assembly, that has their lives and liberty in their power.

The difference from commonwealth by institution. This kind of dominion of sovereignty differs from sovereignty by institution only in this: Men who choose their sovereign do it out of fear of one another and not of the one they institute. But in sovereignty by dominion, men subject themselves to a sovereign because they are afraid of him. In both cases they do it out of fear. This should be noted by those who hold that all covenants are void that proceed from fear of death or violence. If this were true, then no one in any kind of commonwealth would be obliged to be obedient. It is true, however, that once a commonwealth is instituted or acquired, that promises proceeding from fear of death or violence are not covenants and do no create obligations, if what was promised is contrary to the laws. The reason for this, however, is not because the promise was made from fear, but because the one who promised had no right to promise what he did. Also when a person may lawfully perform a promise and does not, he is not absolved by the invalidity of that particular covenant, but rather by the sentence of the sovereign. Otherwise, whenever a man lawfully promises, he unlawfully breaks it, but when the sovereign is the actor who acquits him, then he is acquitted by him that extorted the promise, who is the author of this absolution.

The rights of sovereignty are the same in both. The rights and consequences of sovereignty are the same in both. His power cannot without his consent be transferred to another. He cannot forfeit it. He cannot be accused of injury by any of his subjects. He cannot be punished by them. He is the judge of what is necessary for peace, and the judge of what doctrines can be taught. He is the sole legislator and the supreme judge of controversies. He is the sole judge of the times and occasions to make war and peace. He has the right to choose magistrates, counselors, commanders, and all other officers and ministers, and the right to determine rewards, punishments, honor and order. The reasons for all of this are the same as were stated in the previous chapter on the rights and consequences of sovereignty by institution.

Paternal dominion, how attained. Not by generation, but by contract. Dominion is acquired in two ways: by generation and by conquest. The right of dominion by generation is what parents have over their children and is called paternal. The dominion is not derived from the generation of the children, as if the parent had dominion over his child because he begat him. It derives rather from the child's consent that is either expressly made or is declared by other sufficient arguments. When it comes to generation, God has ordained a helper to man, as there are always two that are equally the parents. The dominion of the child should therefore belong equally to both, and the child should be equally subject to both. But this is impossible for no man can obey two masters. Some have attributed the parental dominion to men only, on account of being the more excellent sex, but this is to make a mistake in reasoning. There is not always that difference of strength and prudence between men and women as that right can be determined without war.[1] In commonwealths this controversy is decided by the civil law. For the most part, but not always, the law decides in favor of the father, because for the most part commonwealths have been erected by the fathers and not the mothers of families. But consider this question of parental dominion in the state of mere nature, where there are no laws of matrimony and no laws for the education of children, but there is just the natural inclination of the sexes to each other and to their children. In the condition of mere nature, either the parents dispose of the dominion over the child by contract between themselves,[2] or they do not dispose of it at all. If they do dispose of the right of dominion, the right passes according to the contract. We find in history that the Amazons contracted with the men in neighboring countries, with whom they had recourse for procreation, that male children would be sent back, but that the female children would remain with the Amazons. In this case the dominion of the females rested with the mother.

On education. If there is no contract, the dominion is the mother's. In the condition of mere nature where there are no matrimonial laws, it cannot be known who is the father, unless it is declared by the mother. Therefore the right of dominion over the child depends on her will and is consequently hers. The infant is from the beginning in the power of the mother, as she may either nourish it or expose it. If she nourishes it, the child owes its life to the mother, and is therefore obliged to obey her rather than any other and as a consequence, the dominion over the child is hers. But if she does expose it and another person finds it and nourishes it, then the dominion belongs to the one that nourished it. The child ought to obey the one who preserved it. The reason is that preservation of life is the end for which one man becomes subject to another. Every man is supposed to promise obedience to the one who has the power to save or destroy him.

Or precedent subjection of one of the parents to the other. If the mother is the father's subject, the child is in the father's power. But if the father is the mother's subject, as when a sovereign queen is married to one of her subjects, the child is subject to the mother, as the father is also her subject.

If a man and a woman who are both monarchs of two different kingdoms have a child together, and if they make a contract who shall have dominion of the child, then the right of dominion is determined by that contract. If they do not make a contract, then the dominion is determined the dominion of the place of residence. The sovereign of each country has dominion over everyone that resides there.

The right of succession follows the rules of the right of possession. The right of succession to paternal dominion proceeds in the same way as does the right of succession in a monarchy, and I have already spoken sufficiently about this in the preceding chapter.

Despotic dominion, how attained. Dominion acquired by conquest or victory in war is what some writers call despotic, from the Greek word, *despotes,* which means a lord or master and is the dominion of a master over his servant. This dominion is acquired by the victor when in order to avoid the present stroke of death, the vanquished covenants, either by express words or by other sufficient signs of his will, to allow himself to serve and be used by the victor, as long as his own life and the liberty of his body be allowed to him. Only after this covenant is made is the vanquished a servant. The term 'servant' may be derived from the Latin *servire* to serve, or from *servare* to save, but I leave this to the grammarians to dispute. In any case 'servant' does not mean a captive that is kept in prison or bonds until his owner, or the one that took him, decides what to do with him. Such people are called slaves and they have no obligations at all, for they may justly break their bonds, escape from prison, or kill or capture their master. However, a person who is captured and is allowed corporal liberty based on the promise not to run away, nor to violently harm his master, does incur an obligation of trust.

Not by the victory, but by the consent of the vanquished. It is therefore not the victory that gives the right of dominion over the vanquished, but the vanquished's own covenant. The vanquished is not obligated to obey the victor because he is conquered, which is to be beaten, taken, or put to flight. Rather, it is because the vanquished came in and submitted to the victor. Nor is the victor obliged to spare an enemy due to his rendering himself without the promise of life based on the enemy's discretion. This action of the enemy does not oblige the victor any more than the victor's discretion shall think fit.

When men demand what is now called quarter (which the Greeks call *zogria* which means taking alive), they are trying to evade the present fury of the victor by submission and compound[3] their life for ransom or service. So one that has received quarter does not have his life given back to him, but this matter is deferred until further deliberation. Asking for quarter is not yielding on the condition of being given life, but rather yielding to the victor's discretion. The vanquished's life is only secure and his service is due to the victor when the victor has trusted the vanquished with corporal liberty. Slaves who work in prisons or fetters do not do it out of duty, but to avoid the cruelty of their taskmasters.

The master of a servant is the master of all that the servant has and may exact the use thereof. That means the master can use the servant's goods, labor, own servants, and children as often as the master thinks fit. The servant only has his life by agreeing to be obedient to the master, and that means that the servant has authorized whatever the master shall do. So if a servant refuses to obey the master, and thus is killed, cast into bonds or otherwise punished, the servant himself is the author of these actions, and so cannot accuse the master of injury.

In sum, the rights and consequences of both paternal and despotic dominion are the very same as those of a sovereign by institution. The reasons are the very same ones that were set down in the preceding chapter. Consider a monarch of diverse nations where he has sovereignty over some by institution of the assembled people, and in others by conquest, where the people submitted to avoid death and bonds. It is ignorance of the rights of sovereignty to demand more from the nation that was conquered than of the other people. A sovereign is absolute over both in the same way; otherwise, there is no sovereignty at all. In this latter case, every man can lawfully protect himself with his own sword if he can, and this is the condition of war.

Difference between a family and a kingdom. It may seem then that a great family, if it is not part of a commonwealth, is like a little monarchy in relation to the rights of sovereignty. It would seem that the father or master is the sovereign, whether the family consists of a man and his children, or a man and his servants, or a man and his children and servants together. Nevertheless, a family is not really a commonwealth unless it has enough power in its own numbers, or by other means, to not be subdued without the hazard of war. Where a group of united men are manifestly too week to defend themselves, every individual may use his own reason in time of danger to save his own life as he thinks best, either by flight or submission to the enemy. In the same manner a very small company of soldiers, surprised by an army, may cast down their arms and demand quarter, or run away rather than be put to the sword. This much suffices for what I find by speculation[4] and deduction of the sovereign's rights, based on the nature, needs and designs of men, in erecting commonwealths and putting themselves under monarchs or assemblies, and entrusting them with enough power for their protection.

The rights of monarchy from Scripture. Let us now consider what the Scriptures teach on these points.[5] The children of Israel said to Moses: "Speak to us and we will hear you, but let not God speak to us, lest we die" (Exodus 20:19) This shows the children of Israel's absolute obedience to Moses. Concerning the right of kings, God Himself said through the mouth of Samuel: "This shall be the right of the king you will have to reign over you. He shall take your sons and set them to drive his chariots, and to be his horsemen, and to run before his chariots, and gather in his harvest, and to make his engines of war and instruments of his chariots, and shall take your daughters to make perfumes, to be his cooks and bakers. He shall take your fields, your vineyards, and your olive-yards, and give them to his servants. He shall take the tithe of your corn and wine, and give it to the men of his chamber and to his other servants. He shall take your man-servants and your maid-servants, and the choice of your youth, and employ them in his business. He shall take the tithe of your flocks and you shall be his servants." (Samuel I, 8:11, 12, etc.) This is absolute power, which is summed up in the last words, "you shall be his servants." When the people heard what power their king was to have, they still consented to it and said, "We will be as all other nations and our king shall judge our causes and go before us to conduct our wars." (Samuel I, 8:19) Here, the rights the sovereign has are confirmed, as concerns both the militia and the judicature which contain all of the absolute power that one man can possibly transfer to another.[6] The prayer of King Solomon to God was this: "Give to thy servant understanding to judge thy people and to discern between good and evil." (Kings I, 3:9) This means that the sovereign has to power to be judge and to prescribe the rules of "discerning good and evil". These rules are laws, and thus the sovereign has the legislative power. Saul sought to kill David, and yet when it was in David's power to slay Saul, and David's servants would have done it, David forbade them saying, "God forbid I should do such an act against my Lord, the anointed of God." (Samuel I, 24:9) Considering obedience to servants, St. Paul says, "Servants, obey your masters in all things" (Colassians 3:20) and "Children, obey your parents in all things." (Colassians 3:22) This implies that there is nothing but simple obedience in cases of paternal or despotic obedience. Again, "The scribes and Pharisees sit in Moses' chair, and therefore all that they shall bid you observe, that you should observe and do." (Matthew 23: 2 and 3) This again is simple obedience. From St. Paul, "Warn them that subject themselves to princes and to those that are in authority, and obey them." (Titus 3:2) This is also simple obedience. Lastly, our Savior himself acknowledges that men ought to pay the taxes imposed by kings when he says, "Give to Caesar what is Caesar's", and He paid such taxes himself. Christ also said that the king's word is sufficient to take anything from any subject when there is a need, and that king is the judge of that need. He himself as the king of the Jews commanded his disciples to take the ass, and the ass's colt to carry him into Jerusalem saying, "Go into the village over against you, and you shall find a she-ass tied, and her colt with her. Untie them, and bring them to me. And if any man asks you what you mean by it, say the Lord has need of them. And they will let you go." (Matthew 21:2 and 3) They will not ask whether this necessity is sufficient reason, nor whether Christ be the judge of that necessity. They will just acquiesce to the will of the Lord.

To the above passages, the following may be added from *Genesis*: "You shall be as gods knowing good and evil." (Genesis 3:5) Also, verse 11, "Who told you that you were naked? Have you eaten of the tree that I commanded you that you should not eat?" As a trial of Adam's obedience, he was forbidden to eat form the fruit of the tree that was named the tree of knowledge, which would provide cognizance and judgment of good and evil. But the devil enflamed the ambition of the woman, to whom the fruit already seemed beautiful, and told her that by tasting it, they would become gods, knowing good and evil. When they did eat it, they did indeed take upon themselves God's office, which is the judgment of good and evil, but they acquired no new ability to distinguish between them aright.[7] It is said that having eaten the fruit, they saw that they were naked. No one has interpreted this passage to mean that they formerly were blind and were not able to see their own skins. Rather, the meaning is plain, and that is that it was then that they first judged their nakedness (which it was how God's will was to create them) to be uncomely. By being ashamed, they tacitly censured God himself. That is why God then says, "Have you eaten, etc." as if saying, do you who owe me obedience, take it upon yourselves to judge my commandments? So it is clearly, though allegorically, signified, that the commands of the one who has the right to command are not to be censured or disputed by their subjects.[8]

It thus appears plainly to my understanding, both from reason and the Scriptures, that sovereign power, whether placed in one man as in monarchy, or in one assembly of men as in popular and aristocratic commonwealths, is as great as possibly men can imagine to make it. Men may think that such unlimited power may have many evil consequences, but the lack of such power, which is the war of every man against his neighbor, is much worse. The condition of man in this life shall never be without inconveniences, but in any commonwealth the inconveniences proceed from the subjects' disobedience and breach of those covenants which are the origin of the commonwealth. Whoever thinks sovereign power is too great and will seek to make it less must subject himself to the power that can limit it, and that means to a greater power.

The greatest objection in practice to this view of sovereign power occurs when men ask where and when have subjects acknowledged that the sovereign has such power. One may respond by asking such men, when or where has there been a kingdom that has been long free of sedition and civil war. In the nations and commonwealths that have had long lives and have not been destroyed by foreign wars, the subjects never disputed the sovereign's power. But any argument based on practice of men is invalid, if it has not sifted the reasons to get to the bottom of matters and with exact reason weighed the causes and nature of commonwealth. People who do not do this suffer daily from the miseries that proceed from ignorance of these matters. It could be that everywhere in the world, men set the foundations of their houses on sand. From this it cannot be inferred that they ought to do so. The skill of making and maintaining commonwealths consists of certain rules as do arithmetic and geometry. It is not like playing tennis, which relies only on practice.

However, poor men do not have the leisure and men who have had the leisure have lacked the curiosity and method to find the rules that apply to commonwealths.

Endnotes

1. Hobbes is challenging here the Scholastic tradition based on Aristotle that men are naturally superior to women.
2. Hobbes' consistency is in question here as he earlier said that contracts in the state of nature are void.
3. Exchange
4. Consideration
5. At this point Hobbes begins the project of trying to show that all of his controversial views about politics are consistent with what is said in the Bible.
6. When Samuel tell the people of Israel that the king will do various things to them, he is not describing the legitimate powers of a monarch, but is trying to dissuade the people from having a king. Thus, this seems to be a cynical use of the Bible to support Hobbes' views about the rights of sovereigns.
7. Correctly
8. This is an especially imaginative interpretation of the Bible on Hobbes' part to support his own views.

CHAPTER 21

Of the Liberty of Subjects

What is liberty. Liberty, or freedom, when properly used, mean the absence of opposition, and by opposition I mean external impediments of motion. These terms can be applied to irrational and inanimate creatures, as well as to rational. For if something is so tied or environed[1] so that it can only move with a certain space that is determined by the opposition of external bodies, we say that the thing does not have the liberty to go further. For living creatures that are imprisoned by walls or chains, we say that they are not at liberty to move as they would if those external impediments were absent. We say the same about water when it is kept in by banks or vessels for without them it would spread itself into a larger space. But when the impediment of motion is in the constitution of the thing itself, we do not say that it lacks liberty, but that it lacks the power to move. Two examples of this are a stone that lays still, or a man that is fastened to his bed by sickness.

What it is to be free. According to this proper and generally received meaning of the word, a free man is one that is not hindered to do what he has a will to do and that he is able to do by his strength and wit. 'Free' and 'liberty' can be applied to any thing, but it is an abuse to apply them merely to physical bodies,[2] for what is not subject to motion is not subject to impediment. And so when someone says that the way is free, it does not mean that the path has liberty, but that those who walk on the path can do so without stopping. And when we say a gift is free, we do not mean that there is any liberty in the gift itself, but that the giver was not bound by any law or covenant to give it. When we say that we speak freely, we are not referring to the liberty of the voice or of pronunciation, but of the speaker whom no law obliged to speak otherwise than he did. Lastly, from the use of the term 'free-will', no liberty can be inferred of the will, desire or inclination of a man, for the liberty refers to the man himself. This liberty consists in that he finds no stop to doing what he has the will, desire or inclination to do.

Fear and liberty are consistent. Fear and liberty are consistent as when a man throws his goods into the sea from fear the ship will sink. This man does these actions willingly, and may refuse to do them if he wills. Therefore throwing the goods is an action of one who is free. Similarly, when a man pays his debts only out of fear of imprisonment, it is the action of a man at liberty, because nobody hindered him from not paying. Generally, all actions which men do in commonwealths from fear of the law are actions which the doers have the liberty to omit.

Liberty and necessity are consistent. Water has not only the liberty, but also the necessity of descending through a particular channel. Likewise, the actions which men voluntarily do proceeds from their will, and so proceeds from liberty. Yet, because every act of men's wills and every desire and inclination proceed from some cause, and that from some other cause in a continual chain, (whose first link is in the hand of God, the first of all causes), every act proceeds from necessity. If someone could see the connection of all of the causes, the necessity of all of men's voluntary actions would be manifest. Therefore God who sees and disposes of all things, also sees that the liberty of men is in doing what they will, which is accompanied the necessity of doing that which God wills, and no more and no less. Men may do many things that God does not command and therefore is not the author of these actions. But men can have no passion, or appetite for any thing, where God's will was not the cause of the appetite. God's will assures the necessity of men's wills and consequently all the things men will depends on Him. Otherwise, the liberty of men would be a contradiction and impediment to the liberty of God. This suffices as an account of that natural liberty which is the only thing that properly may be called liberty.

Artificial bonds or covenants. In order to attain peace and the conservation of themselves, men have made an artificial man, which we call a commonwealth. They have also made artificial chains for themselves by mutual covenants, which are called civil laws. They are fastened the chains at one end to the lips of the man, or assembly, to whom they have given the sovereign power, and the other end to their own ears. Even though these bonds may be weak of their own nature, they may still hold because of the danger, but not the difficulty, of breaking them.

Liberty of subjects consists in liberty from covenants. I will only speak at this point of the liberty of subjects in relation to these bonds. There is no commonwealth in the world where there are rules for regulating all the actions and words of men. To try to do this would be impossible. It thus follows necessarily, that in all kinds of actions that by the laws are pretermitted[3] men have the liberty to do what their own reason shall suggest as to what is most profitable to themselves. If we take liberty in its proper sense to mean corporal liberty, which is freedom from chains and prison, then it is very absurd for men to clamor as they do for the liberty they so manifestly enjoy. If we take liberty to mean an exemption from laws, then it is no less absurd for men to demand liberty as they do, for that would make all other men masters of their own lives. And yet, as absurd as it is, this is what people demand. They do not realize that laws are of no power to protect them without a sword in the hand of a man, or men, who can execute those laws. The liberty of a subject lies only in those things which the sovereign has praetermitted in regulating their actions. This is the liberty to buy and sell, and otherwise contract with one another, to choose their own abode, their own diet, their own trade of life and to raise their children as they see fit, and the like.[4]

Liberty of the subject is consistent with the unlimited power of the sovereign. Nevertheless, we should not think that the sovereign power over life and death is either abolished or limited. It has already been shown that nothing the sovereign representative can do to a subject, on any pretence whatever, can properly be called an injustice or an injury, because every subject is the author of every act the sovereign does. So the sovereign never lacks the right to any thing, except that he himself is subject to God, and thereby bound to observe the Laws of Nature. It may and often does happen in commonwealths that a subject may be put to death by the command of the sovereign, and yet neither does a wrong to the other. This occurred when Jeptha caused his daughter to be sacrificed.[5] In this and in similar cases, the one that died had the liberty to do the action, for which he was without injury, put to death. The same holds for a sovereign prince that puts an innocent subject to death. Even though the action goes against the Law of Nature, as being contrary to Equity, as was the killing of Uriah by David, the injury was not to Uriah, but to God. The injury was not to Uriah, because the right of the sovereign to do what he pleased was given to him by Uriah himself. But the injury was done to God, because David was God's subject, and so was prohibited from all iniquity by the Law of Nature. David himself confirmed this distinction when he repented what he did by saying, "To you only have I sinned."[6] In the same manner, the people of Athens thought they had committed no injustice when they banished the most potent of their commonwealth for ten years. They never thought that these people had committed a crime, but were concerned about the hurt they might do in the future. They even went further, as they were often not even aware of who was to be banished. Every citizen would bring his oyster-shell into the market place, and on it each one had written the name of someone they desired to be banished. Sometimes, this meant they would banish a person such as Aristides, because of his reputation for justice. Sometimes they banished a scurrilous jester, Hyperbolus, just as a jest. Still, no one can say that the sovereign people of Athens lacked the right to banish them, or that an Athenian lacked the right to jest, or to be just.[7]

The liberty which writers praise is the liberty of sovereigns, not of private men. There is frequent and honorable mention of liberty in the histories and philosophy of the ancient Greeks and Romans, and also in the writings and discourse of those that received all of their learning about politics from them. But this is the liberty of the commonwealth and not the liberty of particular men which they would have if there were neither civil laws nor commonwealths. The effects of this latter kind of liberty would be the same in both cases. Among masterless men there is perpetual war of every man against his neighbor. There is no inheritance to transmit to one's son, nor will the son expect it from his father. There is no property of goods or land, and no security, but there is a full and absolute liberty of every particular man. In states and commonwealths not dependent on one another, every commonwealth, but not every individual man, has the absolute liberty to do what it shall judge will most conduce to its benefit. This means that the ones who are judging are the man, or the assembly, that represents the commonwealth. In this situation the commonwealths live in a condition of perpetual war with each other, on the confines[8] of battle, with their frontiers armed and cannon planted against their neighbors round about. The Athenians and Romans were free, that is free commonwealths. It was not that any particular men had the liberty to resist their own representative, but that the representative had the liberty to resist or invade other people. The word 'libertas' is written on the turrets of the city of Luca in great characters at this present day. But no one should infer that a particular man had more liberty there, or immunity from service to the commonwealth, than in Constantinople. Whether a commonwealth be a monarchy or have a popular form, the freedom in both is still the same.

It is an easy thing for men to be deceived by the specious name of liberty, and have the lack of judgment to distinguish, and thus mistake liberty to refer to their private inheritance and birthright, which are only the right of the public. When this same error is confirmed by the authority of men of reputation for their writings on the subject, it is no wonder that sedition and change of government are the result. In these Western parts of the world, we receive our opinions concerning the institution and rights of commonwealths from Aristotle, Cicero and other Greeks and Romans. They derived those rights not from the principles of nature, but transcribed them into their books based on the practice of their own commonwealths, which happened to have the popular form. In the same way grammarians describe the rules of language based on the practice of their time, or the rules of poetry based on the poems of Homer and Virgil. To keep them from the desire of changing their government, the Athenians were taught that they were free men, and that all those that lived under a monarchy were slaves. Aristotle wrote in his Politics (Book 6, chapter 2), "In democracy, liberty is to be supposed, for it is commonly held that no man is free in any other government." Cicero said the same as Aristotle, as did other writers that grounded their civil doctrine on the opinions of the Romans. They were taught to hate monarchy, at first by those who having deposed their sovereign, shared the sovereignty of Rome among themselves. Afterwards the hatred of monarchy was carried on by their successors. By reading these Greek and Latin authors, current men from childhood have gotten a habit under a false show of liberty, of favoring tumults, and of licentiously acting to control the actions of their sovereigns, and then controlling those controllers. This has led to the effusion of so much blood, that I think that I can truly say that never was anything so dearly bought as these Western parts have bought the learning of the Greek and Latin languages.

Liberty of subjects, how to be measured. To discuss the particulars of the true liberty of subjects, we have to see what are the things which subjects can refuse to do without injustice even when commanded by the sovereign. To understand this, we should consider what rights we give up when we make a commonwealth. In other words what liberty do we deny to ourselves, when we own, without exception, all of the actions of the man, or assembly, that we make our sovereign. The act of our submission consists both of obligations and liberty. Based on this, there is no obligation on any man which does not arise from some act of his own, for all men are equally, by free by nature. All arguments on this issue must be drawn from the express words, "I authorize all his actions", or from the intention of those that submit themselves to the sovereign's power. The intention is to be understood by the end that is the goal of the submission. The obligation and liberty of the subject is to be derived either from those words, or their equivalent, or else from the institution or end of the institution of sovereignty, which is the peace of the subjects with each other and their defense against a common enemy.

Subjects have the liberty to defend their own bodies even against those that lawfully invade them. Sovereignty by institution is by the covenant of everyone to everyone, and sovereignty by acquisition is by covenants of the vanquished to the victor or the child to the parent. It is therefore manifest that every subject has liberty in all those things whose right cannot be transferred by covenant. I have shown before in chapter 14, that covenants not to defend one's own body are void.

Subjects are not bound to hurt themselves. Therefore, even if a sovereign commands a justly condemned man to kill, wound or maim himself, or not to resist those that assault him, or to abstain from the use of food, air, medicine, or any other thing necessary for life, the man has the liberty to disobey.

If a man is interrogated by the sovereign, or his authority, concerning a crime done by himself, the man is not bound to confess it without the assurance of pardon. No man can be obliged to accuse himself as I have also shown in chapter 14.

The consent of a subject to sovereign power is contained in these words, "I authorize, or take upon myself, all of his actions." In saying this, the subject makes no restriction at all of his former natural liberty. For by allowing the sovereign to kill me, I am not bound to kill myself when he commands me. It is one thing to say "Kill me or my fellow, if you please", and another thing to say, "I will kill my self, or my fellow."

It follows therefore that no man is bound by the words themselves, either to kill himself, or any other man. The obligation a man may sometimes have to execute a dangerous or dishonorable office upon command of the sovereign does not depend on the words of our submission, but on intention of those words, which is to be understood by their end. Therefore, when our refusal to obey frustrates the end for which sovereignty was ordained, there is no liberty to refuse; otherwise, there is.[9]

Subjects are not bound to warfare, unless they voluntarily undertake it. For these reasons, even though a sovereign commands a soldier to fight against an enemy, and even though the sovereign has the right to punish the refusal to do so with death, the soldier in many cases may refuse without injustice. If the soldier were to substitute someone else who is adequate, then the soldier does not desert his service to the commonwealth. Allowance is also made to those who are naturally timorous, not only to women of whom no such dangerous duty is expected, but also to men of feminine courage. When armies fight, there is on one side or both, a great deal of running away. When people do this out of fear and not treachery, they are considered to be dishonorable, but not unjust. For the same reason, to avoid battle is cowardice, but not injustice. But those who enroll to be soldiers, or take impressed money[10] no longer have the excuse of a timorous nature. They are obliged to not only go to battle, but not to run away from it without their officer's permission. When the defense of the commonwealth requires at once the help of all those able to bear arms, then everyone is obliged to obey. Otherwise, if the people do not have the purpose or courage to preserve it, the institution of the commonwealth was in vain.

No one has the liberty to resist the sword of the commonwealth in defense of another man, no matter whether the man is innocent or guilty. This kind of liberty would take the means of protecting us away from the sovereign and so is destructive to the very essence of government. But consider a case in which a great many men have together already unjustly resisted the sovereign power, or committed some capital crime for which every one of them expects death. Do they have the liberty to join together and assist and defend one another? They certainly do, for they are defending their own lives, which the guilty as well as the innocent may do. Indeed, there was an injustice in the original breach of their duty. But their bearing arms subsequent to that, though it is done to maintain what they have done, is not a new unjust act. If they are only defending their own persons, this new act is not unjust at all. But if they accept an offer of pardon made to them, the plea of self-defense, and their preserving, assisting or defending others, would be unjust.

The greatest liberty of subjects depends on the silence of the law. Other liberties depend on the silence of the law. Where the sovereign has prescribed no rule, the subjects have the liberty to do, or forbear, according to their own discretion. This kind of liberty is more or less in different places, and in some times more, and in some times less, according as a particular sovereign might consider most convenient. For example, there was a time in England where a man might enter his own land and dispossess by force those who wrongfully possessed it. But later, the liberty of forcible entry was taken away by a statute that was made by the king in Parliament. In some places in the world, men have the liberty of having many wives, but in other places no such liberty is allowed.

Suppose that a subject has a controversy with his sovereign about debt, or of the right of possessions of lands or goods, or concerning any service required at the sovereign's hands, or concerning any penalty, corporal or pecuniary grounded on a precedent law. The subject has the same liberty to sue for his right as he would have against another subject, and the suit will be before judges appointed by the sovereign. In this case what the sovereign is demanding is based on a law, and is not based merely on the sovereign's power. What the sovereign is declaring in this case is due to a law. The suit therefore is not contrary to the will of the sovereign. The subject has the liberty to demand a hearing of his cause, and a decision according to the law. But if the sovereign demands or takes anything based on the claim of his power, then in this case there is no action concerning the law. Everything that the sovereign does in virtue of his power is done by the authority of every subject, and so in this case, a subject who brings an action against the sovereign, brings it against himself.

If a monarch, or sovereign assembly, grants a liberty to all or any of his subjects, but this grant disables the sovereign from providing for the safety of the subjects, the grant is void unless the sovereign directly renounces or transfers his sovereignty to another. The sovereign might have openly in plain terms, if it had been his will, transferred or renounced his power, but he did not do that. So it is to be understood that this was not his will, and that the grant proceeded from ignorance of the conflict between liberty and sovereign power in this case. Therefore the sovereign retains his power and all the rest of the powers that are necessary to its exercise, such as the power of war, peace, of judicature, of appointing officers and counselors, or levying money, and the rest named in chapter 18.

In what cases are subjects absolved of their obedience to the sovereign. The obligation of the subjects to the sovereign lasts just as long, and no longer, than his power lasts to protect them. For no covenant can relinquish the right men have by nature to protect themselves when no one else can protect them. Sovereignty is the soul of the body of the commonwealth, and once it departs from the body, the members no longer receive their motion from it. The goal of obedience is protection, and when a man sees it either in his own or another's sword, then nature applies his obedience to it and his endeavor to maintain it. In the intention of those that make sovereignty, it is supposed to be immortal, yet its own nature makes it subject to violent death by foreign war, but also through the ignorance and passions of men. Sovereignty has in it from its very institution many seeds of natural mortality by intestinal discord.

In case of captivity. Suppose a subject is taken prisoner of war or his means of life are held by the guards of an enemy. If the subject's life and corporal liberty are given to him on the condition that he become a subject to the victor, he has the liberty to accept this condition. Once he has accepted it, he is subject to the one that captured him, as he had no other way to preserve himself. It is the same if a subject is detained on the same terms in a foreign country. But if a man is held in prison or bonds or is not trusted with the liberty of his body, he cannot be understood to be bound by any covenant involving subjection. In that case he may escape by any means whatsoever.

In case the sovereign casts off the government from himself and his heirs. If a monarch relinquishes the sovereignty, both for himself and his heirs, his subjects return to the absolute liberty of nature. Nature may declare to a sovereign who are his sons and the nearest of his kin, but who is the sovereign's heir depends on his will as has been stated in a previous chapter. If he therefore decides to have no heir, there is no more sovereignty and no more subjection. The case is the same if he dies without any known kin and without declaring an heir. In that case there is no known heir and so no subjection can be due to anyone.

In case of banishment. If a sovereign banishes a subject, then during the banishment, the person is no longer a subject. But one who is sent on a message, or has permission to travel, is still a subject. This is due to the contract between sovereigns and is not by virtue of the covenant of subjection. For when a person enters another's dominion, they are subject to all of the laws of that dominion unless the person has a special license or a special privilege as a result of the friendship of the respective sovereigns.

In case the sovereign renders himself subject to another. If a monarch who is subdued by war renders himself subject to the victor, then his subjects are delivered from their former obligation and become obliged to the victor. But if a sovereign is held prisoner and does not have the liberty of his own body, he is not understood to have given away his right of sovereignty. The subjects are then obliged to obey the sovereign's magistrates that were formerly placed to govern in the sovereign's name and not in their own. The sovereign's right remains in this case; the only question is one of administration. That means that even if the sovereign does not have the right to currently name magistrates and officers, he approves those whom he had formerly appointed.

Endnotes

1. Surrounded
2. The physical bodies that Hobbes is referring to here are inert things like stones and rocks.
3. What the laws disregard
4. This passage indicates that Hobbes did not think an absolute monarch would have the kind of control that people of later centuries have experienced.
5. The story is in Judges 11. Jeptha made an oath that if he achieved victory in a war, he would sacrifice the first person he met, who unfortunately turned out to be his daughter.
6. In Samuel II David has Uriah killed when he is smitten with Uriah's wife, Bathsheba. The prophet Nathan then condemned David for this act, and David admitted his sin.
7. In the Athenian practice of ostracism a majority could vote to banish anyone without the need to have a justifiable reason for doing so.
8. Edge
9. Who is the one who determines whether the sovereign has ordained an action that frustrates the end for which sovereignty was instituted? The only reasonable answer is that it is the subject who is to make this determination. In that case, does the sovereign power collapse?
10. Mercenaries

CHAPTER 22

Of Systems Subject, Political and Private

The diverse sorts of systems of people. Having spoken of the generation, form, and power of commonwealths, I shall next speak of the parts of commonwealths. But first I will speak of systems which resemble the similar parts of a natural body, like the muscles. By systems I mean any number of men joined in one interest or one business. Some systems are regular and some irregular. The regular ones are those where one man, or assembly of men, is the constituted representative of the whole number. All other systems are irregular.

Of the regular systems, some are absolute and independent, subject to none but their own representative. Commonwealths are systems of this kind as I have already discussed in the previous 5 chapters. Other systems are dependent, which means they are subordinate to some sovereign power to which every one as well as their representative is subordinate.

Of subordinate systems some are political and some are private. The political systems, otherwise called political bodies or persons in law, are those which are made by the sovereign power of commonwealths. The private systems are those which are constituted by subjects among themselves, or by the authority of a stranger. In any territory authority derived from a foreign power within the dominion of another cannot be public. It must be private.

Of the private systems some are lawful and some are unlawful. The lawful ones are those allowed by the commonwealth. All others are unlawful. Irregular systems are those which have no representative and consist only in the concourse[1] of people. If this is not forbidden by the commonwealth nor made for some evil design, then these system are lawful. Examples of them are the conflux[2] of people at markets, or shows, or any other kind of gathering that has a harmless end. But they are unlawful when their intention is evil or unknown and they consist of a considerable number of people.

In all political bodies the power of the representative is limited. In political bodies the power of the representative is always limited by the sovereign power, since unlimited power is absolute sovereignty. The sovereign in every commonwealth is the absolute representative of all the subjects. Therefore, no one else can be the representative of any part of them, but only insofar as the sovereign permits. To permit a political body of subjects to have an absolute representative is to all intents and purposes to abandon the government of the commonwealth. This would be to divide the dominion, contrary to their peace and defense, which the sovereign cannot be understood to do by any grant that does not plainly and directly discharge everyone of their subjection. The consequences of words are not the signs of the sovereign's will when other consequences are signs of the contrary. Rather, when there are these contrary signs, it is more a sign of error and misreckoning to which all mankind is too prone.

The bounds of the power which are given to the representative of a political body are noted by two things. One is their writ[3] or letters from the sovereign, and the other is the law of the commonwealth.

Limitation by patent letters.[4] The institution or acquisition of the commonwealth which is independent need not involve writing, because the power of the representative has no other bounds besides the unwritten Laws of Nature. But in subordinate bodies there are many different kinds which make limitations necessary. These are differences concerning their businesses, times and places. They cannot be remembered without letters or taken notice of without a patent letter that may be read to them and sealed and testified with the seals and other permanent signs of the Sovereign Authority.

Limitation by the laws. It is not always easy, or even possible to describe limitations in writing. So the ordinary laws that are common to all subjects must determine what the representatives may lawfully do in all cases where the letters themselves are silent.

When the representative is one man, his unwarranted acts are his own only. Therefore, in a political body when the representative is one man, whatever he does in the person of the political body that is neither warranted in his letters nor by the laws is his own act, and is not the act of the body nor of any other man besides himself. He represents no one's person but his own further than his letters or the law permits. But what he does according to these limits is the act of everyone in the political body. Everyone is the author of an act of the sovereign, because he is their unlimited representative. The act of one who does not recede⁵ from the letters of the sovereign is the act of the sovereign and therefore of every member of the body that is the author of it.

When it is an assembly, it is the act only of those that assented. But if the representative is an assembly, whatever that assembly decrees that is not warranted by their letters or the laws is the act of the assembly or political body. It is the act of every one by whose vote the decree was made, but it is not the act of any man that being present voted to the contrary, nor is it of any man who is absent, unless he voted it by procuration.⁶ It would be the act of the assembly, because it was voted by the majority. If the act is a crime, the assembly may be punished as much as is capable. Such punishments may be dissolution or the forfeiture of their letters, which would be capital punishment for artificial and fictitious bodies. The punishment would be pecuniary mulct⁷ if the assembly has a common stock in which none of its innocent members own. Nature has exempted all political bodies from corporal penalties. Those that did not vote for an unlawful decree are innocent because the assembly cannot represent any one in things that are not warranted by their letters and are consequently involved in their votes.

When the representative is one man who borrows money or owes it by contract, he is the only liable; the members are not. Suppose the person of a political body is one man who borrows money from a stranger, someone who is not a member of this body. No letters need limit borrowing, as it is left to men's own inclination to limit lending. In this case the debt is just the representative's. If he had the authority from his letters to make the members pay what he borrowed, he would thereby have the condition of sovereignty over them. Therefore, the grant is void as being due to error which is commonly made by human nature and is an insufficient sign of the granter. Or if a member avows the debt, then the representative is sovereign and so does not fit the current discussion which is only about subordinate bodies. Only the representative himself, and not any member, is obliged to pay the debt that was borrowed. The lender is a stranger to the letters and to the qualifications of the body and he understands only who the debtor is who is engaged. The representative can engage himself and so only he is the debtor and must therefore pay the lender out of the common stock if there is any, or if there is none, out of his own estate. If the representative comes into debt by contract or mulct, the case is the same.

When there is an assembly, only those who have assembled are liable. But when the representative is an assembly and the debt is to a stranger, the ones who are responsible for the debt are those that voted to borrow it, or voted for the contract that made it due, or voted to do the act for which the mulct was imposed. Every one of those who voted for it engaged themself for the payment. The one that is author of the borrowing is obliged for the payment, even for the whole debt, although if it is paid by anyone, the author is discharged of his obligation.

If the debt is to one of the assembly, only the body is obliged. If one of the assembly incurs the debt, only the assembly is obliged for the payment out of their common stock if they have any. By having the liberty of voting, anyone that votes that the money be borrowed is voting that it shall be paid. If he later votes later against borrowing, or is absent, because he earlier voted to borrow, he contradicts his former vote and is obliged by the latter vote, and so becomes both a borrower and a lender. Consequently, he can only demand payment from the common treasury and not from any particular man. If this fails, he has no remedy or complaint except against himself.

Protesting against the decrees of political bodies is sometimes lawful, but is never lawful against the sovereign power. It is manifest that in subordinate political bodies subject to a sovereign power, it is not only lawful, but sometimes expedient, for a particular man to make open protest against the decrees of the representative assembly. He may cause his dissent to be registered or to be witnessed, because otherwise he may be obliged to pay the contracted debts and be responsible for the crimes committed by other men. But a particular man does not have this liberty in a sovereign assembly, because protesting there denies the assembly's sovereignty. Also, whatever is commanded by the sovereign power is justifiable as a command to the subject, because the subject is the author of such a command. However, the command might not be justifiable in the sight of God.

Political bodies of the government of a province, colony or town. The variety of political bodies is almost infinite, for they are not only distinguished by the several affairs[8] for which they are constituted of which there is an unspeakable diversity, but also by the times, places and numbers, subject to many limitations. As the their affairs, some of them are ordained for government. First, the government of a province may be committed to an assembly of men, where all of its resolutions shall depend on the votes of the majority. In this case this assembly is a political body and their power is limited by commission. The word 'province' signifies that the one whose business it is commits the charge or care of it to another man to administer it under him. So in one commonwealth where there are diverse countries that have distinct laws or are very distant from one another, the administration of government is committed to different persons. The countries where the sovereign is not resident, but governs by commission, are called provinces. There are, however, few examples of the government of a province by an assembly that resides in the province itself. The Romans, who had the sovereignty of many provinces, always governed them with presidents and praetors,[9] and not by assemblies that they used to govern the city of Rome and its adjacent territories. Similarly, when England sent colonies to plant Virginia and the Summer-Islands, though the government in London was an assembly, the assembly never committed the government of the colony to another assembly. In each case one governor was sent. Every man, where he can be present by nature, desires to participate in the government. Where they cannot be present, they are by nature inclined to commit the government of their common interest to a monarchical form rather than a popular one. This is also evident in the case of men that have great private estates. When they are unwilling to be troubled by the administration of the businesses that belong to them, they would rather trust them to one servant than to an assembly either of their friends or servants. But suppose the government of a province or a colony is entrusted to an assembly. In that case whatever debt is contracted by that assembly, or whatever unlawful act is decreed, is the act only of those that assented and not of any that dissented for the reasons that were previously stated. Also, if the assembly resides outside the boundaries of the colony that they govern, it cannot execute any power over the person or goods of any of the colony. The assembly cannot seize them for debt, or any other duty in any place outside the colony itself. The assembly has no jurisdiction or authority in any other place, but it only has the remedy that the law of the jurisdiction allows them. An assembly has the right to impose a mulct upon any of their members that break the laws they make, but outside of the colony itself, the assembly has no right to execute the mulct. What I have said about the rights of an assembly for the government of a province or a colony is also applicable to an assembly that governs a town, a university, a college, a church, or any other government over the persons of men.

Generally, in all political bodies if any particular member thinks he has been injured by the body itself, the disposition of his cause belongs to the sovereign or to the judges that the sovereign has ordained for that particular cause. The disposition of the case does not belong to the political body itself. For in this case the political body is a subject. In a sovereign assembly it is different, because if the sovereign cannot be a judge in its own cause, there can be no other judge.

Political bodies for the ordering of trade. The most convenient representative in a political body for the well ordering of foreign traffic is an assembly of all the members. That would involve having everyone who adventures his money be present at all deliberations and resolutions of the body where a decision is made. The proof of this is to consider the goal why merchants who buy, sell, export and import their merchandise at their own discretion, nevertheless bind themselves into one corporation. It is true that there are few merchants that with the merchandise they buy at home are able to freight a ship with it in order to export it, or are able to buy abroad in order to import it home. In these cases every man either participates in the gain according to the proportion of his own adventure,[10] or takes his own and sells what he exports or imports at the prices he thinks fit. A collection of such merchants is not a political body, for there is no common representative to oblige them to follow any other law besides those that apply to all subjects. The end of their incorporating is to increase their gain, which is done in two ways: by being the sole buyer or the sole seller, both at home and abroad. To grant a company of merchants to be a corporation or political body is to grant them a double monopoly, which is to be the sole buyers and to be the sole sellers. When a company incorporates for any particular foreign country, they only export the commodities vendible[11] in that country, which amounts to being the sole buyer at home, and the sole seller abroad. At home there is but one buyer, and abroad there is only one that is a seller. Both of these are gainful to the merchant, as he can thereby buy at home at a lower price and sell abroad at a higher one. Abroad there is but one buyer of foreign merchandise, and only one that sells it at home, and both situations are again profitable to adventurers.

Of this double monopoly, one part is disadvantageous to the people at home and another part to foreigners. At home by being the sole exporter, the merchants set what price they please on the husbandry and handiworks of the people. By being the sole importers, the merchants can again set the price they please on the foreign commodities that people need. Both or these situations are harmful to the people. But on the contrary, by being the sole seller of native commodities abroad, they can raise their prices, and by being the sole buyer of foreign commodities abroad, they can lower their price to the disadvantage of the foreigners. Where just one sells, the merchandise is dearer, and where just one buys, it is cheaper. Even though such corporations are monopolies, they would be very profitable to a commonwealth if being bound up in one body in foreign markets, they are at liberty at home where every individual can buy and sell at any price they can.

Consider a body of merchants that have no common stock and they have to contribute individually to the building, buying, provisioning and manning of ships. The end of such a body of merchants is not a common benefit to the whole body, but the particular gain of every individual. That is why it is in the interest that every one of them to be in the assembly and have the power to order expenditures and be acquainted with the accounts. That is why the representative of such a body should be an assembly, where every member of the body may be present at all consultations if they so desire.

If a political body of merchants contracts a debt to a stranger by an act of their representative assembly, every member of the assembly is liable by himself for the whole debt. For a stranger would take no notice of their private laws, but would consider them to be so many individual men, where every one is obliged for the whole payment until the payment by one discharges all of the rest. But if the debt is to just one person in the company, the creditor cannot demand repayment from any individual, but can just demand it from that one person or from the common stock if there is any.

If the commonwealth imposes a tax upon the body of merchants, it is understood to be laid upon every member in proportion to his particular adventure in the company. For in this case there is no other common stock, but what is made from their particular adventures.

If a mulct is laid upon the body for some unlawful act, then the only ones who are liable for it are those that voted for the act, or those who assisted in executing it. For the rest, there is no crime in just being part of the body, which cannot be a crime, since the body was ordained by the authority of the commonwealth.

If one of the members is indebted to the body, he may be sued by the body. But his goods cannot be taken nor can he be imprisoned by the authority of the body. These actions can only be done by the authority of the commonwealth, for if the body can do it by their own authority, they can also make a judgment a judgments by their own authority that the debt is due. In that case they would be the judge of their own cause.

A political body for counsel to be given to the sovereign. The bodies that are made for the government of men or traffic are either perpetual or are for a prescribed time set in writing. But there are also bodies whose times are limited solely by the nature of their business. For example, suppose a monarch, or sovereign assembly, commands the towns or other parts of their territory to send deputies to provide information about the conditions and needs of the subjects, to give advice for making good laws, or for any other cause. As with one person representing the whole country, these deputies would have a place and time for meeting assigned to them and would be at that time a political body representing every subject of the dominion. But their representation only concerns those matters that were propounded[12] to them by the man, or assembly, that had the sovereign authority to send for them. When it is declared that there is nothing more to be propounded or debated, the body is thereby dissolved. If this body were to be considered the absolute representative of the people, then it would be a sovereign assembly and there would be two sovereigns, which is not consistent with peace. So when sovereignty is once established, there can be no other representation of the people. The limits of how far the body of deputies can represent the whole people are set forth in the writing by which they were sent for. The people cannot choose their deputies for any other reason other than what was written to them by the sovereign

A regular private body, lawful as a family. Regular and lawful private bodies are those that are constituted without letters or other written authority, except the laws common to all other subjects. They are regular when they are united in on person who is representative such as are all families, where the father or master orders the whole family. The father or master obliges his children and servants as far as the law permits, but no further, because no one is bound to be obedient in those actions that the laws forbid. As long as they are under domestic government, children and servants are subject to their fathers and masters as their immediate sovereigns. The fathers and masters were the absolute sovereigns of their families before the institution of commonwealths, and so afterwards they have only the authority that the law of the commonwealth leaves for them.

Regular private bodies that are unlawful. Regular private bodies are unlawful when they unite themselves in one representative person without any public authority for doing so. Examples of this are corporations of beggars, thieves and gypsies who unite to better order their trades of begging and stealing. Other examples are corporations of men that unite themselves in another dominion by a foreign person in order to more easily propagate doctrines, and to create a faction against the power of the commonwealth.

Irregular systems that are private leagues. Irregular systems by their natures are leagues, or sometimes just concourses of people, that do not unite for any particular design. They have no obligation to each other, but proceed only from a similarity of wills and inclinations. They are lawful or unlawful according to the lawfulness or unlawfulness of the designs of every particular man in them. The designs are to be understood on the basis of the occasion.

A league of subjects in a commonwealth is for the most part unnecessary and smacks of an unlawful design, because leagues are usually made for mutual defense and a commonwealth is no more than a league of all of the subjects together. For that reason leagues are generally unlawful and are commonly called factions or conspiracies. Leagues are a connection of men by covenants when there is no power given to any one man, or assembly, to compel them to do anything, as occurs in the condition of mere nature. These are valid only if they raise no cause of distrust. Leagues between commonwealths, where there is no human power that is established to keep them all in awe, are not only lawful, but are also profitable for the time they last. But leagues of subjects of one and the same commonwealth, where every one may maintain his rights by the means of sovereign power, are unnecessary to the maintenance of peace and justice. They are unlawful when their design is evil or unknown to the commonwealth. The union of strength of private men is unjust if it is for evil intent. If the intent is unknown, it is unjustly concealed and so is dangerous to the public.

Secret cabals. Suppose the sovereign power is in a great assembly and a number of men, part of the assembly, consult without authority to contrive to guide the rest. This is a faction or unlawful conspiracy and constitutes a fraudulent seduction of the assembly for the faction's particular interest. But it is not unjust if an individual, whose private interest is to be debated and judged in the assembly, makes as many friends as he can. In this case the individual is not part of the assembly. It is also not unjust if he hires such friends with money, unless there is an express law against it. For sometimes, as men's ways are, there can be no justice without money and every man thinks his own cause is just until it is heard and judged.

Feuds of private families. In all commonwealths if a private man has more servants than are required for the government of his estate or that he can gainfully employ, he has made a faction and this is unlawful. Since this private man has the protection of the commonwealth, he does not need the defense of a private force. In nations that are not thoroughly civilized, several large families have lived in continual hostility and have invaded each other with private forces. It is evident that either these families have done so unjustly, or else that there is no existing commonwealth where they live.

Factions for government. As there are factions of kin, there are also factions of government of religion, such as Papists, Protestants, etc., or of the state, such as patricians and plebeians in ancient Rome, and of democrats and aristocrats in ancient Greece. All of these factions are unjust and are contrary to the peace and safety of the people, as they take the sword out of the hand of the sovereign.

The concourse of people is an irregular system, and its lawfulness or unlawfulness depends on the occasion and number of those that are assembled. If the occasion is lawful and manifest, the concourse is lawful, as happens in the usual meeting of men at church or a public show in usual numbers. But if the numbers are extraordinarily large, and the occasion of the gathering is not evident, and if one of the crowd cannot provide a particular and good account of why he is there, then it is to be judged that this person has an unlawful and tumultuous design. It may be lawful for a thousand men to sign a petition to be delivered to a judge or magistrate, but if a thousand men come to present it, there is a tumultuous assembly, as only one or two are needed for that purpose. In such cases there is not a set number that makes the assembly unlawful. It becomes unlawful when the officers that are present are not able to suppress the assembly and bring it to justice.

When an unusual number of men assemble against a man whom they accuse, the assembly is an unlawful tumult, because only a few, or one man, are needed to deliver an accusation to a magistrate. This was the case of St. Paul at Ephesus, where Demetrius and a great number of other men brought two of Paul's companions before the magistrate, saying with one voice, "Diana of Ephesus is great". This was their way of demanding justice against Paul's companions for teaching people their own doctrine that was against the religion and trade of this large group of men. Considering the laws of that people and the occasion, the accusation was just; however, the assembly judged it to be unlawful. The magistrate reprehended the group for bringing it in these words: "If

Demetrius and the other workmen can accuse any man of any thing, there are pleas and deputies, so let them instead accuse one another. And if you have any other to thing to demand, your case may be judged in an assembly that is lawfully called. For we are in danger of being accused in this day's sedition, because there is no way that any man can render any reason for this large congregation of people." (Acts 19:40.) When someone calls for an assembly and he can give no just account for doing so, then there is a sedition and they were responsible for it.

This is all I shall say concerning systems and assemblies of people. They may be compared, as I have said, to the similar parts of man's body. Those that are lawful are like the muscles. Those that are unlawful are like, wens,[13] boils and apostemes,[14] that are engendered by the unnatural conflux of evil humors.

Endnotes

1. The coming together of people
2. Congregation of people
3. Legal written document
4. An official letter stating the rights and privileges of an organization
5. Withdraw
6. By proxy
7. A fine or penalty
8. Reasons
9. Leader of the army
10. Investment
11. Capable of being sold
12. Offered for consideration
13. Tumors of the skin
14. Abscesses

CHAPTER 23

Of the Public Ministers
of Sovereign Power

Who is a public minister. In the last chapter I spoke of the similar parts of commonwealths. In this chapter I shall speak of the organic parts which are the public ministers.

A public minister is someone who the sovereign, whether a monarch or an assembly, employs in any affairs, and who has the authority to represent the person of the commonwealth in that employment. Every man, or assembly, that has sovereignty represents two persons or as is more commonly said, has two capacities. One of them is natural and the other is political. A monarch has the person not only of the commonwealth but also of a man. A sovereign assembly has the person not only of the commonwealth but also of the assembly. Those that are servants to the sovereign in their natural capacity are not public ministers. But those that serve them in the administration of public business are public ministers. Therefore neither ushers, nor sergeants, nor other officers that wait on the assembly for no other reason but for the convenience of the men assembled in an aristocracy or democracy are public ministers. Neither are stewards, chamberlains, cofferers[1] nor any other officers of the household of a monarch are public ministers in a monarchy.

Ministers for general administration. Some public ministers are charged with the general administration either of a part or of the whole dominion. One example of a minister of the whole is a protector or a regent, who may be committed by the predecessor of an infant king during in infant's minority to administer the whole of the kingdom. In this case every subject is obliged to obedience to the ordinances that this minister shall make and the command he shall give in the king's name that are consistent with his sovereign power. When monarchs, or sovereign assemblies, give the general charge to someone to administer a part of their dominion, these ministers are called governors, lieutenants, prae-fects, or vice-roys. Also in these cases also everyone in the province is obliged to follow everything the minister commands in the name of the sovereign that is compatible with the sovereign's right. These protectors, vice-roys and governors only have the rights that depend on the sover-eign's will. No commission that is given to them may be interpreted as a declaration of the will to transfer the sovereignty without the express and perspicuous words to that purpose. These kinds of public ministers resemble the nerves and tendons that move the different limbs of a natu-ral body.[2]

Ministers for special administration, as for the economy. Others are given special administration, as they are put in charge of special business either at home or abroad. At home one kind of special business is the economy of the commonwealth. These public ministers have authority concerning the treasury in matters of tributes, impositions, rents, fines, and whatever public revenue is collected, received, issued or accounted for. These public ministers serve the person representative and can do nothing against his command, or without his authority, and they serve the sovereign in his political capacity.

Secondly, there are public ministers that have authority concerning the militia, which involves the custody of arms, forts, ports, levying, paying and conducting soldiers, or providing any necessary thing for use in war, either by land or by sea. A soldier, though, who has no command over anyone else, though he does fight for the commonwealth, does not there-fore represent its person, because there is no one for him to represent it to. Everyone who has the power of command represents the common-wealth only to those that he commands.

Ministers for instruction of the people. Public ministers also have the authority to teach or to enable other to teach the people their duty to the sovereign power. They also have the authority to instruct people in the knowledge of what is just and unjust, and thereby render the people more apt to live in godliness and in peace among themselves and to resist public enemies. They are public ministers in that they do this, not by their own authority, but by that of another, and because they do it, or should do it, by no authority except the sovereign's. The monarch, or the sovereign assembly, only has the immediate authority from God to teach and instruct the people. And no one but the sovereign receives his authority simply *dei gratia*,[3] that is, from the favor and providence of

God. All others receive their authority from the favor and providence of God as well as from their sovereigns. In a monarchy this is called *die gratia & regis*[4] or *dei providentia & voluntate regis.*[5]

Ministers for judicature. Public ministers are also those to whom jurisdiction is given. In their seats of justice they represent the person of the sovereign and their sentence is his sentence. As has been stated before, all judicature is essentially annexed to the sovereignty and therefore, all judges are but the ministers of the sovereign or those that have sovereign power. As controversies are of two kinds, concerning facts or the law, so are judgments—some are of facts and some are of laws. Consequently, in the same controversy, there may be two judges—one of the facts, and another of the laws.

In both of these controversies a controversy may arise between the judge and the party being judged. Since both parties are subjects to the sovereign, equity demands this controversy to be someone agreed to by both, since no man should be a judge in his own cause. The sovereign has already been consented by both parties to be a judge and so either the sovereign should decide the case himself or appoint a judge that both parties can agree to. This agreement between the parties can be understood to be made in different ways. First, since the complainant has already chosen his own judge, if the defendant is allowed to refuse those judges whose interests are suspect to him, he agrees to those judges that he does not refuse. Second, if the defendant appeals to another judge, he can appeal no further, for his appeal is his choice. Third, if he appeals to the sovereign himself and if the sovereign, or delegates that the parties agree to, gives a sentence, then that sentence is final, for the defendant is judged by his own judges, that is to say himself.

Having considered what is a just and rational judicature, I cannot resist observing the excellent constitution of the courts of justice established in England both for common and public pleas. By common pleas, I mean those where both the complainant and the defendant are subjects. By public pleas, which are also called pleas of the crown, I mean those where the complainant is the sovereign. When there were two orders of men, lords and commons, the lords had the privilege of having only lords be the judges in all cases of capital crimes. The judges would be only those who would be present, and since this was acknowledged as a privilege of favor, the only lords that were present to judge were ones the defendants themselves desired. Every subject in a controversy and every lord in a civil controversy could have judges from the country where the controversy took place. Refusals of judges could be made until twelve men were agreed upon and then those twelve were the judges of the controversy. So, having selected their own judges, neither party could give any reason why the sentence should not be final. These public persons who with the authority of the sovereign power to instruct or judge the people are members of the commonwealth and may be appropriately compared to the voice organs of a natural body.

Ministers for execution. Public ministers also have authority from the sovereign to execute judgments that are made to publish sovereign commands, to suppress tumults, to apprehend and imprison malefactors, and to do other acts tending to the conservation of the peace. Every act that they do by this authority is an act of the commonwealth and their service is comparable to the hands of a natural body.

Public ministers who are abroad represent the person of their own sovereign to foreign states. These are ambassadors, messengers, agents and heralds that are sent by the public authority on public business.

Those that are sent by the authority of some private party of a troubled state are neither public nor private ministers of the commonwealth, even if they are received. None of their actions are authorized by the commonwealth. Likewise, an ambassador sent by a prince to congratulate, offer condolences, or to assist in any other solemnity is a private person, because the business is private and belongs to the prince only in his natural capacity, even though the prince is also the public authority. Suppose a man is sent into another country to secretly explore their counsels and strength. Even though the authority that sent the person is a public one and the business is public, since no one in the other country is supposed to notice him, he is just a private minister, but still is a minister of the commonwealth. He may be compared to an eye in a natural body. Those appointed as public ministers to represent their sovereign and have the office to receive the petitions or other information from the people are comparable to public ears.

Counselors without any other employment but to give advice are not public ministers. Counselors, or counsels of state, are not public persons if they have no authority of judicature or command and only give advice to the sovereign when it is required or offer advice when it is not required. Their advice is only given to the sovereign, when his person cannot be represented by another. But a body of counselors is never without some other authority, either of judicature or of immediate administration. In a monarchy they represent the monarch in delivering his commands to the public ministers. In a democracy the Council or the Senate propounds the deliberations of the Council to the people. When the Council appoints judges, hears causes, or gives audience to ambassadors, it is in the role of a minister of the people. In an aristocracy the Council of the state is the sovereign assembly itself, and it gives counsel only to themselves.

Endnotes:

1. Treasurers
2. In this chapter Hobbes reverts to the image of the state as a human body that he first used in the Introduction. He continues to elaborate on this image through the next chapters.
3. By the grace of God
4. By the grace of God and the king
5. By the providence of God and the will of the king

CHAPTER 24

Of the Nutrition and Procreation of a Commonwealth

The nourishment of a commonwealth consists in the commodities of sea and land. The nutrition of a commonwealth consists in the plenty and distribution of the materials conducing to life. This involves the concoction or the preparation of these materials and their conveyance by convenient conduits for public use.

The amount of matter is limited by nature to those commodities that our common mother provides from her two breasts: the land and the sea. God either gives us these freely or sells them to mankind for our labor.

The matter of this nutriment consists of animals, vegetables and minerals. God has freely laid them before us near the surface of the Earth so we just need our own labor and industry to obtain them. Our achieving plenty thus depends just on our own labor and industry next to God's favor.

This matter, which is commonly called commodities, is partly native and partly foreign. It is native when it exists within the territory of the commonwealth, and it is foreign when it is imported from without. No territory under the dominion of one commonwealth, except if it is of very vast extent, produces all the things needed for the maintenance and motion of the whole body. There are also few commonwealths that do not produce a surplus of something. This surplus for what is needed within does not become superfluous, but it can be used to supply other wants at home by importation from abroad through exchange, just war or by labor. A man's labor is like any other thing, a commodity that is exchangeable for some benefit. That is why there have been commonwealths that have had no more territory than served them for habitation, and nevertheless, not only maintained their power, but increased it. They did this partly by trading from one place to another, and partly by selling things they manufactured, where the materials that made them were brought in from other places.

The right of distribution. The distribution of the materials of this nourishment is the constitution of mine and thine and his. In one word this is 'propriety'[1] and belongs to the sovereign power in all kinds of commonwealths. For where there is no commonwealth, as has already been shown, there is a perpetual war of every man against his neighbor. In this situation everyone that gets something only keeps it by force, and so there is neither propriety, nor community, but uncertainty. This is evident even to Cicero who was a passionate defender of liberty. In a public pleading he attributed all propriety to civil law. He said, "Let the civil law be once abandoned or negligently guarded, not to say oppressed, and there is nothing that any man can be sure to receive from his ancestor, or leave to his children." He also said, "Take away the civil law and no man knows what is his own and what is another man's." The introduction of propriety is an effect of the commonwealth, which is only done by the person that represents it and so it can only be done by the sovereign. Propriety consists of the laws that can only be made by the sovereign power. They knew this in ancient times when they called laws *nomos*, which we call laws, and which involves distribution. The ancients defined justice as distributing to every man his own.

All private estates of land proceed originally from the arbitrary distribution of the sovereign. In this distribution, the first law is the division of the land itself. The sovereign assigns a portion to every man according to how he judges it to conform to equity and the common good. The sovereign makes this decision and not any subject or any group of subjects. The children of Israel were a commonwealth in the wilderness, but lacked the commodities of the Earth until they were masters of the Promised Land. When they conquered it, the land was divided among them. This was not done by their own discretion, but by the discretion of Eleazar the priest, and Joshua, their general. There were twelve tribes made into thirteen by the subdivision of the tribe of Joseph, but only twelve portions of land were given out. The tribe of Levi was given no land, but was assigned a tenth part of all the fruits of the others. This shows that the division of the land was arbitrary. A people who come to possess a land by war do not always exterminate the ancient inhabitants, as did the Jews. Sometimes they let all, or many, or most of the inhabitants keep their estates. Still, it is clear that these estates are still part of the victor's distribution, as the people of England kept all of their estates of William the Conqueror.

Propriety of a subject excludes only another subject but not the dominion of the sovereign. The propriety that a subject has of his lands consists of his right to exclude all other subjects from using them. But it does not exclude the sovereign, whether it is an assembly or a monarch. The sovereign, that is the commonwealth whose person the sovereign represents, orders the common peace and security, and distributing land is understood to be part of this task. Whatever distribution the sovereign makes in prejudice thereof[2] is contrary to the will of every subject that committed his peace and safety to the sovereign's discretion and conscience. Therefore, by the will of every one of the subjects, the distribution is reputed to be void. It is true that a sovereign monarch, or a greater part of a sovereign assembly, may ordain doing many things in pursuit of their passions, which are a breach of trust and of the Laws of Nature. But this is not enough to authorize any subject to either make war against the sovereign or to accuse him of injustice, or to speak evil of him, as the subjects have authorized all of the sovereign's actions and in bestowing the sovereign power have made his actions their own. But the cases where the commands of sovereigns are contrary to equity and the Law of Nature are to be considered later in another place.[3]

A diet is not to be imposed on the public. It may be thought that in the distribution of the land, the commonwealth may possess a portion and have their representative improve it so that it would be sufficient to sustain the whole expense that is needed for the common peace and defense. This thought could be considered if there were any representative that could be conceived who is free of human passions and infirmities. But given human nature as it is, it is vain to set aside any public land or any certain revenue for the commonwealth. Doing so would lead to the dissolution of the government and to the condition of mere nature and war as soon as the sovereign power fell into the hands of a monarch, or assembly, that were too negligent about money or would engage in too much risk handling the public stock in long or costly war. Commonwealths can endure no diet. Their expense is not just a matter of their own appetites, but are also affected by external accidents and the appetites of their neighbors. Thus, the public riches should not be limited by any other limits besides those that emergent occasions may require. In England, William the Conqueror reserved diverse lands for his own use, besides forests and chases[4] for his recreation or for preservation. He also reserved different services on the land he gave his subjects. But these were not reserved for the maintenance of his public capacity, but rather for his natural capacity. For in spite of all he had, he and his successors did lay arbitrary taxes on all of their subjects' land when they judged it necessary. If the public lands and services where ordained as a sufficient maintenance of the commonwealth, it was contrary to the initial institution of the sovereignty. The insufficiency is revealed by the ensuing taxes, and as it appears lately that the revenues of the crown are small and are subject to alienation[5] and diminution. It is therefore in vain to assign a portion of the land to the commonwealth who may sell it or give it away, for this is what the sovereign's representative would do.

The places and matter of traffic depend on the sovereign for their distribution. The sovereign has the right to distribute lands at home and also assign the places and the commodities that subjects will traffic in abroad. If private persons had the right to use their own discretion for these purposes, some of them would be drawn for gain to furnish the enemy with the means to hurt the commonwealth. Or they might hurt it by importing the kinds of things that are pleasing to peoples' appetites, but are nevertheless noxious or at least unprofitable to them. Therefore, the sovereign has the right to approve or disapprove of the places and matter of foreign traffic.

The laws transferring propriety also belong to the sovereign. It is not enough for the sustenance of the commonwealth that every man has the propriety of a portion of land or of some natural commodities. Neither is it enough that every man has the natural ownership of some useful art, for there is no one art in the world that is necessary either for the being or well-being of every particular man. It is therefore necessary that men distribute what they can spare and transfer their propriety mutually to one another by exchange and mutual contract. Therefore the sovereign of a commonwealth has the right to determine the manner of all kinds of contracts between subjects that are to be made in matters of buying, selling, exchanging, borrowing, letting,[6] and hiring. The sovereign should determine what words and signs make such contracts valid, so that to the extent he can arrange it, the matter and distribution of nourishment to the members of the commonwealth will be sufficient.

Money, the blood of the commonwealth. Concoction means the reduction of all commodities to something of equal value that is portable, that are presently not consumed and are reserved for nourishment in future time. This is done to not hinder men from moving from place to place, so that a man can have nourishment in any place. This involves gold, silver and money. Gold and silver happen to be highly valued in almost all countries and so are a convenient measure for different nations of the value of things. Money, or whatever is coined by a sovereign, is a sufficient measure of the value of all other things for the subjects of a commonwealth. By the means of these measures, all moveable and immoveable commodities accompany a man wherever he lives, within and without the place of his ordinary residence. Commodities pass from man to man within a commonwealth and go round about, nourishing every part as they pass through. This kind of concoction can be called the sanguification[7] of the commonwealth. In the same manner natural blood is made from the fruits of the earth and by circulating, it nourishes every member of a man's body.

Silver and gold have value from their own matter and so they have the privilege that their value cannot be altered by one, or a few, commonwealths. First, silver and gold are the common measure of all commodities in all places. But money may be easily enhanced or abased. Secondly, silver and gold have the privilege of making commonwealths, when they need to, move and stretch out their arms into foreign countries to supply private subjects that travel and whole armies with provisions. But money in the form of coins is not useful for this purpose. It is unable to endure the change of air and so it only has its effect at home. Even there it is subject to the change of laws and to have its value diminished, often to the detriment of those that have it.

The conduits and ways of money for public use. There are two sorts of conduits and ways that money is conveyed for public use. One way that it is conveyed is by means of public coffers. The other is when it is issued for public payments. The first sort involves collectors, receivers and treasurers, and the second also involves treasurers and the officers that are appointed for payment by public and private ministers. This is another way that the artificial man, the commonwealth, resembles a natural man. In the natural man the veins receive the blood from the several parts of the body, and carry it to the heart, where it is made vital again, and then the arteries send it out again to enliven the body's members and enable them to move.

The children of a commonwealth are colonies. The procreation, or children of a commonwealth, are called plantations or colonies. These are numbers of men sent out from the commonwealth sent out from a commonwealth under the leadership of a conductor or governor to inhabit a foreign country that is void of inhabitants or is made void of them by war. In some case the colony when it is settled is either a commonwealth itself or is discharged from the subjection of the sovereign that sent them. This has been done by many commonwealths in ancient times. When it happens, the commonwealth from which they were sent is called their metropolis or mother, and requires no more of them than a father requires of children that he has emancipated and made free from his domestic government. What is required in these cases is only honor and friendship. If the colonies remain united to their metropolis, as occurred in ancient Rome, then they are not commonwealths themselves. Instead, they are provinces and parts of the commonwealth that sent them. Besides the honor and league colonies owe their respective metropolises, their rights depend wholly on the license and letters that the sovereign authorized them to plant.

Endnotes

1. Property
2. In conflict with the sovereign's role to maintain peace and security.
3. It is not clear what other place in the *Leviathan* Hobbes is referring to. This paragraph does hint that a sovereign may be so unjust that the subjects may justly not obey his commands.
4. Groves
5. Transfer to others
6. Renting
7. Circulation of the blood

CHAPTER 25

Of Counsel

What is counsel. It is very fallacious to judge the nature of things by the ordinary and inconstant use of words. This is evident in the confusion between 'counsel' and 'command', that arises from the imperative manner that is used in speaking of both of them on many occasions. For example, the words 'do this' are the words used not only of one who commands, but also of someone who is giving counsel or is giving an exhortation. But there are very few people who see that these are very different things, even though most people can see the distinctions between them when they see who is actually speaking and to whom and on what occasion. But when people find these phrases in men's writing, readers often make mistakes distinguishing the precepts of counselors for the precepts that are commands by not being able or willing to consider the circumstances of the utterances. These readers then look at these cases in ways that would agree with the conclusions and actions that they themselves approve of. To avoid these kinds of mistakes and to give the terms 'commanding', 'counseling' and 'exhorting' their proper meanings, I define them as follows.

Differences between command and counsel. A command occurs when a man says, "Do this", or "Do not do this", and the hearer does not expect to be provided with any reason given besides the will of the one who says it. It follows manifestly, that the one who commands pretends[1] thereby only his own benefit. For the reason behind a command is only the speaker's own will and the proper object of every man's will is some good to himself.

Counsel occurs when a man says, "Do this", or "Do not do this", and the speaker deduces the reasons for the action from the benefit that should arrive to the one hearing the utterance. From this it follows that the one giving counsel, whatever he intends, claims to provide for the good of the one hearing the utterance.

Therefore, the one great difference between command and counsel is that command is directed at a speaker's own benefit and counsel is directed to the benefit of the hearer. Based on this point, there is another difference. A person is obliged to do what he is commanded, as when he makes a covenant to obey. But a person has no obligation to follow someone's counsel, because the hurt of not following it just belongs to the receiver of the counsel. If the person hearing the counsel covenants to obey it, then the counsel possesses the nature of a command. A third difference between them is that no man can pretend a right to another man's counsel, because he should not pretend a benefit by the counsel to himself. To demand the right to the counsel of another indicates a will to know the other person's designs or to gain some other good for himself. As I said before, the good for oneself is the proper object of every man's will.

It is also part of the nature of counsel that whoever asks for it cannot with equity, punish someone who gives it. To ask for counsel from another is to permit the other to give the counsel the other thinks is best. Consequently, it would be unjust to punish someone who gives counsel to a sovereign when he asks for it, whether the sovereign is a monarch or an assembly. This applies whether or not the counsel given is agreed to by most or is a matter of debate. If the sense of an assembly can be noted before the debate is ended, the assembly should neither ask nor take any further counsel. The sense of an assembly is the resolution of the debate and the end of all deliberation. Generally, the one that asks for counsel is the author of the request and so cannot punish it, and what the sovereign cannot do, no one else should do. But if a subject counsels another to do something contrary to the laws, that counsel is punishable by the commonwealth, whether the counsel proceeds from evil intent or only from ignorance. Ignorance of the law is no excuse, where every man is bound to take notice of the laws to which he is subject.

What are exhortation and dehortation. Exhortation and dehortation[2] are kinds of counsel that are accompanied by signs of the one providing it, that indicate a vehement desire that the counsel be followed. To say this more concisely, these are counsels vehemently pressed. One who exhorts is not just deducing the consequences of what he is advising or promoting this by the vigor of true reasoning. Rather, he is encouraging the one that is counseled to action. Those who offer dehortations are trying to deter someone from action. When exhorter and dehorters deduce their reasons in their reasons, they have a common regard for the common passions and opinions of men. They both make use of similes, metaphors examples and the other tools of oratory to persuade their hearers of the utility, honor and justice of following their advice.

What can thus be inferred is first, that exhortation and dehortation are directed to the one that gives the counsel and not to the one that receives it. This is contrary to the duty of a counselor, who according to the definition of 'counsel' ought to think of the benefit of the one he advises and not his own benefit. A person that directs his counsel to his own benefit, when he does this with long and vehement urging, only provides counsel by accident that is of benefit to the one who asked for it. Usually, there is no benefit at all to the one that asked for counsel.

Secondly, exhortation and dehortation are only of use when a man is speaking to a multitude. When such a speech is directly addressed to an individual, the person may interrupt the speaker and examine his reasons more rigorously than can be done by a multitude. In the latter case there are too many to enter into a dispute and a dialogue with someone who is speaking to a number of people all at once.

Thirdly, those who exhort and dehort when they are required to give counsel are corrupt counselors, who are, in effect, bribed by their own interests. For even if a counselor gives good advice, he is no more a good counselor than a judge who gives a just sentence for a reward is a just judge. In those cases where a man lawfully commands, as a father in a family or a leader in an army, exhortations and dehortations are not lawful, but are necessary and laudable. But in these cases they are not counsels, but commands, and when they are for the execution of some sour labor, they are sometimes necessary. In these cases humanity always requires that instead of the harsher language of command, they should be encouraged by deliveries of the sweetened tune of the phrases of counsel.

There are examples of the differences between command and counsel that are found in forms of speech that express them in Holy Scripture. "Have no other gods but me; make no grave images for yourself, do not take God's name in vain; sanctify the Sabbath, honor your parents, do not kill; do not steal; etc." are commands, because the reason why we are to obey them is drawn form the will of God our king, whom we are obliged to obey. But the words, "Sell all that you have; give it to the poor and follow me," are expressions of counsel. The reason given for why we are to do so is drawn from our own benefit, which is that we shall have "treasure in heaven". The words, "Go to the village over against you, and you shall find an ass tied and her colt; loosen her and bring her to me" are a command. The reason is the fact that they are drawn from the will of their Master. But the words, "Repent, and be baptized in the name of Jesus" are expressions of counsel. The reason why we should do so, does not tend to the benefit of God Almighty, who would still be the king no matter how we rebel. The reason is rather for the benefit of ourselves, who have no other means of avoiding the punishment hanging over us for our sins.

Differences between fit and unfit counselors. The differences between counsel and command have been deduced from the nature of counsel. These consist of deducing the benefit, or hurt, that may arise to the one that is counseled by the necessary or probable consequences of the actions that were advised. The differences between apt and inapt counselors can be derived from the same considerations. Experience is the memory of the consequences of similar actions that were formerly observed, and counsel is the speech by which this experience is made known to another. Thus, the virtues and defects of counsel are the same as the intellectual virtues and defects. Counselors serve the person of the commonwealth as their memory and mental discourse. But there is one difference of great importance between a commonwealth and a natural man. That is that in the case of a natural man, he receives his experience from the natural objects of sense that work on him without passions or interests of their own. But those who give counsel to the representative person of a commonwealth may, and often, have their own particular ends and passions that render their counsel always suspicious and many times, unfaithful. This is the basis as the first condition of good counselors: A counselor's ends and interests should not be inconsistent with the ends and interests of the one whom he counsels.

Secondly, the office of a counselor is to truly inform the one counseled about the consequences of an action that is being considered. To do this, the counselor ought to provide his advice in the form of speech that would make the truth appear evident. That means he should speak with as much firm ratiocination,[3] brevity and proper and meaningful language as the evidence will permit. What are thus repugnant to the office of a counselor are rash and unlikely inferences, such as inferences that are far-fetched and only come from examples, the authority of books, or witnesses of fact and opinion, and are not from arguments about what is good or evil. What are also repugnant are obscure, confused and ambiguous expressions, as well as all metaphorical speech that tends to stir up the passions. Such reasoning and expressions are useful only to deceive or to lead the one counseled to other ends besides his own.

Thirdly, the ability to counsel proceeds from experience and long study. No one is presumed to have experience in all those things that the administration of a great commonwealth should know. Thus, no one is presumed to be a good counselor, except in the business that he has greatly meditated upon and considered, as well as being greatly versed in it. The business of a commonwealth is to preserve the people at peace at home and defend them from foreign invasion. This requires great knowledge of the dispositions of mankind, of the rights of government, and the nature of equity, law, justice and honor. These can only be obtained with study. A commonwealth also has to know the strength, commodities and places, both of their own country and of their neighbors. The commonwealth must also know the inclinations and designs of all nations that may in any way annoy them. These latter things can only be attained with much experience. The whole sum of them, but also every particular, requires years of observation and more than ordinary study. As I said in chapter 8, the kind of wit required for counsel is judgment. The differences in men's judgment derives from different educations in different studies and businesses. In matters that involve infallible rules, such as with engines, edifices and geometry, all of the experience in the world will not provide better counsel than one who has learned or found the relevant rule. But when there is no such rule, then the one with the most experience in that particular kind of business has the best judgment and is the best counselor.

Fourthly, consider the situations in which someone is asked to give counsel to a commonwealth that concerns another commonwealth. In order to do this, it is necessary to be acquainted with the intelligence and letters that come from the other commonwealth. It is also necessary to see the all the records of treaties and other state transactions between them. No one can do this except those that the representative thinks are fit to do so. This shows that those who are not asked to be counselors can have no good counsel in such cases to obtrude.[4]

Fifthly, suppose there are a number of counselors. In that case the one who is to be counseled would be better served to hear them apart from each other than in an assembly. This is so for many reasons. First, in hearing them apart one has the advice of every man. But to hear them in an assembly, many of them will deliver their advice by just saying, "Aye" or "Nay" or voting with their hands or feet. They would not be expressing their own sense, but rather would be influenced by the eloquence of another, or from fear of displeasing some, or the whole assembly that have already spoken. Or they may fear appearing duller in apprehension than those that have already applauded the contrary opinion. Secondly, in an assembly of many there will always be some whose interests are contrary to the public interest. Such people with passionate interests will produce passionate eloquence and this eloquence will draw others to provide the same advice. The passions of men which may be moderate when asunder, as in the heat of one brand, are like many brands that enflame one another in an assembly. This is especially the case when they blow on one another by their orations and are apt to set the commonwealth on fire under the pretence of counseling it. Thirdly, when one hears every man apart, one may examine when there is need the grounds of their advice by frequent interruptions and objections. This cannot be done in an assembly, where in every difficult question, where a person trying to get counsel would be bewildered and dazzled by the variety of opinion being presented, rather than being informed about the course he ought to take. In any assembly of many there will always be some that have the ambition to be thought eloquent and learned in politics. These people will not give careful advice on the business in question, but will rather be concerned to be applauded for their motley orations made from the diverse colored threads or shreds of various authors. This is at the very least an impertinence that takes away time from serious consultation, and can be easily avoided by having consultation in secret and apart from others. Fourthly, the counsels of many in assemblies are dangerous in matters of deliberation that ought to be kept secret, of which there are many occasions in public business. That is why large assemblies have to commit such affairs to smaller numbers, and to such people that are most versed in the matter and whose fidelity they can trust.

To conclude, would anyone desire the counsel of a large assembly of counselors on matters such as the marrying of one's children, the disposing of one's land, the governing of one's household, or the managing of one's private estate? And what if some of the assembly were known not to desire one's prosperity? A man that does his business with the help of many prudent counselors, would do it best when every one is consulted about just that element that he knows best. In the same way it is best to use seconds when playing tennis when each one is placed at their proper station. It is even better to use one's own judgment and not have any seconds at all. But worst of all is to be carried back and forth in some business by a framed counsel that cannot move except by the plurality of consenting opinions, which often cannot be determined because of those who dissent out of envy or interest. This is similar to one who is playing some ball game, but is carried to the ball in a wheelbarrow or other heavy machine. Even though those who are carrying the wheelbarrow are good players themselves, the motion is retarded by their conflicting judgments and desires. The more people involved in driving the wheelbarrow, the more retarded will be the motion, and most of all, when there is one among them that wants the person to lose the game. While it is true that many eyes see more than does one, this only applies when there is a final resolution in one man as to what they all see. Otherwise, because many eyes see the same thing in diverse lines,[5] they are apt to squint in order to see their own private benefit. Those that desire to hit the target, though they look about with two eyes, never aim but with one. That is why no large popular commonwealth has ever survived except by a foreign enemy that united them, or the reputation of some one eminent man among them, or by the secret counsel of a few, or by the mutual fear of equal factions. Open consultations in an assembly have never led to the survival of a large popular commonwealth. As for little commonwealths, whether they are monarchies or democracies, there is no human wisdom that can uphold them if they have potent neighbors that are jealous of them.

Endnotes

1. Claims
2. Dissuading someone
3. Reasoning
4. Put forward
5. Different perspectives

CHAPTER 26

Of Civil Laws

What is civil law. Civil laws are those laws that men are bound to observe not because they are members of a particular commonwealth, but because they are members of any commonwealth. The knowledge of particular laws belongs to those who profess the study of their particular countries. But the knowledge of civil law, in general, belongs to any man. The ancient law of Rome was called their civil law, from the word 'civitas', which means a commonwealth. Those countries that have been under the Roman Empire and were governed that their laws still call the laws they retain from that empire the civil law to distinguish them from their own civil laws. But I do not intend to speak of that portion of Roman law. My design is not to show what is the law here and the law there, but as Plato, Aristotle, Cicero and other have done, I intend to show what law is in general.

First, it is manifest that law in general is not a type of counsel, but a type of command. It is not a command from one man to another, but it is the command of one to another who has been formerly obliged to obey him. The civil law only adds the name of the commanding person, which is *persona civtatis,* that is, the person of the commonwealth.

Thus, I define civil law in the following manner. The civil laws are the rules that the commonwealth has commanded to every subject either by word, writing or other sufficient sign of his will. These laws distinguish right from wrong in terms of what is contrary or in agreement with the rules.

Everything is clearly evident in this definition. Every man sees that some laws are addressed to all subjects in general, and some to particular provinces, some to particular vocations, and some to particular men. Therefore all laws are commands directed to some men and to no one else. The laws are the rules of what is just and unjust, as nothing can be considered unjust that is not contrary to some law. Only the commonwealth can make laws, because our subjection is only to the commonwealth. Commands are to be signified by sufficient signs, for otherwise, people do not know what they are to obey. Whatever can be deduced from this definition as a necessary consequence should be acknowledged as the truth. From this definition I now deduce the following:

The sovereign is the legislator. 1) The sovereign is the only legislator in a commonwealth, whether the sovereign is one man as in a monarchy, or an assembly, as in a democracy or aristocracy. The legislator is the one that makes the laws. Only the commonwealth prescribes and commands the observation of those rules that are called the laws. Therefore the commonwealth is the legislator. But the commonwealth is not a person and does not have the capacity to do anything. The person is the representative, which is the sovereign, and therefore the sovereign is the sole legislator. For the same reason no one can abrogate a law except the sovereign. A law can only be abrogated by another law that forbids the execution of the former one.

The sovereign is not subject to civil law. 2) The sovereign of a commonwealth, whether it is one man or an assembly, is not subject to civil laws. The sovereign has the power to make and repeal laws, and so when he pleases, he can free himself from any subjection by repealing the laws that trouble him and making new ones. This means that he was free from the law before he repealed it, as someone is free when he can be free when he so wills. It is also not possible for any person to be bound to himself, because if a person can release his bounds, as happens when a person is bound to himself, he is not really bound at all.

The use of a law is not by virtue of time, but of the sovereign's consent. 3) When the authority of a law is obtained[1] by long use, it is not the length of time that makes the authority, but the will of the sovereign signified by his silence. Silence is sometimes an indication of consent. Something is not a law if the sovereign is silent about that. If the sovereign has a question of whether his present rights are grounded upon his present will or a law that was formerly made, the length of time the law has been established is no prejudice to his rights. The question shall be judged instead by equity. Many unjust actions and unjust sentences go uncontrolled for a longer time than any man can remember. Our lawyers say that the only customs that are laws are ones that are reasonable and that evil customs are to be abolished. But the judgment of what is reasonable and what is to be abolished belongs only to the one that makes the laws, which is a sovereign assembly or a monarch.

The Law of Nature and the civil law contain each other. 4) The Law of Nature and the civil law contain each other and are of equal extent. As I said before in chapter 15, the Laws of Nature, which consist of equity, justice, gratitude and the other moral virtues that depend on these in the condition of mere nature, are not properly laws. They are rather qualities that dispose men to peace and obedience. Once a commonwealth is settled, and not before, they actually become laws. At that point they are the commands of the commonwealth, and therefore are also civil laws, for it is the sovereign power that obliges men to obey them. There is the need of ordinances of sovereign power to punish those who have been determined to break them, as private men have different views of what are equity, justice and moral virtue. These ordinances are therefore part of the civil law. The Laws of Nature are therefore part of the civil laws in all commonwealths of the world. Reciprocally, the civil law is part of the dictates of nature. Justice, which involves the performance of covenants and giving every man what he's due, is a dictate of the Law of Nature. Every subject in a commonwealth has covenanted to obey the civil law. They do this with each other when they assemble to make a common representative, or with the representative, one by one, when they are subdued by the sword and promise obedience so that their lives may be spared. Therefore obedience to the civil law is also part of the Law of Nature. Civil and Natural Law are not different kinds, but different parts of the law. The written part is called civil, and the unwritten is called natural. The right of nature, that is the natural liberty of man, may be abridged and restrained by the civil law. Actually, the end of making laws is just such a restraint, for without it there cannot be any peace. The only reason laws were brought into this world was to limit the natural liberty of particular men so that they might not hurt, but assist one another, and join together against a common enemy.

Provincial laws are not made by custom, but by the sovereign power. 5) Suppose a sovereign of one commonwealth subdues a people that have lived under some written laws, and afterwards this sovereign governs them by these same laws. Even so, these are the civil laws of the victors and not of the vanquished of this defeated commonwealth. The legislator is not the authority that first made the laws, but is one by whose authority they continue to be laws. Suppose there are different provinces within the dominion of a commonwealth, and the different provinces has a diversity of laws that are commonly called customs of each province. Such customs do not have their force only from the length of time they have been in effect. There were originally ancient laws that were written or otherwise known in the constitutions and statutes of the sovereigns of these territories. Now they are laws, not by virtue of the prescription of time, but by the constitutions of their present sovereigns. If there is an unwritten law in all provinces of a dominion that is generally observed, and no iniquity appears in its use, then that law can only be a Law of Nature and so is equally obliging on all mankind.

Some foolish opinions of lawyers concerning the making of laws. 6) In monarchies and sovereign assemblies all laws have their authority and force from the will of the commonwealth which is the will of the representative. This might lead one to wonder what is the source of the opinions found in the books of some eminent lawyers in several commonwealths that claim that the legislative power depends on private men or subordinate judges. For example, consider the following view, "The common law has no controller but the Parliament." This is true only when the Parliament has the sovereign power and cannot be assembled, nor dissolved, but by its own discretion. If there is a right to dissolve the Parliament, there is a right to control it and to consequently to control its controllings. If there is no such right, then the controller of the laws is not the Parliament, but *Rex in Parliamento.*[2] If a Parliament is sovereign, then even if it should assemble many wise men from the countries that are subject to it, no one will believe that this assembled group has thereby acquired legislative power. Consider also the view that there are two arms of a commonwealth, force and justice, and the king is the first arm and the other is deposited in the hands of the Parliament. This view implies that a commonwealth could exist where the force is in one hand and that justice does not have the authority and command to govern.

7) Our lawyers agree that the law can never be against reason. That means that every construction of the law is not the letter of the law, but that the law is the intent of the legislator. While this is true, there is the doubt raised, which is whose reason determines what is the law. This cannot mean that the reason involved is that of private men, for then there would be as much contradiction in the laws as there are in the schools. Nor can it mean as Edward Coke says, "An artificial perfection of reason, gotten by long study, observation and experience" (as his was). (Sir Edward Coke, Littleton, book 2, chapter 6, folio 97b) It is possible that long study may increase and confirm erroneous sentences, and when men build on false grounds, the more they build, the greater the

ruin. When many different people study and observe with equal diligence in equal time, their resolutions are, and will remain, discordant. This shows that it is not *juris prudentia*, the wisdom of subordinate judges that makes the laws, but the reason of the artificial man, the commonwealth. Since the representative of the commonwealth is but one person, there cannot easily arise any contradiction in the laws. If there is a contradiction, the same reason is able to take it away by interpretation or alteration. The sovereign, that is the person of the commonwealth, is the one that judges in all courts of justice. The subordinate judges ought to regard the reasons that moved the sovereign to make their laws and adjust their own sentences accordingly. If they do this, then their sentences are those of the sovereign's, but otherwise the sentences are their own and are unjust.

Laws that are not made known, are not laws. 8) Laws are commands and commands consist of declarations or manifestation of the will of the one that commands. The laws are made by voice, writing, or other signs sufficient to indicate the will of those who command. It follows that the command of the commonwealth is only a law to those that have the means to notice it. There is no law for fools, children, mad-men or brute beasts. None of them can be called just or unjust, because they do not have the power to make any covenant or to understand a covenant's consequences. They do not authorize the actions of any sovereign, as do those who do make a commonwealth for themselves. Men are excused from following the laws in general if nature or accident takes away their capacity to take notice of them. If an accident takes away from a man the means to note a particular law, if the accident is not the man's fault, then he is excused if he doesn't observe the law. Speaking properly, that law is not a law to him. So it is important to consider what arguments and signs are sufficient to indicate the knowledge of what is the law, which is the will of the sovereign in monarchies and other forms of government.

The unwritten laws are the Laws of Nature. First, if a law obliges all subjects without exception and is not written or published where people may notice it, this law is a Law of Nature. For what men are supposed to take to be knowledge of the law that is not based on other men's words, but is only based on every individual's reason, must be in agreement with the reason of all men. Such laws can only be the Laws of Nature. The Laws of Nature do not need to be published or proclaimed. Indeed, they are contained in this one sentence that is approved by all of the world: do not do to another what you think is unreasonable for another to do to you.

Secondly, if there is a law that only obliges some kinds of men, or one particular man, but it does not have to be written or published by word, then it also is a Law of Nature. It would be known by the same arguments and signs that distinguish the particular kinds of men from other subjects. For when whoever makes a law does not write it or publish it in some way, then it can only be known through the reason of those who are to obey it, and is therefore a Law of Nature and not just a civil one. For example, if a sovereign employs a public minister and does not provide him with written instructions, the minister is obliged to use the dictates of reason to determine his instructions. If the sovereign makes a judge, the judge is to take notice that his sentences accord with the reason of his sovereign. This reason is always understood to be equity, and so the judge is bound by the Law of Nature. In all things that an ambassador does that are not defined by written instructions, the ambassador should use his reason to determine what is conducive to the sovereign's interest. Similar considerations apply to all public and private ministers of a sovereignty. All of the instructions of natural reason may be subsumed under the name of fidelity, which is a branch of natural justice.

Aside from the Laws of Nature, it is the essence of all other laws that they be made known to every man obliged to obey them, either by word, writing, or some other act known to proceed from sovereign authority. The will of a person cannot be understood except by his own word, act, or conjecture taken from his scope and purpose. When the person is the commonwealth, the conjecture is always supposed to be consonant with equity and reason. In ancient times before writing was in common use, the laws were often put into verse. This was done so that common people would more easily retain them in their memories by taking pleasure in singing or reciting them. For the same reason Solomon advises men to bind the Ten Commandments to their ten fingers. (Proverbs 7:3.) When Moses spoke to the people when he renewed the covenant, (Deuteronomy 11:19) he bid them to teach it to their children, by speaking of it both at home and upon the way, when going to bed and when rising from bed, and it write it upon the posts and doors of their houses, (Deuteronomy 31:12) and to assemble the people, men, women and children to hear it read.

There is no law where the legislator cannot be known. The difference between authorizing and verifying. It is not enough that the law be written and published. There must also be manifest signs that it proceeds from the will of the sovereign. When private men have, or think they have, the force to secure their unjust designs and safely convoy them to their ambitious ends, they may publish what they please as laws without, or even against, the legislative authority. So it is not just requisite to declare the law, but also to produce the signs of author and authority. The author, or legislator, is supposed to be evident in every commonwealth. He is the sovereign who as been constituted by the consent of everyone and should be known by every man. However, the ignorance and security of men is such that for the most part they do not remember the first constitution of their commonwealth. When this happens, they do not consider whose power defends them against their enemies, protects their industry, or rights the wrongs done to them. But no man who considers these matters can question who has this power, and so no excuse can be derived from ignorance concerning who is sovereign. It is a dictate of natural reason and so a Law of Nature that no man should weaken that power. Every man asked for this power and wittingly received it against others. No matter what evil men suggest, there can be no doubt in anyone, except through his own fault, about who is the sovereign. But there is a real difficulty in seeing the evidence of the authority derived from the sovereign. Whether this difficulty can be removed depends on the knowledge of public registers, public counsels, public ministers, and public seals. All of these provide that the laws are sufficiently verified. I said "verified" and not "authorized", as verification is the testimony and record, and not the authority of the law. The latter consists only in the command of the sovereign.

When the law if verified by a subordinate judge. Suppose that a man has a question about an injury that depends on a Law of Nature, that is, on common equity. The sentence of the judge that by commission has the authority to judge in such cases is a sufficient verification of the Law of Nature in that particular case. The advice of one that professes the study of law may be useful for avoiding contention in these cases. Still this is only advice and it is the judge that must determine what is the law when hearing the controversy.

By the public registers. Suppose the question is a matter of injury or crime that is based on a written law. Every person has recourse to the registers, either by himself or through others, so that he can be sufficiently informed, if he chooses, to know before he does the action whether it is considered an injury or a crime. Indeed, he ought to do so, for if a man doubts whether an act he is considering is just or unjust, if he can inform himself about it and does not, then his doing the act is unlawful. Suppose that a person thinks himself to be injured in a case that is covered by a written law that he, or others, may read and consider. If the person complains before he has consulted the law, he does so unjustly, and betrays a disposition to vex other men, rather than be one who demands his own rights.

By patent letters and public seals. Suppose the question is one of obedience to a public officer. It is a sufficient verification of the authority of the officer to see his commission with the public seal and to hear it read, or to have other means of being informed of it. Every man is obliged to try to do his best to inform himself of all written laws that may concern his own future actions.

The interpretation of the law depends on the sovereign power. Even if the legislator is known and the laws are sufficiently published by writing or the light of nature, there is still another very material circumstance that must hold to make them obligatory. For the law consists not in its letter, but in its intention or meaning, which is the authentic interpretation of the law, that is the sense the legislator gave it. The interpretation of all laws depends on the sovereign authority and the interpreters can only be those whom the sovereign appoints. Otherwise, the craft of an interpreter can make a law bear a sense contrary to the sovereign's intent, which would make the interpreter the legislator.

All laws need interpretation. All written and unwritten laws need interpretation. The interpretation of the unwritten Laws of Nature should be very easy to do without partiality and passion, because they just require natural reason and so violators of them have no excuse. But there are very few, and perhaps no one, that are not blinded by self-love or some other passions in some cases. So of all laws, the Laws of Nature have become the most obscure and thus the ones in greatest need of able interpreters. If a written law is very short, it is easily misinterpreted because of the different meanings of a word or two. If a written law is long, it is even more obscure because of the different meanings of many words. In either case no written law can be well understood without a perfect understanding of the final cause for which the law made, but the final knowledge of this final cause exists in the legislator. For a legislator there cannot be any knot in any law that is insoluble, either by finding the ends that will undo the knot, or by just formulating the ends that he wills by legislative power, as Alexander did with his sword to the Gordian knot. These are things no interpreter can do.

The authentic interpretation of the laws is not provided by writers. The interpretation of the Laws of Nature in a commonwealth do not depend on books of moral philosophy. Even if their opinions of the laws are true, the authority of writers without the authority of the commonwealth does not make their opinions the law. What I have written in this treatise concerning the moral virtues and their necessity for procuring and maintaining peace is evidently true, but even so, it is not presently the law. It is only the law if it is part of the civil law in all commonwealths. Even if what I have written is by nature very reasonable, it is only by sovereign power that it can become the law. Otherwise, it would be a great error to call the Laws of Nature the unwritten law, as we see so many volumes published about them that contain so many contradictions of the claims of each other, and even of themselves.

The interpreter of the law is the judge giving the sentence out loud, in every particular case. The interpretation of the Law of Nature is the sentence of the judge that is constituted by the sovereign authority to hear and determine a relevant controversy. The interpretation is the application of the law to the present case. In an act of judicature the judge does no more than consider whether the demand of the party is consonant to natural reason and equity. The sentence the judge gives is therefore the interpretation of the Law of Nature. This interpretation is authentic, not because it is his private sentence, but because he gives it by authority of the sovereign. It thus becomes the sovereign's sentence, which is the law for that time to the two parties that are pleading.

The sentence of a judge does not bind him, or other judges, to give like sentences in like cases ever after. Any subordinate judge or sovereign may err in a judgment concerning equity. If later the same judge in a similar case finds it more consonant with equity to give a contrary sentence, then he is obliged to do it. For the same reason a judge's sentence does not become a law to other judges, even though they are sworn to follow the law. Suppose by the authority of a sovereign a wrong sentence is given for a mutable law. A judge may realize this and still follow it in a case where there is the constitution of a new law or in cases where every little circumstance is the same. But it is different with immutable laws such as the Laws of Nature. There are no laws that are the same as these or other judges who should judge the same in like cases for ever after. Princes succeed one another and one judge passes and another comes up. Even heaven and earth shall pass away, but not one title[3] of the Law of Nature shall pass away, for it is the eternal law of God. Therefore all the sentences of previous judges that have ever been made cannot together make a law contrary to natural equity. Nor can any examples of former judges warrant an unreasonable sentence, nor discharge a present judge from the trouble of using the principles of his own natural reason to study what is equity. For example's sake, consider the Law of Nature that says that one should not punish the innocent. An innocent person is one that is acquitted judicially and is acknowledged as innocent by a judge. Now consider the example of a man who is accused of a capital crime and seeing the power and malice of some enemy and the corruption and partiality of the judges, he runs away out of fear of an unjust verdict. Suppose that later he is captured and brought to a legal trial and makes it sufficiently appear that he was not guilty of the crime and is therefore acquitted. Nevertheless, he is condemned to lose his goods. This would be a clear condemnation of the innocent. There is no place in the world where this can be a proper interpretation of the Law of Nature or be made into a law by sentences of previous judges that had done the same. The first one who condemned this man to punishment judged unjustly and no injustice should be a pattern of judgment to succeeding judges. A written law may forbid innocent men from fleeing and they may be punished for fleeing. But when fleeing for fear of injury is taken as a presumption of guilt, once a man is already judicially absolved of the crime, it would be contrary to the nature of a presumption to still punish him. For such presumptions have no place after judgment is given. And yet this is not what a great lawyer sets down as the common law of England. He says, "If a man that is innocent, be accused of a felony, and from fear, flees, even though he is judicially acquitted of the felony, if it is determined that he did flee when accused of the felony, he shall be punished, even if he is innocent. He shall forfeit his goods, chattel, debts and duties. He forfeits them because the law will admit no exception to the presumption in law, grounded upon his flight."[4] Notice the phrases, "an innocent man", "judicially acquitted", "even if he is innocent" (when there is no written law that forbids him from fleeing) after his acquittal, "the presumption in law" which is the basis of his losing all the goods he has. If the law bases on his flight a presumption of the fact (that he committed a capital crime), the sentence ought to have been capital. But if the presumption does not ground the fact, then why should he lose his goods? Therefore, this can be no law of England, nor is condemnation grounded upon a presumption of law; rather the condemnation is grounded on the presumption of judges. It is also against the law to say that no proof shall be admitted against a presumption of law. But for all judges, sovereign and subordinates, if they refuse to hear proof, they refuse to do justice. Even if a sentence is just, if judges condemn without hearing the offered proofs, they are unjust judges and their presumptions are merely prejudice. No man should bring prejudice to the seat of justice whatever the precedent judgments are or whatever examples he pretends to follow.

There are other things of this nature where men's judgments have been perverted by trusting precedents. This however, should be enough to show that even though the sentence of a judge will be a law to the pleading party, it does not make it a law to any judge that shall succeed him in that office.

Similarly, a commentator on the question of the meaning of the written laws is not the one who is the interpreter of them. For commentaries are commonly more subject to being caviled about than is the text itself. Commentaries therefore need other commentaries and this would mean no end of interpretation. The interpreters must be the ordinary judges, unless there is an interpreter authorized by the sovereign that subordinate judges must follow. This is the same situation that applies to the unwritten law. The sentences of judges in such cases are to be taken by those that plead as the law in their particular cases, but they do not bind other judges in like cases to give like judgments. A judge may err in the interpretation even of written laws, but no error of a subordinate judge can change a law that is the general sentence of the sovereign.

The difference between the letter and the sentence of the law. Men used to distinguish between the sentence and letter of the law for written laws. This is a good distinction when the letter of the law is taken to mean whatever can be gathered from the bare words of the law itself. The meanings of almost all words in themselves are either ambiguous or can be used metaphorically. They may thus be used in arguments to make many different meanings; however, there is only one sense for a law. But if the letter of the law is taken to mean the literal sense of the law, then the letter and the sentence and the intention of a law are all the same. The literal sense is what the legislator intended and should be signified by the letter of the law. The intention of the legislator is always supposed to be equity, as it would be a great contumely[5] for a judge to think otherwise of a sovereign's intent. If the word of the law does not fully authorize a reasonable sentence, a judge should supply it with the Law of Nature, but if this is difficult to do, then the judge should delay making a decision until he has received more ample authority. Suppose for example, that a written law ordains that one, who is thrust out of his house by force, should be restored by force. Then consider a man who negligently leaves his house empty and upon returning is kept out be force. In this case there is no special law that is applicable. However, it is clear that the previously mentioned law contains this case; otherwise the person would have no remedy at all and that goes against the intention of the legislator. Again, the word of the law commands the judge based on the evidence before him. Suppose a man is falsely accused of a fact that the judge himself saw was done by another and not by the one who is accused. In this case the letter of the law should not be followed if it means the condemnation of an innocent person. Nor shall a judge give a sentence that goes against the evidence of witnesses, just because the letter of the law orders the contrary. In this case the judge should ask the sovereign to make someone else the judge, so that the former could be a witness in the case. There is an inconvenience in following the bare words of a law to find the law's intent, for sometimes the bare words do not lead to the best interpretation. But no inconvenience can warrant a sentence that is against the law. For every judge of what is right and wrong is not the judge of what is commodious or incommodious to a commonwealth.

The abilities required in a judge. The abilities required in a good interpreter of the law, a good judge, are not the same as those of an advocate, which is the study of the laws. As a judge should just base his view of the facts only on witnesses, so he should only base his view of the laws only on the statutes and constitutions of the sovereign that are raised by those who are pleading. A judge should not investigate beforehand the matter he is to judge. He should just determine the facts by the witnesses and what he says about the point of the laws should be determined by what those who are pleading cite as the relevant laws and cite as the authority to interpret these laws. The lords of the Parliament in England were judges, and they heard and decided the most difficult cases. Yet very few of them were well versed in the study of the laws and fewer made this their profession. Even though they consulted with lawyers who were appointed to be present for that purpose, the lords alone had the authority to give the sentence. Similarly, in ordinary trials twelve men of the common people are the judges that give the sentence, not only about the facts, but also of what is right. By pronouncing for the complainant or defendant, they are the judges of the facts and of what is right. In questions of crime these twelve people not only determine whether the crime was done or not, but also whether it is a murder, homicide, felony, assault and the like. These are determinations of law, but since they do not know the law themselves, there is a person who has the authority to inform them about it in the particular cases they are to judge. But if they do not judge according to what this person has told them, they not subject to any penalty, unless it can be shown they did so against their consciences or they had been corrupted by some reward.

The things that make for a good judge, or interpreter of the laws, are first, a correct understanding of the principle Law of Nature called equity. This depends on the goodness of man's own natural reason and meditation and not on the reading of other men's writings. This ability is presumed to occur in those that have the most leisure and the greatest inclination to meditate about equity. The second thing needed for a good judge is the contempt of unnecessary riches and preferments. The third is to be able in judgment to divest oneself of all fear, anger, hatred, love and compassion. The fourth and last is to have the patience to hear, the diligence to pay attention to what is heard, and the memory to retain, digest and apply what has been heard.

Divisions of law. The different divisions of the laws has been made in different ways according to the different methods of those men that have written on them. The divisions of the law do not depend on nature, but on the scope of the writer and so these divisions are subservient to every man's proper method. In the institution done by Justinian, there are several kinds of civil laws. 1) The edicts, constitutions and epistles of the princes, or the emperor, as he contained the whole power of the people. These are similar to the proclamations of the kings of England.

2) The decrees of the whole people of Rome, meaning the Senate, when they were put to the question by the Senate. These were the laws which were made at first by virtue of the sovereign power residing in the people. Those laws that were not later abrogated by the emperors remained laws by the imperial authority. All laws that are binding are understood to be laws if they are not repealed by the authority that has the power to do so.

3) The decrees of the common people (excluding the Senate) when they were put to the question by the tribune of the people. Again, these laws that were not abrogated by the emperors, remained laws by imperial authority. These laws are similar to the orders of the House of Commons in England.

4) *Senatus consulta,* or the orders of the Senate. When the people of Rome became so numerous that it was inconvenient to assemble them, the emperor thought fit that men should consult the Senate instead of the people. These laws have some resemblance to the Acts of Counsel.

5) The edicts of Praetors[6] and in some cases of the aediles.[7] These are similar to the chief justices in the courts of England.

6) *Responsa Predetum,* which were the sentences and opinions given by lawyers to whom the emperor gave authority to interpret the law and to give answers to matters of law that required their advice. According to the constitutions that the emperors made, judges were obliged to observe these answers when giving their judgments. They are similar in England

to the reports of judged cases, whether other judges are bound to observe them by the law of England. The judges of the common law of England, are not strictly judges, but are *juris consulti*.[8] According to the law, the lords and twelve men on a jury when they act as judges are supposed to ask the *juris consulti* for advice.

8) Unwritten customs, which in their own nature are an imitation of the laws. These are laws if they have the tacit consent of the emperor and are not contrary to the Laws of Nature.

Another way to categorize laws is by natural and positive. The natural ones are those that have been laws for eternity and are also called moral laws. They consist of the moral virtues, such as justice, equity and all habits of the mind that conduce to peace and charity, that I have already discussed in the fourteenth and fifteenth chapters.

The positive laws are those that have not existed from eternity, but have been made laws by the will of those that have had sovereign power over others. They are either written or made known to men by some other argument of the will of the legislator.

Another division of law. The positive laws are divided into the humane and the divine. The humane positive laws are divided into the distributive and the penal. The distributive laws are those that determine the rights of the subjects. They apply to all subjects and state what the laws are for acquiring and holding propriety of land or goods and what people have the right or liberty to do. The penal laws are those that state the penalties that shall be inflicted on those that violate the laws. These laws speak to the ministers and officers that are ordained to execute the laws. Although every one should be informed beforehand of the punishments that are ordained for any transgression, the command of the penal laws is not addressed to the delinquents, who cannot be supposed will faithfully punish themselves. They are rather addressed to the public ministers who are appointed to see that the penalties are executed. The penal and distributive laws are usually written together and are sometimes called judgments. All laws are general judgments or sentences of the legislator, as every particular judgments is a law to the one whose case is judged.

Divine positive law—how it is made known to be the law. The natural laws are all eternal and universal and are hence, all divine. The divine positive laws are commandments of God that are not eternal or universally addressed to all men, but only to certain people or person. These are the laws that are declared by those that God has authorized to declare them. But can it be known that God has given His authority to a man to declare these positive divine laws? God may command a man by supernatural means to deliver laws to other men. However, it is the essence of law that those who are obliged to follow them are assured of the authority of those that declare the law. Since we cannot naturally observe that God has given His authority, how can a man without supernatural revelation be assured of the revelation received by the declarer? And how then can a man be bound to obey these laws? In regard to the first question, it is impossible for a man to be assured of the revelation of another without having his own revelation. A man may be induced to believe another's revelation by seeing him do miracles, from seeing the extraordinary sanctity of his life, seeing his extraordinary wisdom or the extraordinary felicity of his actions. All of these are the marks of God's extraordinary favor, but they are not assured evidence of special revelation. Miracles are marvelous works, but what is marvelous to one may not be so to another. Sanctity may be feigned and the visible felicities of this world are very often the work of God by natural and ordinary causes. Therefore a man can only believe and not infallibly know by natural reason that another has had a supernatural revelation of God's will. The signs of God's will appear greater or lesser according to whether a person has a firmer or weaker belief.

But it is not so hard to answer the second question, which was who can a man be bound to obey. If a law is declared which is not against the Law of Nature (which is undoubtedly God's law) and a man undertakes to obey it, he is bound by his own act to obey. I said that he is bound to obey it, but he is not bound to believe it. Men's beliefs and other interior cogitations are not subject to commands, but are only subject to the operation of God, both ordinary and extraordinary. Faith in the supernatural law is not fulfilling it, but only assenting to it. It is not a duty that we exhibit to God, but a gift that God freely gives to whomever he pleases. In the same way unbelief is not a breach of any of His laws, but a rejection of them all, except for the Laws of Nature. My views will be made clearer by the examples and testimony concerning this point in Holy Scripture. The covenant that God made with Abraham was supernatural in manner: "This is the covenant which you shall observe between me and you and your seed after you." (Genesis 17:10) Abraham's seed did not have this revelation as they did not yet exist. Yet they were still a party to the covenant and were bound to obey what Abraham declared was God's law. This was so by virtue of the obedience that they owed their parents. Since they were subject to no other earthly power as was Abraham, their parents had sovereign power over them. Another example is where God says to Abraham, "Abraham, in you shall all the nations of the earth be blessed. For I know you will command your children and your house after you to keep the way of the Lord, and to observe righteousness and judgment." It is clear from this passage that the obedience of the family, that had no revelation, depended on their former obligation to obey their sovereign. At Mount Sinai only Moses went up to God. The people were forbidden to approach Him on pain of death and still they were bound to obey all that Moses told them was God's law. The basis for their doing so was their own submission to Moses, "Speak to us and we will hear you, but do not let God speak to us, lest we die." These two places appear sufficient to show that in a commonwealth, a subject that has no certain and assured revelation for himself of what is the will of God should obey the command of the commonwealth. If men were at liberty to their own dreams and fancies or those of other private men to be God's commandments, there would be scarcely any two men that would agree about what God actually commanded. As a result every man would despise the commandments of the commonwealth. My conclusion is therefore that in all things that are not contrary to the moral law (the Law of Nature), all subjects are bound to obey what the laws of the commonwealth declare to be the divine laws. This is also evident to any man's reason, for whatever is not against the Law of Nature may be made the law in the name of those who have the sovereign power. There is no reason that men should be less obliged to obey the laws when they are propounded[9] in the name of God. There are no places in the world where men are permitted to pretend that there are other commandments of God besides those that are declared by the commonwealth. Christian states punish those that revolt from the Christian religion and all other states forbid religions other than the ones they set up. Men are equally at liberty to do whatever is not regulated by a commonwealth. This follows equity which is the Law of Nature and thus the eternal law of God.

Another division of laws. Another distinction of laws is between those that are fundamental and those that are not fundamental. However, I have never seen an author clearly explain the meaning of a fundamental law. Still, one may reasonably distinguish laws in this manner.

What is a fundamental law. A law is fundamental when if it is taken away from a commonwealth, the commonwealth fails and is completely dissolved, as what happens to a building when the foundation is destroyed. So a fundamental law is one that the subjects are bound to uphold whatever power is given to a sovereign, whether it is a monarch or sovereign assembly. Without such a law the commonwealth will not be able to stand. These are the laws that give the sovereign the power of war and peace, of judicature, of selection of officers, and of doing whatever is thought necessary for the public good. A law is not fundamental when abrogating it does not lead to the dissolution of the commonwealth. These are the laws that concern the controversies between subject and subject. So much for this particular kind of division of laws.

Difference between law and right. I find that even the most learned authors use the terms, '*lex civilis*' and '*jus civile,* which mean law and civil right promiscuously for the same thing. This should not be so. Rights are liberties that the civil laws leave us. But civil law is an obligation and takes away from us the liberty that the Law of Nature gave us. Nature gave a right to every man to secure himself by his own strength and to invade a suspected neighbor to prevent harm to themselves. The civil law takes away that liberty in all cases where the protection of the law may be safely made. In that way *lex* and *jus* are as different as obligation and liberty.

The difference between a law and a charter. Similarly, laws and charters are promiscuously considered to be the same thing. But charters are donations of the sovereign and are not laws, but are instead exemptions from the law. The phrases that indicate a law is "*Jubeo, Injungo*" which mean, I command and I enjoin. The phrases that indicate a charter are "*Dedi, Concessi*" which mean I have given or I have granted. What is given or granted to a man is not forced upon him by a law. A law may be made to bind all the subjects of a commonwealth. A liberty, or charter, is given only to one man or some one part of a people. To say that all people in a commonwealth have liberty in any case whatsoever, is just to say that in such cases no law has been made or else having been made, is now abrogated.

Endnotes

1. Attained
2. King in Parliament
3. Very small part
4. This passage quotes from the book Institutes of Law by the same Edward Coke, who was previously quoted in this chapter.
5. Insult
6. Magistrates
7. A kind of judge in Rome
8. Those who have the capacity to be consultants about the law
9. Put forward

CHAPTER 27

Of Crimes, Excuses and Extenuations

What is a sin. A sin is not only a transgression of a law, but also is any expression of contempt of a legislator. Such contempt is a breach of all of his laws at once. Sin, then, consists not only in the commission of a fact or in the omission of what the law commands, but also in the intention or purpose that is behind an act of transgression. When a person has the purpose to break some law, it includes to some degree contempt for the one who is supposed to see that the laws are executed. One does not breach the law that states, "You shall not covet" by only being delighted by imagining possessing another man's goods, servants and wife but has no intention of actually taking them by force or fraud. It is also not a sin to get pleasure from imagining or dreaming of the death of someone from whose life one only expects damage and pain. But resolving to put some act into execution does tend to sin. It is a passion of both humans and every other living creature to be pleased by a fiction that would be pleasant if it were real. This is so much a part of our nature that if it is a sin, it is a sin to be human. These considerations have made me think that it is too severe, both to oneself and others, to maintain that the first motions of the mind are sins, even when they are checked by the fear of God. But I admit that it is safer to err on that side of the issue than on the other.

What is a crime. A crime is a sin that consists of committing by word or deed, an act that the law forbids, or it is an omission of an act that the law commands. Every crime is a sin, but not every sin is a crime. To intend to steal or kill is a sin, though the act never appears in word or fact. God that sees the thoughts of man can legitimately charge a person for his intentions. But it cannot be called a crime by a human judge until the intention becomes evident by something done or said. The Greeks observed this distinction in their terms, '*hamartema*', '*egklema*' and '*aitia*'. The first one is translated as 'sin' and signifies any swerving from the law. The latter two terms that are translated as 'crime' signify the kind of sin where one man can accuse another of committing. There is no place for a human accusation to be made about intentions that never appear by any outward act. In the same manner in Latin '*peccatum*' which means 'sin' signifies any kind of deviation from the law, but '*crimen*' which derives from '*cerno*' and means to perceive, means only those sins that are not mere intentions, but are such that one can be brought before a judge.

Where there is no civil law, there is no crime. From these relations of sin to the law and of crime to the civil law, it may be inferred, first, that where a law ceases to function, sin also ceases. But the Law of Nature is eternal and so the violation of covenants, ingratitude, arrogance and all actions contrary to moral virtue never cease to be sins. Secondly, one can infer that if the civil laws cease, then crimes do cease to exist. If there is no other law remaining besides that of nature, there is no place for accusation, as every man is his own judge and thus can be accused only by his own conscience and only cleared by the uprightness of his own intention. If therefore, his intention is right, his action is not a sin. If otherwise, his action is a sin, but not a crime. Thirdly, when the sovereign power ceases, crime also ceases for where there is no such power, there is no protection one can have from the law. In that case every man may protect himself by his own power, for no man in instituting the sovereign power can be supposed to be giving away the right of preserving his own body. All sovereignty was ordained for the sake of peoples' safety. This point can only be understood to apply to those that do not contribute to taking away the power of the sovereign that protected them. To do this is a crime from the beginning.

Ignorance of the law excuses no one. The source of every crime is some defect of the understanding, some error in reasoning or some sudden force of the passions. A defect in understanding is ignorance and a mistake in reasoning is an erroneous opinion. Ignorance is of three kinds: of the law, of the sovereign and of the penalty. Ignorance of the Law of Nature is not an excuse for anyone. Every man who has attained the use of reason is supposed to know that he ought not to do to another what he would not have done to himself. Therefore, wherever a man shall go, if he does something contrary to the Law of Nature, it is a crime. Suppose a man comes here from the Indies and persuades men here to receive a new religion, or teaches them anything which would lead them to disobedience to the laws of this country. Even if he is completely per-suaded of the truth of what he teaches, he is committing a crime and may be justly punished for it. This is so not only because his doctrine is false, but also because he does something that he would not approve another's doing, namely, coming from here and trying to alter the religion there. Ignorance of the civil law, however, does excuse a man in a foreign coun-try until the man be told the law. Until that time no civil law is binding.

Ignorance of the civil law is sometimes an excuse. Similarly, if an action is not against the Law of Nature and is a civil law in man's own country, but it has not been sufficiently declared so that he can know it if he wills, then ignorance is a good excuse. But in other cases ignorance of the civil law cannot be excused.

Ignorance of the sovereign does not excuse. If a man is ignorant of the sovereign power in the place of his ordinary residence, this does not excuse him. A man should take notice of the power that is protecting him there.

Ignorance of the penalty does not excuse. Ignorance of the penalty, where the law is declared, is not a legitimate excuse. A law that could be broken without the fear of the penalty to follow would be not be a law, but would be vain words. The person who breaks the law should undergo the penalty even if he does not know what it is. Anyone who voluntarily does an action accepts all the known consequences of it, and punishment is a known consequence of the violation of the laws in every commonwealth. If the punishment is already determined by law, the law-breaker is subject to that. If it is not determined, then he is sub-ject to arbitrary punishment. It is reasonable that one who does an injury without any other limitation besides that of one's own will, should suffer punishment without any limitation of the will whose law was violated.

Punishments that are declared before an action, excuse one from greater punishments after it. A delinquent is excused from a greater penalty, when a penalty is either annexed to the crime in the law itself or has been usually inflicted in like cases. If a punishment is known before-hand and is not great enough to deter men from the action, it becomes an invitation to commit the crime. When men compare the benefit of their injustice with the harm of the punishment, by the necessity of nature they choose what appears best to themselves. When they are therefore pun-ished more than the law had formerly determined or more than others were punished for the same crime, it is the law itself that tempted and deceived them.

Nothing can be made a crime by law made after an act. No law can make an action a crime if the law is made after the action is done. If the act was against the Law of Nature, then the law existed before the act. A positive law cannot be known before it was made and therefore it cannot be obligatory beforehand. But when a law that forbids an act is made before the act is done, the person who does the act is liable to the penalty even if it is ordained after the act is done. This would be the case if there is no lesser penalty that was made known before by writing or by example, for the reasons that were previously stated.

False principles of right and wrong that are the cause of wrong. Men are prone to violate the laws from defects in reasoning and from error in three ways. The first is by the presumption of false principles. This occurs when men have observed in all places and all ages that potent men have broken through the cobweb of laws in their countries and their unjust actions have been authorized by their force and victories. Weaker men, who have failed in their unjust enterprises, have been considered to be only criminals. Some people have used these examples to ground the follow reasoning: that justice is but a vain word; that whatever a man can get by his own industry and luck is his own; that the practice of all nations is just; that examples of former times are good arguments for doing the same again; and many more of the same kind. If these are granted to be true, then no act in itself can be a crime, but can only be so by the lack of success of those who commit it and not by law. The same act could be virtuous or vicious as fortune pleases. Then what Marius does is a crime, but when Sylla does it, it is meritorious, and Caesar's doing it, turns it into a crime again. This will lead to the perpetual disturbance of the peace of the commonwealth.

False teachers misinterpret the Law of Nature. Secondly, false teachers may misinterpret the Law of Nature and thereby make it conflict with the civil law. They also can say that laws are their own doctrines or traditions of former times. These are errors if they are inconsistent with the duties of a subject.

Teachers can make false inferences from true principles. Thirdly, errors can be made by erroneous inferences from true principles. This commonly happens to men that are hasty and who precipitously conclude and resolve what to do. People are prone to this error if they have both a great opinion of their own understanding and the belief that things of this nature do not require time and study, but only common experience and good natural wit. Everyone thinks they are well provided with this characteristic. But no man pretends to the knowledge of right

and wrong without great and long study even though it is no less difficult. None of the defects of reasoning can excuse a crime, although it
may provide the extenuation that a man pretends is done in the administration of his own private business. An error in reasoning is even less of
an excuse in those that undertake a public charge. Those that pretend to
reason try to base their excuse on the lack of it.

By their passions. One of the passions that is most frequently a cause
of crime is vain-glory, which is the foolish over-rating of one's worth.
This leads to people thinking that their difference in worth is an effect or
their wit, riches, blood, or some other natural quality, and does not
depend on the will of those that have sovereign authority. This leads such
people to a presumption that the punishments ordained by the laws and
extended generally to all subjects should not be inflicted on them with
the same rigor that that they are applied to poor, obscure and simple
men, who are called the vulgar.

Presumption of riches. It often happens that people who value themselves because of the greatness of their wealth adventure to commit
crimes. They hope to escape punishments by corrupting public justice or
by obtaining pardon by money or other rewards.

And friends. Those who have a multitude of potent kin and popular
men who have gained a reputation among the multitude, become coura-
geous about violating the law. They hope to oppress the power that has
the right to execute the laws.

Wisdom. Those that have a great and false opinion of their own wisdom reprehend[1] and call into question the authority of those that govern. They unsettle the laws with their public discourse, so that nothing
shall be a crime but what their own designs require should be so. These
same men are prone to the crimes that are based in craft and in deceiving
their neighbors. They believe their designs are too subtle to be perceived.
I say that all of these faults are the effects of a false presumption of their
own wisdom. Those who are the first movers in the disturbance of a
commonwealth, which can never happen without a civil war, are seldom
left alive to see the establishment of their new designs. So even if they are
the ones who would least wish for it, the benefit of their crimes is mainly
redounds[2] to their posterity. This shows they were not as wise as they
thought they were. Those that deceive others with the hope they will not
be observed, commonly deceive themselves, as the darkness in which
they think they lie hidden is just their own blindness. They are really
no wiser than children that think everyone is gone when they hide their
own eyes.[3]

Generally all vain glorious men are subject to anger unless they are also timorous. They are more prone than others to interpret the ordinary liberty of conversation as contempt. There are few crimes that are not produced by anger.

Hatred, lust, ambition and covetousness can cause crimes. It is obvious in every man's experience and understanding that the passions of hate, lust, ambition and covetousness are apt to cause crimes. Nothing really need be said about them, except that these infirmities are so annexed to the nature of men and other living creatures that their effects cannot by hindered but by the extraordinary use of reason or a constant severity in punishing them. When men hate things, they find that these things are continually and unavoidably molesting them. In that case men should have everlasting patience or they can only comfort themselves by removing the power of the thing that is molesting them. The former is very difficult and the latter may be impossible without some violation of the law. Ambition and covetousness are passions that are also perpetually incumbent[4] and pressing. Since reason is not perpetually present to resist them, whenever the hope of impunity appears, the effects of these passions proceeds. As for lust, what it lacks in lasting, it makes up with its vehemence. This is sufficient to weigh down a person's apprehension of all obvious and uncertain punishments.

Fear sometimes is a cause of crime, when danger is neither present nor corporeal. The passion that least inclines men to break the laws is fear. Besides those that have a generous nature[5], fear is the only thing that makes men keep the laws when there is an appearance of profit or pleasure in breaking them. Still, in many cases a crime may be committed through fear.

Not every fear justifies the action it produces. The only cases that are justified would be the fear of corporeal injury, which is called bodily fear. In these cases men cannot see how to be delivered from the injury except by action. Suppose that a man is assaulted and fears that he will be killed. He sees no way to escape, except to wound the person who is assaulting him. If the wound is deadly, it is not a crime, because no man in agreeing to the commonwealth abandons the right to defend his life or limbs in cases where the law does not arrive in time to assist him. But if there is time and means to demand protection from the sovereign, then it is a crime for me to kill someone who is threatening by words or deeds to kill me. Suppose a man is subject to words of disgrace or some other little injuries. Say that there are no laws that assigned punishments for these things, as they were considered to be things a reasonable man would ignore. But suppose the victim of these actions is afraid that unless he takes revenge for them, he will become an object of contempt and thus liable to suffer similar injuries from others. To avoid this kind of situation, he breaks the law and protects himself in the future by the terror of his private revenge. This is a crime for the injury was not corporeal, but phantastical[6] and so slight that it would be ignored by a gallant man who is assured of his own courage. Even so, in this corner of the world private revenge has become a custom among those who are young and vain. Suppose a man is afraid of spirits, either through his own superstition or through giving too much credit to other men. These other men tell him of strange dreams and visions, and the man then thinks the spirits will hurt him for doing or omitting different things which are against the law. If this person then does or omits these things, he has committed a crime, and is not to be excused by the fact he did it from fear. As I have shown in the second chapter, dreams are naturally just fancies that remain in sleep after our senses have received impressions while we were awake. It does happen that sometimes by some accident men are not sure that they were sleeping, and they think they have had a real vision. However, it would be against the Law of Nature to allow someone to break a law of the commonwealth on their own, because of another's dream or pretended vision, or upon the fancy of the power of invisible spirits. It is a clear offense against the Law of Nature to follow one's own imagery or that of another private man's brain. No one can ever know whether these images signify anything or nothing, or whether the one who tells his dream is saying something that is true or is a lie. If anyone has the right to follow these images, then according to the Law of Nature, everyone has the same and in this case no law could be made to hold and the commonwealth would be dissolved.

Crimes that are not equal. The different sources of crimes shows that the Stoics of ancient times were mistaken when they maintained that all crimes have the same allay.[7] There is a place for excuses where what seemed to be a crime is proved not to be, and also for extenuation, where what appeared to be a great crime is shown to be a lesser one. The Stoics were right that all crimes do equally deserve to be considered an injustice, as all deviation from a straight line equally can be considered to be crooked. But it does not follow that all crimes are equally unjust, no more than all crooked lines are equally crooked. The Stoics did not observe the difference and thus held that it is as great a crime when one kills a hen against the law as it is to kill one's father.

Total excuses. If something totally excuses an action and thus the action no longer has the nature of a crime, the same thing will take away the obligation to obey the law that is involved. For if an action when done is against the law, if the one who committed it is obliged to follow the law, the act must be a crime.

The lack of the means to know the law is a total excuse. It is not obligatory to follow a law if a man has no means to inform himself of it. But the lack of diligence to inquire about a law is not considered as a lack of means. Also, if any man claims to have enough reason to govern his own affairs, then he cannot be supposed to lack the means to know the Laws of Nature. These laws are known by the reason that the person pretends to have and only children and madmen are excused from offenses against the Law of Nature.

Suppose a man is a captive or in the power of an enemy. A man in the power of an enemy has power over his person or his means of living. If the man's becoming a captive was not his fault, then his obligation to obey the law ceases, as he must obey the enemy or die. This kind of obedience is not a crime, for no man is obliged not to protect himself by the best means he can when the protection of the law fails.

If a man is compelled to do an act because of the terror of his present death, he is totally excused. No law can oblige a man to abandon his own preservation. Suppose there was a law that commanded a man to abandon his own life. The man could then reason, if I do not do the act, I will die now, but if I do it, I will die later. Therefore by doing it, I gain some life. Nature would then compel a man to do the act.

Suppose that a man is destitute of food or some other thing necessary for his life. He cannot preserve himself in any other way, but by doing some action against the law. This could happen in a great famine, when he might take food by force or stealth when he cannot obtain any charity or money. If in defense of his life, he snatches away another man's sword, he is totally excused for the reasons that were previously stated.

Excuses against the author. Actions that are done against the law by the authority of another are excused if the act is done against the one who gave the authority. This is so because no man should be accused of committing his own act, when another actually did it, but only as an instrument of the one authorizing it. But if someone acts on the authority and injures a third person, it is not excused. It is a violation of the law and both the author and actor are criminals. It follows that when a man, or assembly, that has the sovereign power commands a man to do what is contrary to a former law, the act of the man obeying the command is totally excused. The man should not condemn the act himself, as he is actually its author and what cannot justly be condemned by the sovereign cannot justly be punished by anyone else. Also, when the sovereign commands anything to be done that is against a former law, the command to do that particular act abrogates the former law.

Suppose that a man, or an assembly, that has the sovereign power disclaims a right that is essential to sovereignty. By doing so a subject gains a liberty which is inconsistent with sovereign power that is the very being of a commonwealth. If a subject now refuses to obey the sovereign's command about anything, even given the liberty that was granted, the disobedience is a sin and is against the duty of a subject. The subject ought to realize what is inconsistent with sovereignty, because it was erected by his own consent and for his own defense. When some liberty is granted that is inconsistent with sovereignty, it could only have been granted through ignorance of the evil consequences it would lead to. But if a subject not only disobeys a sovereign's command, but also resists a public minister who is executing the command, the disobedience is a crime. The subject could have corrected the situation without any breach of the peace by making a complaint.

The degrees of crime are determined and measured on different scales: first, by the malignity of the source or cause; secondly, by the contagion of the example; thirdly, by the mischief of the effect, and fourthly, by the concurrence of times, places and persons.

Presumption of power increases the degree of crime. Suppose an act is done against the law and it proceeds from a presumption of strength, riches or friends who will help to resist those who execute the law. This is a greater crime than one that proceeds from the hope of not being discovered or of escaping detection by flight. A contempt of all laws always springs from the root of the presumption of impunity by force. But when men try to avoid detection, the apprehension of danger which makes them flee also renders them more obedient for the future. A crime that one knows to be so is a greater than the same crime that proceeds from a false persuasion that it is lawful. One that commits a crime against one's own conscience presumes on this basis, or other power, and is encouraged to do the same thing again. But he that commits a crime by error, after the error is shown to him, will then conform to the law.

Evil teachers extenuate the degree of crime. If an error proceeds from the authority of a teacher or from an interpreter of the law that is publicly authorized, it is not as faulty as one who errs because of a peremptory[8] pursuit of his own principles and reasoning. Teaches who have public authority are just presenting what the commonwealth teaches. What they say resembles the law until the commonwealth takes control of those teachers. Crimes committed on this basis do not involve a denial of sovereign power and are not against an evident law, and so are totally excused. But one that bases his action on one's own private judgment should stand or fall according to the rectitude or error of one's own reasoning.

Examples of impunity extenuate the degree of crime. The same action is a greater crime if it has been constantly punished in other men than if there have been many examples of impunity. The sovereign himself is providing many to hope for impunity by those examples. Anyone who furnishes someone with the hope and presumption of mercy encourages him to offend, and thus has part of the responsibility for the offense. In these cases, the sovereign cannot reasonably charge the offender with the whole responsibility.

Premeditation increases the degree of crime. A crime that arises from a sudden passion is not as bad as when the same crime arises from a long meditation. In the former case there is extenuation in the common infirmity of human nature. But one who does a crime with premeditation has used circumspection and has cast his eye on the law, on the punishment and on the consequences to human society. In committing the crime, this person thus expresses contempt and postposed[9] all of this to his own appetite. But the suddenness of passion is not sufficient to be a total excuse. The time between the first knowing of the law and the commission of the act should be considered a time of deliberation. Meditating on the law should rectify the irregularity of one's passions.

Suppose the law is publicly and with assiduity[10] read and interpreted before all of the people. In that case an act done against it is a greater crime than one where men are left without such instruction and can only inquire about it with difficulty, uncertainty and the interruption of their callings and then only be informed of it by private men. When this happens part of the responsibility for a crime falls on the infirmity of making the law available. But when the law is properly taught, breaking it is a sign of negligence and usually of some contempt for the sovereign power.

Tacit approbation of the sovereign extenuates the degree of crime. Those actions that the law expressly condemns, but that the law-maker tacitly approves by some manifest signs of his will, are lesser crimes than the same actions that are condemned both by the law and the law-maker. The law is supposed to be the will of the law-maker, so if they do not agree, there appear to be two contradictory laws. In a situation like this, men would be totally excused for they would be asked to notice the sovereign's approval by other means than are expressed by his commands. There are punishments consequent, in this situation, not only for the transgression of the law, but also for observing of it. This shows that the sovereign is part of the cause of the transgression, and therefore he cannot reasonably impute the whole responsibility for the crime to the delinquent. For example, the law condemns duels and the punishment for them is capital. But on the other hand, one who refuses a duel is subject to contempt and scorn without remedy. Sometimes the sovereign himself thinks such a person is unworthy to have any charge or preferment in war. If this person then agrees to duel, he should not be rigorously punished, as all men lawfully endeavor to obtain the good opinion of those that have sovereign power. Part of the fault then should be discharged to the punisher. If the sovereign does not wish people to have the liberty of private revenge or any other kind of disobedience, he should take care not to obliquely countenance the acts he directly forbids. When people see examples of what princes do, it has a far more potent effect on their actions than the laws themselves. Even though it is our duty to do what the princes say and not do what they do, our duty will not be performed until it pleases God to give men an extraordinary and supernatural grace to follow that precept.

Comparison of crimes based on their effects. Let us compare crimes by the mischief of their effects. First, the same action is a greater crime when it leads to the damage of many than it leads to the hurt of a few. Similarly, an action that hurts people in the present and future is a greater crime than one the only hurts people in the present. The former is a fertile crime and multiplies the hurt of many; the latter is barren. Maintaining a doctrine contrary to the established religion of the commonwealth is a greater fault in an authorized preacher than in a private person. The same holds for living profanely and incontinently or doing any irreligious act whatsoever. It is a greater crime for a professor of law to maintain any point or do any act that tends to weaken the sovereign power than it is for another man to do these things. It is worse for a man to act against the law that has a reputation for wisdom so that his counsel is followed and his actions are imitated by many than the same act would be for another man. These supposed wise men not only commit crimes, but they also teach them as the law to all other men. Generally, all crimes are great by the scandal they produce. These crimes become stumbling-blocks to the weak, who are not really looking at the path they are walking on, but just look at the light that other men carry before them.

Crimes that damage the majesty. Actions of hostility against the present state of the commonwealth are greater crimes than the same acts done to private men. The damage of the former extends itself to all. Examples of these are the betraying of the strengths and the revealing of secrets of the commonwealth to an enemy. Other examples are attempts upon the representative of the commonwealth, whether it is a monarch or assembly, and all attempts by word or deed to diminish their authority in the present or in the future. In Latin these crimes are called *crimina laesea majestatis*[11] and consist in designs or acts that are contrary to the fundamental law.

Bribery and false testimony. The crimes that render judgments ineffective are worse than crimes that injure one or a few persons. To receive money in order to give a false judgment or testimony is a greater crime than deceiving a man of the same or even of a greater sum of money. Not only does the person who has taken bribes made wrong judgments, but he has also rendered all judgments useless, and has encouraged the use of force and private revenge.

Depeculation. Robbery and depeculation[12] of the public treasure or revenues is a greater crime than robbing or defrauding a private man, because to rob the public is to rob many men at once.

Counterfeiting authority. Counterfeit usurpation[13] of the public ministry, counterfeiting public seals or the public coin is worse than counterfeiting a private man's person or his seals. The fraud in the former case extends the damage to many others.

Comparison of crimes against private men. In acts against the law that are committed against private men, the greater crime is the one where the damage is most clear in the common opinion of men. And therefore,

To break the law when killing someone is a greater crime than any other injury that nevertheless does not result in death.

To kill with torment is a greater crime than simply killing.

Mutilating a limb is a greater crime than spoiling a man's goods.

Spoiling a man's goods through terror of his death or wounds is a greater crime than by clandestine surreption.[14]

The violation of chastity by force is worse than by flattery.

The violation of a married woman is worse than of an unmarried woman.

All of these things are commonly valued in the same degree, although some men are more, and some are less, damaged by the same offense. The law, however, regards the general inclination of mankind and not the particular case.

The laws of the Greeks, Romans and ancient and moderns commonwealths have been silent about the offense of insults in words or gesture that produce no other harm but the present grief of the one who is reproached. The silence is based on the supposition that the true cause of the grief consists not in the insult, which would not affect men who are conscious of their own virtue, but in the pusillanimity[15] of the one that is offended by it.

A crime against a private man can be greatly aggravated by the factors of who the victim is and the time and place. To kill one's parent is a greater crime than to kill someone else. The parent ought to have the honor of the sovereign because he had it originally in nature, even though he surrendered it to the power of the civil law. To rob a poor man is a greater crime than to rob a rich man, because it is greater damage to the poor man.

Crimes committed in the time or place of devotion are greater than if committed at some other time or place, for such crimes proceed from a greater contempt for the law.

There are many other cases of aggravation and extenuation that could be added, but it is obvious from those that I have already set down how to assess the importance of any other crime.

What are public crimes.   Lastly, because in almost all crimes there is an injury done, not only to some private man, but also to the commonwealth. When the accusation is made in the name of the commonwealth, it is a public crime, and when it is made in the name of a private man, it is a private crime. The pleas that are made about these crimes are called public, *judicia publica,* pleas of the crown, and private pleas, respectively. In an accusation of murder, if the accuser is a private man, the plea is a private plea. If the accuser is the sovereign, the plea is a public plea.

Endnotes

1. Criticize
2. Accrues
3. This is actually a better answer to the fool than the ones Hobbes offered in Chapter 15.
4. Hanging over one
5. People with generous natures would be those that do not do everything for their own self-interest. Hobbes says here that there are such people.
6. Emotional or mental
7. Status
8. Self-assured
9. Subordinated
10. Diligence
11. Crimes that damage the majesty
12. Embezzlement
13. Stealing
14. Acts done secretly
15. Cowardly spirit

CHAPTER 28

Of Punishments or Rewards

The definition of punishment. A punishment is an evil inflicted by a public authority on one that has done, or omitted to do, something that is judged by the authority to be a transgression of the law. The end of punishment is that the will of men may thereby be better disposed to obedience.

The derivation of the right to punish. Before I proceed to infer anything from this definition, there is a prior question of great importance: by what door did the right or authority of punishing come in for any case? From what has been said before, no man can be supposed to be bound by a covenant not to resist violence. No one can intend to give another the right to lay violent hands upon his person. In making the commonwealth every man does give away the right of harming another, but not of defending himself. Also, a person does oblige himself when making the commonwealth to assist the sovereign in punishing another, but he does not oblige to assist in punishing himself. To covenant to assist the sovereign to hurt another person is not to give the sovereign the right to punish, unless the one who is covenanting also has a right to hurt another. It is clear then that the commonwealth's or its representative's right to punish is not grounded on any concession or gift of the subjects. As I have formerly shown, before the institution of the commonwealth, every man has the right to every thing and the right to do whatever he thinks is necessary for his own preservation. This includes subduing, hurting or killing any man. This is the foundation of the right of punishment which is exercised in every commonwealth. The subjects did not give the sovereign that right, but only in laying down their own rights, strengthened the sovereign to his rights as he should think fit for the preservation of all. So the right was not given to sovereign; rather, it was left to him, and to only him. Except for the limits set by the Law of Nature, the sovereign is entirely within the condition of mere nature, where there is a war of every one against his neighbor.

Private injuries and revenge are not punishments. From the definition of 'punishment', I infer, first, that neither private revenge nor the injuries of private men can properly be called "punishment", since they do not proceed from public authority.

Denial of preferment is not punishment. Secondly, to be neglected or not preferred for some public favor is not punishment. This would not inflict any new evil on a man, as he is only left in the estate that he was in before.

Pain inflicted without a public hearing is not a punishment. Thirdly, the evil that is inflicted by a public authority, without a preceding public condemnation, is not to be called "a punishment". This is rather a hostile act, because an act for which a man is punished should be first judged by a public authority to be a transgression of the law.

Pain inflicted by a usurped power is not a punishment. Fourthly, the evil that is inflicted by usurped powers and judges without authority from the sovereign is not punishment. These again would rather be hostile acts, because they are the acts of a usurped power, and so the author of them is not the person who is victimized, as they would be if they were the acts of a public authority.

Pain inflicted without respect to the future good is not punishment. Fifthly, all evil that is inflicted without intention, or the possibility of disposing the delinquent, or other men by his example to obey the laws, are also but acts of hostility. Without the end of producing obedience, no hurt that is done should be considered to be punishment.

Natural evil consequences are not punishment. Sixthly, there are certain actions that naturally have different hurtful consequences. For example, a man who is assaulting another is slain or wounded himself or when someone who is doing an unlawful act falls into sickness. These injuries may be considered divine punishment as being inflicted by God who is the author of nature. But they are not punishment with respect to men, because the injuries were not inflicted by the authority of man.

If the hurt inflicted is less than the benefit of transgressing, it is not punishment. Seventhly, if the harm that is inflicted is less than the benefit or contentment that naturally follows from the commission of a crime, the harm does not fit the definition of 'punishment'. Rather it is more the price or redemption of the crime than its punishment. The nature of punishment is to have for its end the disposing of men to obey the law. This end is not attained.when the harm is less than the benefit of the transgression, and in fact, the effect in this case would be the opposite.

Where the punishment is annexed to a law, a greater hurt is not punishment, but hostility. Suppose that a punishment is determined and prescribed in a law itself. After a crime is committed, a greater punishment is inflicted on the transgressor. This excess is not punishment, but is an act of hostility. The aim of punishment is not revenge, but is terror. The terror of a great unknown punishment is taken away by the declaration of a lesser punishment and so the unexpected addition of injury is not part of the punishment. But when there is no specific punishment determined by the law, whatever injury is then inflicted on transgressors has the nature of punishment. Those who go about violating the laws that do not contain any determined penalty expect an indeterminate, which means an arbitrary punishment.

Hurt that is inflicted for an act done before a law is established, is not punishment. Ninthly, harm that is inflicted for an action done before there was a law that forbad it is not punishment, but is an act of hostility. Before there is a law, there is no transgression of the law. Punishment presupposes that an action has been judged to be a transgression of the law. So harm inflicted before the law is made is not punishment, but is an act of hostility.

The representative of the commonwealth is unpunishable. Tenthly, hurt that is inflicted on the representative of the commonwealth is not punishment, but is an act of hostility. The nature of punishment is that it is that public authority that inflicts it and this is the authority only of the representative itself.

The hurt that is done to a subject who revolt is done by the right of war, and is not punishment. Lastly, harm that is inflicted upon one that is a declared enemy does not fall under the definition of punishment. Those that were never subject to a law cannot transgress it. Those who were subject to the law, but now profess no longer to be so, thereby deny that they have transgressed the law. Thus, all harms that can be done to them should be taken as acts of hostility. In declared situations of hostility inflicting any evil is lawful. So if a subject by act or word wittingly and deliberately denies the authority of the representative of the commonwealth, he may lawfully be made to suffer whatever the representative wills or whatever penalty has been formerly ordained for treason. By denying that he is a subject, he denies the punishments that the law ordains and therefore suffers as an enemy of the commonwealth, which is according to the will of the representative. The punishments set down in the laws are for subjects, not for enemies and enemies are those that have been subjects and by their own acts deliberately revolt and thus deny the sovereign power.

The first and most general distinction of punishments is into divine and human. I shall speak of the former in forthcoming chapters.[1]

Human punishments are those that are inflicted by the commands of men. They can be corporal, pecuniary, ignominy, imprisonment, exile, or a mixture of these.

Corporal punishments. Corporal punishments are those inflicted directly on the body and according to the intention of the one inflicting it. They are stripes,[2] wounds or deprivations of bodily pleasures that were before lawfully enjoyed.

Capital punishment. The corporal category can be divided into capital and less than capital. Capital is the infliction of death, either simply or with torment. Less than capital are stripes, wounds, chains, and any other corporal pain that is not mortal in its own nature. Suppose that during the infliction of a punishment, death does follow, but not due to the intention of the one inflicting it. This case is not to be considered as capital punishment, even though the harm did prove to be mortal by an unforeseen accident. In this case death is hastened, but is not inflicted.

Pecuniary punishment. Pecuniary punishment consists not only of the deprivation of a sum of money, but also of lands or any other good which are usually bought and sold for money. There are some cases of laws that ordain such a punishment, but are not made with the aim of gathering money from those that transgress the law. These cases should not properly be considered to be punishment, but are more cases of providing a price or privilege and exemption from the law. This kind of law does not absolutely forbid a particular act, but only forbids it to those that are not able to pay the money. The exception to this is if the law involved is natural or part of religion. In those cases the fine does not provide for an exemption from the law, but is for transgressing it. Consider a law that exacts a pecuniary mulct[3] for those who take the name of the God in vain. The payment of the mulct is not the price of a dispensation to swear, but is the punishment of the transgression of an indispensable law. In a similar manner, if the law imposes a sum of money to be paid to one that has been injured, this is to satisfy the hurt done to him, and extinguishes the accusation of the injured party. It does not extinguish the crime of the offender.

Ignominy. Ignominy is the infliction of evils that are considered dishonorable or the deprivation of goods that are made honorable by the commonwealth. There are some things that are honorable by nature, such as the effects of courage, magnanimity, strength, wisdom and other abilities of the body and mind. Others are honorable by action of commonwealths, such as badges, titles, offices or other singular marks of the sovereign's favor. Those things, which are honorable by nature, though they may fail by nature or accident, cannot be taken away by law and so their loss is not punishment. But when it comes to the other kind of honor, the public authority that made them honorable can take them away and that is a punishment. This occurs when men are degraded by taking away their badges, titles and offices, or declaring them ineligible to receive them in the future.

Imprisonment. Imprisonment occurs when a public authority deprives a man of liberty. This can happen for two different reasons. The first is to keep a man who is accused in safe custody. The second is to inflict pain on a condemned man. The former is not a punishment, because no man is to be punished before he has been heard by a judge and declared guilty. That is why it is against the Law of Nature to hurt a man who is made to suffer by bonds and restraint beyond what is necessary to assure his custody before his case is heard. The same thing would be punishment, however, because it would be an evil inflicted by a public authority, or by someone that has the same authority, on a person that has been judged to have transgressed a law. The word 'imprisonment' means the restraint of motion caused by an external obstacle. If the obstacle is a building, it is called "a prison". The obstacle can be an island when men are confined to it or it can be a place where men are set to work. In ancient times men were condemned to quarries or galleys by chains or other impediments.

Exile. Exile, or banishment, is punishment for a crime when a man is condemned to leave the dominion of the commonwealth or a certain part of it. The person is not allowed to return for a certain set time or forever. It seems that of its own nature without other considerations, this is not a punishment, but rather an escape or a public command to avoid punishment by flight. Cicero says no such punishment was ordained in the city of Rome and he calls it a refuge for men in danger. If a man is banished and he is still permitted to enjoy his goods and the revenue of his lands, the mere change of air is not really a punishment. It does not tend to benefit the commonwealth by conforming men's wills to the observation of the law and this is the purpose why punishments are ordained. In fact, banishment seems many times to do damage to the commonwealth, as a banished man is a lawful enemy of the commonwealth that banished him, as he is no longer a member of it. If he is deprived of his lands or goods, then the punishment does not consist in his exile, but is to be reckoned among the pecuniary punishments.

The punishment of an innocent subject is contrary to the Law of Nature. All punishments, great or little, of innocent subjects are against the Law of Nature. Punishment can only be for a transgression of the law and so there can be no punishment of the innocent. First, it would be a violation of the Law of Nature that forbids all men in their revenge to consider anything but some future good. No good can come to a commonwealth in the future by punishing an innocent person. Secondly, it would violate the Law of Nature that forbids ingratitude. The sovereign power is originally given consent by every one of the subjects for the purpose of protection as long as they are obedient. Thus, the punishment of the innocent would be rendering evil for good. Thirdly, it would violate the Law of Nature that commands equity, which is giving an equal distribution of justice. Punishing the innocent does not observe this law.

The harm done to an innocent in war is not against the Law of Nature. But it is not a breach of the Law of Nature to inflict any evil whatsoever on an innocent man that is not a subject, if it is for the benefit of the commonwealth and is not a violation of any former covenant. All men who are not subjects are either enemies or else they have ceased being so by some preceding covenants. It is lawful by the original right of nature for a commonwealth to make war against any it judges capable of doing it damage. The only consideration for victors is the good of one's own people and not the distinction between nocent[4] and innocent or any consideration of mercy. In this way the sword does not judge. For the same reasons vengeance is lawfully extended against subjects who deliberately deny the authority of the established commonwealth. It is even lawful to extend vengeance not only to the fathers, but also to the third and fourth generations that do not yet exist and consequently are innocent of the acts for which they will be afflicted. The nature of this type of offence consists in renouncing subjection and that means a relapse into the condition of war, which is commonly a rebellion. Those that offend in this way suffer not as subjects, but as enemies, as rebellion is but a renewal of war.

Rewards are either salaries or grace. A reward is given as a gift or by contract. When it is by contract, it is called a salary or wages, which is a benefit due for a service that is performed or promised. When a reward is a gift, it is a benefit proceeding from the grace of those that bestowed it. People do this to encourage or enable others to do them service. When the sovereign of a commonwealth establishes a salary for any public office, the one that receives it is bound by justice to perform his office. If there is no established salary, the person is only bound to perform by honor or by an acknowledgment that the sovereign will endeavor to pay. When men are commanded to quit their private business and to serve the public without reward or salary, they have no lawful remedy. They are not bound to do so, however, by the Law of Nature or by the institution of the commonwealth unless the service cannot be done in any other way. It is supposed that the sovereign may use anyone for the commonwealth, but still those used may demand a salary just as the most common soldier may demand the wages as a debt for his use in warfare.

Benefits bestowed for fear are not rewards. It is not properly a reward when a sovereign bestows a benefit on a subject out of fear of the subject's power and ability to harm the commonwealth. This is not a case of a salary since there is no contract, as every man is already obliged not to do any disservice to the commonwealth. This is also not an example of grace for the benefit is extorted by fear, which should not be one of the effects of sovereign power. These situations should be considered as sacrifices that the sovereign makes to appease the discontent of one that he thinks more potent than himself and that he does in his own natural person and not in the person of the commonwealth. This kind of action does not encourage obedience, but on the contrary, it leads to the continuation and increase of further extortion.

Certain and casual salaries. Some salaries are certain and proceed from the public treasury. Others are uncertain and casual and they proceed from the execution of an office for which the salary is ordained. The latter can be damaging to the commonwealth as in the case of judicature. There are two inconveniences when the benefits of judges and the ministers of a court of justice are related to the multitude of cases that are brought to their cognizance. One is the nourishing of suits, for the more suits, the greater the benefit. The other inconvenience is related to the first one and it involves contention over jurisdiction. Each court draws to itself as many cases as it can. The offices of execution do not have these inconveniences, because their employment cannot be increased by any endeavor of their own.

This will suffice as a discussion of the nature of punishments and rewards. They are, as it were, the nerves and tendons that move the limbs and joints of the commonwealth.

So far I have set forth the nature of man, whose pride and other passions have compelled him to submit himself to government. I have also shown the great power of man's governor that I compared to a

Leviathan. I took this comparison out the last two verses of the forty-first chapter of Job where God, having set forth the great power of the Leviathan, calls him the king of the proud. He says, "There is nothing on earth to be compared to him. He is made so as not to be afraid. He sees every high thing as below him, and is king of all the children of pride." But he is still moral and subject to decay, as are all earthly creatures. There is also one in heaven, though not on earth, that he should stand in fear of, and whose laws he ought to obey. In the following chapters I shall speak of his diseases and the causes of the Leviathan's mortality, and of the Laws of Nature he is bound to obey.

Endnotes

1. The reference is to chapters 31, 38 and 44.
2. Lashes of a whip
3. A fine
4. Guilty

CHAPTER 29

Of Those Things That Weaken, or Tend to the Dissolution of a Commonwealth

Dissolution of commonwealths proceeds from their imperfect influence. Nothing can be immortal that mortals make. But if men had the use of reason they pretend to, they would at least secure their commonwealths from perishing from internal diseases. By the nature of their institution, commonwealths are designed to live as long as mankind or as long as the Laws of Nature or justice itself, which is what gives them life. So when commonwealths come to be dissolved, when it is not due to external violence but by intestinal disorder, the fault is not in men in the sense that they are the matter of the commonwealths, but it is men's fault in the sense that they make and order them. Men become at last weary of the irregular jostling and hewing of one another and desire with all their hearts to conform themselves into one firm and lasting edifice. But men lack the art of making fit laws by which to square their actions. They also lack the humility and patience to let the rude and cumbersome points of what they think is their present greatness be shaved off. Thus, they cannot without the help of a very able architect be compiled into anything other than a crazy building that will hardly last out their own time and will assuredly fall upon the heads of their posterity.

Among the infirmities of a commonwealth I will first reckon those that arise from an imperfect institution and resemble the diseases of a natural body that proceed from a defective procreation.

Lack of absolute power. The first is that when a man obtains a kingdom, he is sometimes content with less power than is required for the peace and defense of the commonwealth. In these cases when it comes to pass that the exercise of power is used for public safety to be resumed, it has the appearance of an unjust act. This disposes great numbers of men to rebel when the occasion presents itself. In the same way the bodies of children who were conceived by diseased parents are subject either to an untimely death or to purge their bad qualities derived from their vicious conception, by breaking out into boils and scabs. When kings deny themselves some necessary power, it is not always, but sometimes, out of ignorance of what is necessary to the office they undertake. Many times they hope to recover their power at their pleasure. This is not good reasoning, because foreign commonwealths will help maintain those that will hold the kings to their former promises. Foreign commonwealths will let slip few occasions to weaken the estate of their neighbors in order to promote the good of their own subjects. An example is Thomas Becket, the Archbishop of Canterbury, who was supported against Henry the Second by the Pope. William the Conqueror gave away the subjection of the ecclesiastics at his reception when he took an oath not to infringe on the liberty of the Church. Another example is William Rufus. He increased the power of the barons to have their help in transferring the succession from his elder brother to himself. This increase of power to the barons was inconsistent with his own sovereign power and later the French supported their rebellion against King John.

Nor does this happen only in monarchies. The style[1] of ancient Roman commonwealth was the senate and the people of Rome. Neither one pretended the whole power. This first caused the seditions of Tiberius Gracchus, Caius Gracchus, Lucius Saturninus and others. Afterwards it led to the wars between the senate and the people, under Marius and Sylla, and again under Pompey and Caesar, until at last the democracy was extinguished and a monarchy was set up.

The people of Athens bound themselves from only one action and that was that no man on pain of death should recommend the renewal of the war for the Island of Salamis. If Solon had not caused the people to think he was mad, and recommended this in verse to the people that flocked about him, the Athenians would have had an enemy that was in perpetual readiness at the gates of their city. All commonwealths are forced to shift to avoid damage when their power is limited.

Private judgment of good and evil. In the second place there are the diseases of a commonwealth that derive from the poison of seditious doctrines. One is that every private man is the judge of good and evil actions.[2] This is true in the condition of mere nature where there are no civil laws and also in civil governments, in those situations that are not covered by laws. But otherwise, it is manifest that the measure of good and evil actions is the civil law and the legislators and the judges who are the representatives of the commonwealth. From this false doctrine men are disposed to debate with themselves and dispute the commands of the commonwealth. Afterwards they obey or disobey the commands as they think fit. In this way the commonwealth is distracted and weakened.

Erroneous conscience. Another doctrine that is repugnant to civil society is the view that it is a sin to do something against one's conscience. This view depends on the presumption that an individual is the judge of good and evil. For a man's conscience and his judgment are the same thing, and judgment, and also conscience, can be erroneous. One that is not subject to civil law may sin in everything that he does if all of his actions are against his conscience and he has no other rule to follow but his own reason. But it is quite different in a commonwealth, because the law is the public conscience by which a person has already undertaken to be guided. There is such a diversity of private consciences, which are but private opinions, that a commonwealth would become distracted, as no one would dare to obey the sovereign power farther than it would seem good in his own eyes.

Pretence of inspiration. It has also been commonly taught that faith and sanctity are not to be attained by study and reason, but by supernatural inspiration or infusion. If this is granted, I do not see why any man should provide a reason for his faith or why every Christian should not also be a prophet. I also do not see based on this view why any man should take the law of his country for his rule of action, rather than his own inspiration. We fall once more into the mistake of taking it upon ourselves to be the judges of good and evil. We make the judges of good and evil to be private men who pretend to be supernaturally inspired and this leads to the dissolution of all civil government. Faith derives from hearing and hearing derives from those accidents that guide people to those who speak to them. These accidents are all contrived by God Almighty, but they are not supernatural. They are just unobservable for the great number of them that agree to what they hear. Faith and sanctity are indeed quite uncommon, but even so, they are not miracles. They are brought about by education, discipline, correction and the other natural ways that God works them into the elect at the times that He thinks fit. The three above opinions are pernicious to peace and government. They have proceeded chiefly from the tongues and pens of unlearned divines. These divines join the words of Holly Scripture together, in ways that are not agreeable to reason, and thus do what they can to make men think that sanctity and natural reason cannot stand together.

Subjecting the sovereign power to civil laws. A fourth opinion that is repugnant to the nature of a commonwealth is the following: The person that has sovereign power is subject to civil laws. It is true that sovereigns are all subject to the Laws of Nature, because these laws are divine and cannot be abrogated by any man or commonwealth. But the sovereign is not subject to the laws that the sovereign, that is the commonwealth, makes. To be subject to laws is to be subject to the commonwealth, and that means that the sovereign representative would be subject to himself. This is not subjection, but is rather freedom from the laws. This error sets the laws above the sovereign and thus also sets a judge above the sovereign that has the power to punish him. This, in effect, is to make a new sovereign, and then again a third, to punish the second one. This would go on continually without an end and would result in the confusion and dissolution of a commonwealth.

Attributing absolute propriety to subjects. A fifth doctrine that tends to the dissolution of commonwealths is that every private man has an absolute propriety of his goods, which excludes the right of the sovereign. It is true that every man has indeed a propriety that indeed excludes the right of every other subject. But he has it only on the basis of sovereign power. Every man has an equal right to the protection of the sovereign in this regard. But if the sovereign is also excluded from individuals' propriety, he cannot perform the office that the subjects have put him into. This is to defend them both from foreign enemies and from the injuries of one another and consequently, if the sovereign is also excluded from individuals' propriety, there will no longer be a commonwealth.

If the propriety of the subjects does not exclude the right of the sovereign representative to their goods, then it also doesn't exclude those that represent the sovereign himself, such as the offices of judicature and execution.

Division of the sovereign power. A sixth doctrine that is plainly and directly contrary to the essence of a commonwealth is the view that the sovereign power may be divided. To divide the power of a commonwealth is just to dissolve it, for divided powers mutually destroy each other. These doctrines are professed mainly by those who make their profession from the laws and are thus endeavoring to make others dependent on their own learning and not upon the legislative power.

Imitation of neighboring nations. The examples of different governments in neighboring nations are like false doctrines in that they dispose men to alter a form of government that is already settled. The Jewish people were stirred up to reject God and call upon the prophet Samuel to provide a king for them after the manner of other nations. Also, the smaller cities of ancient Greece were continually disturbed by seditions of aristocratic and democratic factions. One part of the city desired to imitate the Lacedaemonians and the other, the Athenians. Many see the late troubles of England growing out of an imitation of the Low Countries. Some think that the only thing needed to grow rich is to change England and adopt the Low Countries' form of government. The constitution of man's nature is itself subject to the desire for novelty. So when people are provoked by this desire and see others in their neighborhood that have grown rich by changing, it is almost impossible for them to not follow those that solicit them to change. This leads to a love of the first beginnings of the change, though eventually there will be grief over the continuance of disorder. This is like hot blood that once having caused an itch, leads people to tear themselves with their own nails until they can no longer endure the pain.

Imitation of the Greeks and Romans. One of the most frequent causes of rebellion against monarchy in particular is reading the books of policy and histories of the ancient Greeks and Romans. Young men and others who are not provided with the antidote of solid reason receive a strong and delightful impression of their great exploits of war achieved by the leaders of their armies. These readers are also pleased by the other things that the Greeks and Romans did and they think that their great prosperity did not proceed from the emulation of particular men, but from the virtue of their popular form of government. The frequent seditions and civil wars produced by the imperfections of their policies are not considered. Based on the reading of these books, men have undertaken to kill their kings, because the Greek and Latin writers made it lawful and laudable to do so in their books and discourses on policy. All that was required was to call the king a tyrant, as then they can say they performed tyrannicide, which is the lawful killing of a tyrant, and not regicide, the killing of a king. The same books lead those who live in a monarchy to the opinion that those that are subjects in a popular commonwealth enjoy liberty, but the subjects in a monarchy are all slaves. Those that live in a monarchy form this opinion, but not those who live under a popular government, for the latter find no such liberty. I cannot imagine how any thing can be more prejudicial to a monarchy than allowing the public reading of these books, without applying the correctives of discrete masters who would be able to take away their venom.

This venom can be compared to the bite of a mad dog, which is the disease that physicians call hydrophobia or fear of water. The one that is bitten has a continual torment of thirst and yet abhors water, and is in such an estate that the poison seems to be endeavoring to convert him into a dog. Sometimes monarchies are bitten to the quick by those democratic writers that continually snarl at the monarchical form of government. At this time they need a strong king to combat tyrranaphobia, the fear of being strongly governed. When such a king is present, the democratic writers abhor him, even as they need him.

There have been doctors[3] that have held that there are three souls in a man. There are also those that think that there is more than one soul, that is more than one sovereign, in a commonwealth. They then set up a supreme authority against the sovereignty, canons against the laws, and a ghostly authority against the civil authority. These doctors work on men's minds with words and distinctions that really mean nothing, but indicate by their obscurity that another kingdom, that some think is invisible, walks in the dark—as it were, a kingdom of fairies. It is clear, however, that the civil power and the power of the commonwealth is the same thing. The supreme authority and the power to make canon laws and to grant faculties imply the power of a commonwealth. So it follows that where one is sovereign and another is supreme, and where one can make laws and another can make canons, there is the situation of having two commonwealths for the same group of subjects. This is a kingdom divided against itself and it cannot stand. Even though the distinction between temporal and ghostly is meaningless, there would still be two kingdoms and every subject would be subject to two masters. When the ghostly power challenges the right of the sovereign to declare what is a sin, it therefore challenges the right to declare what is a law, as a sin is nothing but a transgression of the law. The ghostly power would also be challenging the civil power's to declare laws and so every subject would have two masters who both will give commands that are to be observed as the law. This is an impossible situation. If there is to be one kingdom, the civil power of the commonwealth must be subordinate to the ghostly and then there is no sovereignty but the ghostly one. Or else, the ghostly must be subordinate to the temporal one and then there is no supremacy but the temporal one. When these two powers oppose one another, the commonwealth is in great danger of civil war and dissolution. The civil authority is more visible and stands in the clearer light of natural reason and so at all times, a considerable part of the people will be drawn to it. But the spiritual authority will also draw a party sufficient to trouble and sometimes to destroy a commonwealth. For even if the spiritual authority stands in the darkness of Scholastic distinctions and unintelligible words, the fear of darkness and ghosts is greater than other fears. This is a disease that can appropriately be compared to epilepsy or the falling-sickness in a natural body that the Jews took to be one kind of possession of spirits. In this disease there is an unnatural spirit, or wind, in the head that obstructs the roots of the nerves and moves them violently. This takes away the motion that they naturally should have from the power of the soul in the brain and thereby causes violent and irregular motions in the parts of the body that are called convulsions. One that is seized by this disease falls down sometimes into water and sometimes into fire, as a man deprived of his senses. The same kind of thing happens in the political body. Sometimes the spiritual power moves the members of a commonwealth by means of the terror of punishments and the hopes of rewards, which are the nerves of the commonwealth. In these cases, the commonwealth is not moved by the civil power, which is the soul of the commonwealth, as it ought to be. Strange and difficult words then suffocate the understanding and distract the people. When this happens, the people are either overwhelmed in the commonwealth by oppression or are cast into the fire of a civil war.

Mixed government. Sometimes in a civil government itself, there is more than one soul.[4] This occurs when the power of levying money, which is the nutritive faculty, depends on a general assembly. The power of conduct and command, which is the motive faculty, depends on one man, and the power of making laws, which is the rational faculty, depends on the accidental consent, not only of the first two, but also a third body. This endangers the commonwealth sometimes for the lack of consent to make good laws, but more often for the lack of the nourishment necessary for life and motion. Few perceive that such a government is not a government at all, but a division of the commonwealth into three factions. It is called a mixed monarchy, but in truth, it is not one independent commonwealth, but three independent factions. It is not one representative person, but is rather three. In the kingdom of God there may be three independent persons, that do not breach the unity of the God that reigns,[5] but where men reign that are subject to the diversity of opinion, it cannot be so. If a king bears the person of the people, and the general assembly also bears this person of the people, and another person bears the person of a part of the people, they are not one person, nor one sovereign, but three persons and three sovereigns.

I do not know of a disease in the natural body of man that is similar to this irregularity of commonwealths. But I have seen a man that had another man growing out of his side that had a head, arms, breast and stomach of his own. If this man had another man growing out of his other side, the comparison to the irregularity described above would have been exact.

Lack of money. I have so far named the diseases of a commonwealth that are the greatest and that are the most dangerous at present. There are others, which being not as bad, still need to be observed. The first is the difficulty of raising money for the necessary uses of the common-wealth, especially in the approach of war. The difficulty arises from the opinion that every subject has the propriety of his own lands and goods that excludes the right of the sovereign to use them. A sovereign may foresee some dangers approaching the commonwealth, but finds people tenaciously obstructing the passage of money to the public treasury. The sovereign should extend itself to encounter and prevent the coming dangers at their beginnings. Instead, the sovereign contracts itself as long as it can and when this no longer works, it struggles with the people through the stratagems of law to obtain small sums. If these do not suffice, he must at last violently open the way to increase the supply of money or he will perish. In this extremity the sovereign can at last make the people give money or else the commonwealth will perish. This kind of distemper can be compared to the ague. In this disease the fleshy parts become congealed or are obstructed by venomous matter. The veins, then, cannot follow their natural course which is to empty themselves into the heart, as they are not supplied by the arteries as they ought to be. The result is a cold contraction and a trembling of the limbs, and afterwards, a hot and strong endeavor of the heart to force the passage of the blood. But before it can do that, the heart contents itself with small refreshments that will cool it for a time. It does this until if nature is strong enough, it breaks the last contumacy[6] of the obstructed parts and it dissipates the venom into sweat. But if nature is too weak to do this, the patient dies.

Monopolies and abuses of tax collectors. There is a disease that sometimes occurs in commonwealths that resembles pleurisy. This occurs when the treasure of a commonwealth, flowing out as it does in its due course, is gathered together in too much abundance in one, or a few private men, by monopolies, or by farms of the public revenues. In the same manner, in pleurisy, blood gets into the membrane of the breast and causes an inflammation accompanied by a fever and painful stitches.

Popular men. The popularity of a potent subject is a dangerous disease, unless the commonwealth has a good grasp of his fidelity. People should receive their motions from the authority of the sovereign, but sometimes they are drawn away from their obedience to the laws by the flattery and the reputation of an ambitious man. They follow this man whose virtues and designs they do not know. This is commonly a greater danger in a popular government than in a monarchy, because an army is of such great force and multitude, that it may easily believe that it is the people. This is the way that Julius Caesar, who was set up by the people against the senate, won for himself the affections of the army and thus made himself the master of the senate and the people. This kind of activity of popular and ambitious men is plain rebellion and may be compared to the effects of witchcraft.

Excessive greatness of a town or multitude of corporations. There is another infirmity of commonwealths which occurs when it contains a very large town that can furnish the number and expense of a whole army out of its own resources. The same kind of problem can occur when there are a great number of corporations in the commonwealth. These corporations can act like lesser commonwealths in the bowels of a greater one, like worms in the entrails of a natural man. Another problem occurs when there are many pretenders who claim political prudence and they have the liberty to dispute against the absolute power. These people are usually bred in the lees[7] of the people and animated by false doctrines, they are perpetually meddling with the fundamental laws to the detriment of the commonwealth. They are like the little worms that physicians call "ascrides".

We may further add the infirmities of insatiable appetite, or bulimia,[8] which is the insatiable enlarging of the dominion. Another problem is the incurable wounds that are often delivered by an enemy. There are also wens[9] which are conquests that cannot be united and are often a burden that are less dangerous when lost, than when kept. Other infirmities are the lethargy of ease and the consumption produced by riot and vain expenses.

Dissolution of the commonwealth. Sometimes in wars, both foreign and internal, the enemies get the final victory. When this happens the forces of the commonwealth can keep the field no longer and can no longer protect the loyal subjects. At that point the commonwealth is dissolved and every man is at liberty to protect himself by any means his own discretion suggests to him. The sovereign is the public soul that gives life and motion to the commonwealth. When it expires the members are no longer governed by it and they are like the carcass of a man when its immortal soul has departed. The right of a sovereign monarch cannot be extinguished by the act of anyone else, but the obligation of the members may be extinguished. Anyone who lacks protection may seek it anywhere, and when he gains it, he is obliged to protect his protector as long as he is able. If a person makes the claim that that he only submitted to this new protector out of fear, the claim is fraudulent. When the power of an assembly is suppressed at some time, the right of that assembly perishes completely, because the assembly itself is then extinct and consequently there is no possibility for sovereignty to be revived.

Endnotes

1. The kind
2. In this and the following paragraph, Hobbes is criticizing the views of John Calvin.
3. Scholastic philosophers
4. Hobbes is using 'soul' here in its Aristotelian sense, of being a faculty of a living organism. Thus according to Aristotle, humans have a nutritious soul, an active one, and a rational one.
5. Hobbes is referring here to the concept of the trinity in Christianity. According to some Christian views, God is a trinity which is three different persons, who are nevertheless one unified being.
6. Stubborn and willful resistance
7. Sediments, lowest aspects
8. Hobbes is clearly using 'bulimia' differently than its current use.
9. Tumors, cysts

CHAPTER 30

Of the Office of the Sovereign Representative

The agent of the good of the people. The office of the sovereign, whether a monarch or an assembly, is the end for which he is entrusted with sovereign power.

This end is the procuration[1] of the safety of the people and the sovereign is obliged by the Law of Nature to give an account of doing this to God and only to Him who is the Author the Law of Nature. Safety does not mean here the bare preservation of life, but also refers to all other of life's other goods, which every man shall acquire for himself by lawful industry and without any danger or hurt to the commonwealth.

By instruction and laws. This end is not to be accomplished by care applied to each individual further than providing protection to them when they shall complain. Instead, the sovereign should provide it by creating a general providence that is contained in public instruction of both doctrine and example, and also by making and executing good laws that individuals may apply to their own cases.

Against the duty of a sovereign to relinquish any essential right of sovereignty. It is his duty to see that people are taught the grounds of these rights. As was specified before in the eighteenth chapter, if the essential right of sovereignty is taken away, the commonwealth is thereby dissolved. Then, every man returns into the condition and calamity of war with every other man, which is the greatest evil that can happen in this life. It is the office of the sovereign to maintain his complete rights, and consequently it is first of all against his duty to transfer them to another or to give any of them away. If he deserts the means, he deserts the end, and he deserts the means of being the sovereign, if he acknowledges himself to be subject to the civil laws. There are other ways that he can desert the means of sovereignty. These include renouncing the following: the power of supreme judicature and of making war and peace by his own authority; judging the necessities of the commonwealth; levying money and soldiers as his own conscience shall judge necessary; making officers and ministers of war and peace; and appointing teachers and examining the doctrines that are conformable or contrary to the defense, peace and good of the people. Secondly, it is against the sovereign's duty to let the people be ignorant or misinformed of the grounds and reasons of these essential rights. If he does not teach the people of these matters, it becomes easy for the people to be seduced and drawn to resist him at those times that the commonwealth requires the sovereign to use and exercise these rights.

The grounds of these rights have the need to be diligently and truly taught, because they cannot be maintained by any civil law or terror of legal punishment. A civil law that would forbid rebellion, which is all resistance to the essential rights of sovereignty, is not an obligation as are other civil laws. It is only an obligation by virtue of the Law of Nature that forbids the violation of faith. If men do not know this natural obligation, they cannot know the right of any law that the sovereign makes. They would then consider punishment to be merely acts of hostility and if they have strength enough, they will avoid these acts by acts of hostility of their own.

The objection of those that say there are no principles of reason for absolute sovereignty. I have heard some say that justice is but a word without substance. These people say that whatever a man can acquire for himself by force or art is his own, not only in the condition of war, but also in a commonwealth. I have already shown this to be false. There are also those that maintain that there are no grounds or principles of reason to sustain the essential rights that makes sovereignty absolute. They say that if there were such, there would have already been discovered in some place or other. But we see that there has not yet been any commonwealth where those rights have been acknowledged or challenged. This is a very poor argument. It would be the same as if the savage people of America would deny there are any grounds, or principles of reason, to build a house that would last as long as its materials, because they never yet saw one so well built. Every day time and industry produce new knowledge. The art of building is derived from principles of reason that have been observed by industrious men that have long studied the nature of materials and the different effects of figure and proportion. Discoveries of these principles occurred long after men began making their original very poor buildings. In the same way, long after men began to constitute their first imperfect commonwealths that were apt to relapse into disorder, principles of reason can be discovered by industrious meditation of how to make constitutions everlasting, except for destruction by external violence. These are the principles that I set forth in this discourse. I am very little concerned on this day whether those that have the power to use them shall see them and use them or neglect them. Even if these principles of mine are not such principles of reason, I am sure that they are the principles that have the authority of Scripture. I will show this when I shall speak of the kingdom of God over the Jews, his peculiar[2] people by covenant, that was administered by Moses.[3]

Objection from the incapacity of the vulgar. Some say that although the principles are correct, the common people do not have enough capacity to understand them. Actually I would be glad if the rich and potent subjects of a kingdom, or those who are considered to be the most learned, were as incapable as the vulgar. Everyone knows that the obstacles to promoting my doctrine are the interests of those who should learn them and not the difficulty of the matter. Potent men have trouble digesting anything that sets up a power to bridle their affections and learned men do not take to anything that points out their errors and thereby lessens their authority. The minds of common people are like clean paper, unless they are tainted by dependence on the potent or scribbled over with the opinions of the doctors. The common people are fit to receive whatever the public authority shall imprint on them. After all, whole nations are brought to acquiesce to the great mysteries of the Christian religion that are above reason. Millions of men are made to believe that the same body may be in innumerable places at one and the same time and this is against reason. If men can be taught these things, they should also be able to be learn principles taught and preached by those protected by the law that are consonant with reason, and that any unprejudiced man needs no more to learn them than to hear them. I conclude that there is no difficulty when a sovereign uses his entire power in instructing the people in the essential rights of sovereignty, which are the natural and fundamental laws. Any difficulty in this regard proceeds from his own fault or the fault of those that he trusts with the administration of his commonwealth. Consequently, it is sovereign's duty to instruct the people to be instructed. Further, it is to his benefit to do so as security against the danger that may come to his natural person by means of rebellion.

Subjects are to be taught not to affect a change of government. These
are the particulars that the people should be taught. First, that they
should not love any form of government that they see in their neighboring nations more than their own. They should not desire to change their
own form of government, even if they see neighboring nations that have
a different form of government are more prosperous. The prosperity of a
people ruled by an aristocratic or democratic assembly does not come
from aristocracy or democracy. Rather, it comes from the obedience and
concord of the subjects. In the same way people do not flourish in a
monarchy because one man has the right to rule them. They flourish
because they obey him. If you take away in any kind of state the obedience, which is the concord of the people, the state will not flourish, and
in fact, in a short time it will be dissolved. Those who are disobedient in
an attempt to reform a commonwealth shall find that they are just
destroying it. In the same way in the fable the foolish daughter of Peleus
had the desire to renew the youth of her decrepit father. To do so, she followed the counsel of Medea, and cut her father into pieces and boiled
him together with strange herbs. By doing this, she did not make him
into a new man. This desire for change is like a breach of the first of
God's commandments. In that commandment God says, "Non habebies
deos alienos" which means that you shall not have the gods of other
nations. In another place the Bible says when referring to kings, that they
are gods.

Subjects should not adhere against the sovereign to popular men. Secondly, the people should be taught that they should not give honor and
obedience appropriate to the sovereign to anyone else. This includes
those individuals who have admirable virtue and stand very high and
shine conspicuously in a commonwealth. It also applies to any assembly
besides the sovereign assembly. The people should not be influenced by
such individuals or assemblies, except when they convey the influence of
the sovereign authority to the people. A sovereign cannot be thought to
love his people, unless he is jealous of them. The sovereign suffers when
the people are seduced from their loyalty to him by the flattery of popular men. This happens not only secretly, but also in the open, as when
preachers proclaim marriage to the people *in facie eccleiae*[4] and by publishing such things in the public streets. This point may be aptly compared to the second of the Ten Commandments.

Subjects are not to dispute the sovereign power. Thirdly, the people
should be informed that it is a great fault to speak evil of the sovereign
representative, whether it is one man or an assembly of men. It is a fault

to argue and dispute his power, or to use his name irreverently. This leads to contempt for the sovereign from his people and their obedience is thus slackened, and that means the safety of the commonwealth is compromised. This point resembles the third of the Ten Commandments.

Days should be set aside for subjects to learn their duties. Fourthly, it is difficult for people to be taught these things, or when it is taught to remember them, and after one generation has past to know who has the sovereign power. So it is helpful to set aside a part of the peoples' ordinary labor and designate certain times that they are to attend to those that are appointed to instruct them. It is necessary that some times be determined when people should assemble together and after prayers and praises are given to God, the sovereign of sovereigns, they should hear someone tell them all of their duties. This would include the positive laws that concern them all, which should be read and expounded and they should be told of the mind of the authority that makes them the law. For these ends, the Jews made every seventh day the Sabbath, when the law was read and expounded. In the solemnity of this day they were made to think that their king was God, and that having created the world in six days, He rested on the seventh. By resting from their labor on the seventh day, the Jews were reminded that God was their king and He had redeemed them from their servile and painful labor in Egypt. This gave them a time, after they had rejoiced in God, to take joy also in themselves by lawful recreation. Thus, the first table of the Ten Commandments sets down a summary of God's absolute power, not only as God, but also as king by a peculiar pact, of the Jews. These commandments also provide light to those that have sovereign power conferred on them by the consent of men, and they show what doctrine the sovereigns ought to teach their subjects.

Subjects are to honor their parents. The first instruction of children depends on the care of their parents. It is necessary that children should be obedient to them while they are under their parents' tuition[5], not only in the present, but afterwards, as gratitude requires. The children should thus acknowledge the benefit of their education by external signs of honor. In the same way people are to be taught that originally the father of every man was also his sovereign lord that had the power of life and death over him. When people instituted a commonwealth, the natural fathers resigned that absolute power to the father of families. But in doing this fathers did not lose the honor that was due them for the education of their children. Relinquishing this right to get such honor was not necessary for the institution of the sovereign power. There would not be any reason why a person would desire to have children, to take care to nourish and instruct them if afterwards the person would have no more benefit from them than would any other person. This accords with the fifth of the Ten Commandments.

Subjects are to avoid doing any injury. Every sovereign should be sure that justice is taught which consists in teaching that no man should take what is not his. People should not deprive their neighbors by violence or fraud of anything that the sovereign authority deems to be theirs. Of the things that are held in propriety, those that are dearest to men are first their life and limbs, and to a lesser degree their conjugal affections, and after that, their riches and means of living. People should thus be taught to abstain from violence to one another's person by private revenge, to abstain from the violation of conjugal honor and from forcible rape, and also from the fraudulent surreption[6] of another's goods. It is also necessary to show the people the evil consequences of false judgment by means of the corruption of judges and witnesses. These cause the distinction of propriety to be taken away and justice to have no effect. All of these things are intimated in the sixth, seventh, eighth and ninth of the Ten Commandments.

And to do all this sincerely from the heart. Finally, subjects should be taught that injustice involves not only doing unjust actions, but also having the designs and intentions to do them, even if the actions are hindered by accident. Injustice consists in the depravity of the will as well as in the irregularity of the act. This is the intent of the tenth of the Ten Commandments and the summary of the second table, which is reduced all to the one commandment of mutual charity, which is that you shall love your neighbor as yourself.[7] The summary of the first table is reduced to the love of God, whom the Jews had just received as their king.

The use of universities. To find the means and conduits for teaching these instructions, we should first find why so many opinions have been so deeply rooted in people that are contrary to the peace of mankind and that are based on weak and false principles. These are the principles I specified in the preceding chapter. These include the following: men should judge what is lawful and unlawful by their own consciences and not by the law itself; subjects sin in obeying the laws of the commonwealth unless they themselves first judge them to be lawful; subjects' propriety over their riches excludes the dominion that the commonwealth has over them; it is lawful for subjects to kill what they call a tyrant; and the sovereign power may be divided. How do these false precepts come to be instilled in the people? The greatest part of mankind consists of two sorts. The first are those whom through necessity or covetousness only attend to their own trades and labor. The second are on the other side, who through superfluity[8] and sloth just pursue sensual pleasures. Both groups of people are diverted from the deep meditation that is necessarily required to learn the truth, not only in matters of natural justice, but also in the other sciences. So they learn the notions of their duty mainly from divines in the pulpit and partly from their neighbors or familiar acquaintances who discourse readily and plausibly, and seem wiser than themselves in cases of law and conscience. The divines, and others who make a great show of learning, have derived their knowledge from universities and from the schools of law or from books that eminent men in those schools and universities have published. It is clear that the instruction of the people depends completely on the correct teaching of the youth in the universities. Some may ask, are not the universities of England learned enough to do that? And are you the one who will undertake to teach the universities? Hard questions. For the first question I have no doubt what is the answer. Until the later end of the reign of Henry the Eighth, the universities principally upheld the power of the Pope that was always upheld against the power of the commonwealth. So many preachers and lawyers who were taught at the universities held these doctrines that it is a sufficient basis for saying that even though the universities were not the authors of the false doctrines, they did not know how to plant the true ones. Given all the contradictory opinions that were taught, the preachers and lawyers were not sufficiently instructed on the correct ones. They thus retained a relish of that subtle liquor that first seasoned them to be against the civil authority. As for the second question, there is no need for me to say yes or no. Any man that sees what I am doing can easily perceive what I think the answer is.

The safety of the people further requires that the sovereign power, one man or many, administer justice equally to all degrees of people. The poor and obscure as well as the rich and mighty should be righted when injuries are done to them. The great should have no greater hope of impunity when they do violence, dishonor or injury to meaner[9] men than when one of the latter does the like to one of the former. This is equity that is a precept of the Law of Nature and a sovereign is as subject to it as any of the meanest of his people. All breaches of the law are offenses against the commonwealth, but there are some that are also offenses against private persons. Those that concern only the commonwealth may be pardoned without a breach of equity, for every man may pardon what is done against himself according to his own discretion. But an offense against a private man cannot be pardoned in equity without the consent or reasonable satisfaction of the one that was injured.

The inequality of subjects[10] proceeds from the acts of the sovereign power and therefore have no more place in the presence of the sovereign in a court of justice than the inequality between kings and their subjects has in the presence of the King of Kings. The honor of great persons should be given only for the value of their beneficence and the help they give to men of inferior rank. The violence, oppression and injuries that honored persons do are not extenuated, but are aggravated, by their rank, as they have the least need to commit them. The consequences of this partiality towards the great proceeds in this manner: impunity leads to insolence, insolence to hatred, and hatred to an endeavor to pull down all oppressing and contumelious[11] greatness through the ruins of the commonwealth.

Equal taxes. Equal justice also involves the equal imposition of taxes. The equality of taxes does not depend on equal riches, but on the equality of debt that every man owes to the commonwealth for his defense. It is not enough for a man to labor for the maintenance of his life, but also to fight, if there is a need, to secure the fruits of his labor. People must do as the Jews did after their return from captivity, when in rebuilding the temple, they built with one hand and held a sword in the other. Or else people must hire others to fight for them. The impositions that are laid on the people by the sovereign power are the wages due to those who hold the public sword and thereby defend private men in the exercise of several trades and callings. The benefit that everyone receives is the enjoyment of life, which is equally dear to the poor as to the rich. The debt which a poor man owes to those who defend his life is the same that a rich man owes for the defense of his. But the rich, who have the service of the poor, may thus be debtors, not only for themselves, but also for many others. So the equality of imposition consists in the equality of what is consumed, rather than the equality of the riches of the persons that consume the same amount. What reason would there be to charge more from a person who labors a great deal and consumes little sparing the fruits of his labor, and charging less of one that lives idly, gets little and spends all that he gets? After all, the one does not have more protection from the commonwealth than does the other. When impositions are laid upon those things that men consume, then every man pays equally for what he uses. Then the commonwealth is not defrauded by the luxurious waste of private men.

Public charity. Many men become unable to maintain themselves by their own labor due to inevitable accidents. These men should be provided the necessities that nature requires by the laws of the commonwealth and not have to rely on the charity of private persons. As it is uncharitable for any man to neglect the impotent, it would be the same for the sovereign of a commonwealth to expose unfortunate people to the hazard of uncertain charity.

Prevention of idleness. But it is different for those that have strong bodies, as they should be forced to work. There should be laws that encourage all manner of the arts, such as navigation, agriculture, fishing, and all other kinds of manufacture that requires labor, so that there will be no excuse that the able cannot find employment. If the multitude of poor, and yet strong people is still increasing, they should be transplanted into countries that are not sufficiently inhabited. But in this case the transplanted people should not exterminate those that already live there, but should be constrained to live close together and not to range over a great deal of ground. They should not snatch whatever they find, but instead should cultivate each little plot with art and labor to provide them with sustenance for the seasons. However, when all the world is overcharged with inhabitants, the last remedy is war, which provides for every man by victory or by death.

What are good laws. One of the duties of the sovereign is making good laws. But what is a good law? By a good law I do not mean a just law, for no law can be unjust. The law is made by the sovereign power and all that is done by that power is warranted and owned by every one of the people. That which every man will have as so, no man can say it is unjust. The laws of the commonwealth are just like the laws of gambling. Whatever they all agree on is not an unjust to any of them. A good law is one that is needful,[12] for the good of the people, and is perspicuous.

Laws that are necessary. The use of laws, which are simply authorized rules, is not to keep people from performing voluntary actions. Rather laws are to keep people from hurting themselves by their own impetuous desires, rashness or indiscretion. The laws should be hedges that are set to keep travelers on their way, but not to stop them. A law that is not needful does not have the true goal that laws should have, and so is not good. A law may be conceived to be good when it is for the benefit of the sovereign, even though it is not necessary for the people. But this is incorrect. The good of the sovereign and the good of the people cannot be separated. A weak sovereign is one that has weak subjects, and a weak people is one whose sovereign lacks the power to rule over them at his will. Unnecessary laws are not good laws, but are traps for money. Where the right of the sovereign power is acknowledged, these kinds of laws are superfluous. Where the right of the sovereign power is not acknowledged, these laws are insufficient to defend the people.

Laws that are perspicuous. The perspicuity of a law does not consist that much in the words of the law itself, but rather in the declaration of the causes and motives for which it was made. The causes and motives are what show us the meaning of the legislator and once the meaning of the legislator is known, the law is more easily understood in a few, rather than many, words. All words are subject to ambiguity and so the multiplication of words in the body of the law is a multiplication of ambiguity. Also having a large number of words implies that those who have too much diligence can evade the words and thus be outside the compass of the law. This sort of thing is a cause of many unnecessary processes. When I think of how short the ancient laws were and how they grew longer by degrees, it indicates to me that there was contention between the writers and the pleaders of the law. The former were trying to circumscribe the latter and the latter were trying to evade the circumscriptions, and in this struggle the pleaders gained the victory. In commonwealths the legislator is the supreme representative, whether it is one man or an assembly and it belongs to his office to make the reasons for the law perspicuous. The legislator should make it clear why the law was made and the body of the law itself should be as short as can be and use just proper and meaningful terms.

Punishments. The office of the sovereign has the duty to make the right application of punishments and rewards. The proper end of punishment is not revenge and the discharge of anger, but the correction of the offender or of others by his example. The severest punishments should be inflicted for the crimes that are of the greatest danger to the public. These are crimes that proceed from malice to the established government, those that spring from contempt for justice and those that provoke indignation in the multitudes. Finally, these dangerous crimes include those which when unpunished, seemed to be authorized, as when they are committed by the sons, servants or favorites of men in authority. Indignation causes men to act not only against the actors and authors of injustice, but also against all power that are likely to protect them. An example of this is the case of Tarquin. He was driven out of Rome and the monarchy was dissolved because of the insolent act of one of his sons. However, there is a place for leniency without prejudice to the commonwealth in cases of crimes of infirmity. These are crimes that proceed from great provocation, from great fear, great need, or from ignorance, whether an act is a great crime or not. The Law of Nature requires leniency when there is the place for it. When there is a great commotion, it would profit the commonwealth more to punish the leaders or teachers of the commotion as examples, rather than the poor seduced people. To be severe to the people is to punish their ignorance, which may in a great part be imputed to the sovereign who is responsible that the people were not better instructed.

Rewards. Similarly, it is the duty of the office of the sovereign to always apply rewards for the benefit of the commonwealth. This is the use and end of rewards, and rewards serve the commonwealth best when they are given with as little expense to the common treasury as is possible. The payments, when done properly, will encourage others to serve the commonwealth faithfully and to study the arts so they can become better at them. It is not a reward when money or preferment is used to influence a popular and ambitious subject to be quiet and to desist from making ill impressions in the minds of the people. Rewards should be ordained for services done in the past, not for disservice. Money given to keep people quiet is not a sign of gratitude, but of fear, and it does not benefit, but rather it damages the public. Rewards of this kind become a contention with ambition. They are like the case of Hercules in his struggles with the monster Hydra that had many heads and for every one that Hercules vanquished, three grew up in its place. Similarly, when the stubbornness of one popular man is overcome with a reward, the example will cause many others to arise that will do the same mischief in the hope of the same benefit. All sorts of manufactures increase by being venible,[13] and the same is true for malice. Sometimes a civil war can be deferred by these ways, but even then the danger will grow even greater and the public ruin will be more certain. It is therefore against the duty of the sovereign in whom the public safety is committed to reward those that aspire to greatness by disturbing the peace of their country. The sovereign should instead oppose such men at the beginning when there is little danger, rather than at a later time when the danger is greater.

Counselors. Another business of the sovereign is to choose good counselors. I mean by this those people whose advice he should take in the government of the commonwealth. The word 'counsel', *'consilium'* in Latin, which is corrupted from *'considium'* is of great significance and applies to all assemblies of men that sit together.

It applies when they deliberate what is to be done in the future, but also when they judge past actions and when they make laws for the present. When I talk about counsel here, I mean it only in the first sense. In this sense there in no choice of counsel in democracies or aristocracies, because the person counseling are members of the person who is counseled. The choice of counselors properly only occurs in a monarchy, in which the sovereign would not discharge his office as he should do if he does not choose those who are the most able. The most able counselors are those that have the least hope of benefit by giving evil counsel and have the most knowledge of those things that conduce to the peace and defense of the commonwealth. It is a difficult matter to know who expects to benefit from public troubles. But there are signs. One that is a good reason for suspicion is when men whose estates are not sufficient to pay for their accustomed expenses begin to soothe the people in their unreasonable or irremediable grievances. This can easily be observed by anyone who is concerned to see it. But it is even harder to know who has the most knowledge of public affairs. Those that have the knowledge need it a great deal less. To know who knows the rules of any art often requires knowledge of that art itself, because no man can be assured of the truth of another's rules unless he is first taught to understand them. The best signs of knowledge of any art are being able to talk about it and showing good effects from using it. Good counsel does not come from lot or inheritance. There is no more reason to expect good advice from the rich or noble in matters of state than in delineating the dimensions of a fortress, unless we think there is no more method in the study of politics but only to be an on-looker. This is not so, just as it is not the case for the study of geometry. Politics is even a harder subject than geometry. In some parts of Europe certain persons think that through inheritance they have the right to be the highest counselors of a state. This view is derived from the conquests of the ancient Germans. Many absolute lords would not join a confederacy to conquer other nations without the privileges that would be marks of difference in future times. These marks would distinguish their posterity from the posterity of their subjects. Even though the sovereign may seem to maintain these favors, these privileges are inconsistent with sovereign power. They have the right to contend for these privileges, but when the need arises they should let them go by degrees and then have no further honor, but what they deserve to have according to their abilities.

No matter how able a counselor may be in any affair, the benefit of the counsel is greater when they give their advice and the reason for it to individuals apart from others, rather than give it in an assembly. It is also better to provide the advice when they give a speech that they have premeditated rather than just speak on the sudden.[14] In both cases the coun-selors have more time to survey the consequences of action and are less subject to be carried away into contradiction through envy, emulation or any other passion that arises from differences of opinion.

Consider situations that do not concern other nations, but only the laws that look inward and deal with the ease and benefit the subjects may enjoy. The best counsel in such cases should be taken from the gen-eral information and complaints of the people in each province. They are the ones who are best acquainted with their own wants and should be diligently taken notice of, as long as they demand nothing that conflicts with the essential rights of sovereignty. As I have said before, without these essential rights, the commonwealth cannot subsist at all.

Commanders. If a commander-in-chief of an army is not popular, he will not be beloved or feared as he ought to be, and thus, he will not be able to perform his office with good success. In order for the commander to be loved and be thought sufficient by his soldiers, he should be indus-trious, valiant, affable, liberal and fortunate. This amounts to popularity and breeds in the soldiers the desire and courage to recommend them-selves to his favor. It also protects the severity of the general when he has to punish mutinous or negligent soldiers. But one must be cautious about the fidelity of the commander, because the love of his soldiers is a dan-gerous thing to a sovereign power, especially if the sovereign is in the hands of an assembly that is not popular. For the safety of the people, it is therefore important that the sovereign should commit the armies to one who is not only a good conductor of men, but is also a faithful subject.

When the sovereign himself is popular and reverenced and beloved by his people, then there is no danger at all from the popularity of a subject. Soldiers are not that unjust that they would side with their captain, even though they love him, against a sovereign when they love not only his person, but also his cause. That is why those before they have settled into the sovereign's place, those who have tried to suppress the power of the lawful sovereign by violence, have first taken the trouble to give them-selves a title to save the people from the shame of receiving them. If someone has a known right to sovereign power, that is such a popular quality, that the person with this power can turn the hearts of his subject to him if they can see him absolutely able to govern his own family. If an enemy sees a sovereign disbanding the enemy's own armies, the enemy will also turn to the sovereign. For the greatest and most active part of mankind has never been well contented with the present.

The law of nations concerns the offices of one sovereign to another. I will not say anything about this because the law of nations and the Law of Nature are the same thing. Every sovereign has the same right to procure the safety of his people that any particular man has in procuring the safety of his own body. The same law that dictates to men that have no civil government what they ought to do, and what to avoid in regard to one another, dictates the same to commonwealths. In these cases the consciences of sovereign princes and sovereign assemblies determine what should be done. There is no court of natural justice except in peoples' consciences. Where men do not rule, God does, and his laws oblige all of mankind. God is the author of nature and since He is the king of kings, His laws are the Laws of Nature. I shall speak in the rest of this discourse of the kingdom of God, as the king of kings, and also His being king of a peculiar people.

Endnotes

1. To be the agent for
2. Special
3. This is one of the topics of the third part of Leviathan.
4. In the presence of the church
5. Instruction
6. Theft
7. Hobbes implies that 'you should love your neighbor as yourself is the tenth commandment. Actually, it is not. The tenth commandment is that you should not covet your neighbor's goods.
8. Having too much
9. Very poor
10. The inequalities that Hobbes is referring to here are those that result from the sovereign giving certain people titles and honors.
11. Insulting and humiliating
12. Necessary
13. Capable of being sold
14. Off the cuff

CHAPTER 31

Of the Kingdom of God by Nature

The scope of the following chapters. Those that are in the condition of mere nature have absolute liberty as they are neither sovereigns nor subjects. This is a state of anarchy and is the condition of war. The precepts which guide men to avoid this condition are the Laws of Nature. A commonwealth without sovereign power is but a word and cannot stand. Subjects owe their sovereigns simple obedience in all things where their obedience is not repugnant to the laws of God. I have sufficiently proved all of these points in what I have already written. In order to have the complete knowledge of our civil duty, it is necessary to fill in the only thing that is missing and that is the knowledge of the laws of God. Without this knowledge a man will not know whether or not something that he is commanded to do by the civil power is contrary to the laws of God. A man might by too much civil obedience offend the Divine Majesty, or through fear of offending God transgress the commandments of the commonwealth. It is thus necessary to know what the divine laws are in order to avoid both of these rocks. As the knowledge of all law depends on the knowledge of the sovereign power, I shall say something in what follows about the kingdom of God.

Who are the subjects in the kingdom of God. The Psalmist says, "God is the king; let the earth rejoice" (Psalms 96:1) He also says, "God is the king though the nations be angry. He sits by the cherubim, though the earth be moved." (Psalms 98:1) Men are always subject to divine power whether they will to be or not. When men deny the existence or providence of God, they may shake off their ease, but not their yoke. However, it is a metaphorical use of the word 'kingdom' to refer to the power of God which extends itself not only over man, but also over beasts, plants and inanimate bodies. It is only proper to say that someone reigns when they govern their subjects by their words and by promises of rewards to those who obey them and threatening punishment to those who do not obey. Inanimate bodies and irrational creatures are not subjects in the kingdom of God because they do not understand any precepts as being His. Atheists are also not subjects of God, nor are those who think that God has no concern for the actions of mankind, as they acknowledge no words to be His and do not have any hope of His rewards, or fears of His threats. God's subjects are those that believe that God governs the world and has given it precepts and has offered rewards and punishments to mankind. Those who are not God's subjects are to be considered His enemies.

A threefold word of God: reason, revelation and prophecy. To rule by words requires that the words be manifestly known, for otherwise, the words are not laws. The nature of laws requires a clear promulgation that is sufficient for taking away the excuse of ignorance. When it comes to the laws of men, there is only one way to provide this promulgation and that is by the proclamation by the voice of man. But God declares his laws in three ways: by the dictates of natural reason, by revelation and by the voice of some man who is credited by others by his performance of miracles. This is the basis of the triple word of God: rational, sensible and prophetic. Corresponding to this is the triple hearing: right reason, supernatural sense and faith. No universal laws have been given by supernatural sense, which consists of revelation or inspiration. God only speaks in that manner to particular persons and to different people about different things.

A twofold kingdom of God: natural and prophetic. On the basis between the other two kinds of God's words, rational and prophetic, a twofold kingdom may be attributed to God: natural and prophetic. The natural is one where God governs as many of mankind as acknowledge His providence by the natural dictates of right reason. The prophetic is one where God has chosen one peculiar nation, the Jews, to be His subjects. He governed them, and only them, by positive laws which He gave them from the mouths of holy prophets, and not just by natural reason. I shall speak of the natural kingdom in this chapter.

The right of God's sovereignty is derived from his omnipotence. The right of nature whereby God reigns over men and punishes those that break His laws is not derived from his creating them. Obedience is not required as gratitude for his benefits. Obedience arises from His irresistible power. I have previously shown how the sovereign right arises from a pact. To show how this same right may arise from nature, I just have to show in what cases it can never be taken away. When all men by nature had a right to all things, every one had the right to reign over all the rest. But this right could not be obtained by force and it concerned the safety of every one, who set aside that right to establish a sovereign authority by consent that would rule and defend them. If there had been any man who had irresistible power, there is no reason why that man should have not used that power to rule, and defend both himself and others according to his own discretion. Someone who has irresistible power naturally has dominion over all others as a result of the excellence of their power. It is because of that power, that God Almighty if the king over men and has the right to afflict men at His pleasure. This is not because He is gracious or our creator, but because He is omnipotent. Punishment is only deserved for sin, because 'punishment' means the affliction of sin, but the right of afflicting it, which is not derived from men's sin, but from God's power.

Sin is not the cause of all afflictions. The question, why evil men often prosper and good men suffer adversity has been much disputed by the ancients. This is the same question as the current one, by what right does God dispense the prosperities and adversities of life? These are difficult questions that have not only shaken the faith of the vulgar in divine providence, but even more, it has given difficulty to the saints. David said, "How good is the God of Israel to those that are upright in heart; and yet my feet were almost gone and my treading had well-nigh slipped, for I was grieve at the wicked when I saw the ungodly in such prosperity." (Psalms 72:1,2,3) And Job so earnestly expostulates with God for the many afflictions he suffered, even though he was so righteous. The question in the case of Job is decided by God himself, not by arguments from Job's affliction due to his sin, but rather on the basis of His own power. Job's friends drew their arguments from the afflictions due him because of his sins, and Job defended himself by proclaiming his innocence. God Himself took up the matter and justified the affliction by arguments based on His power. God says, "Where were you when I laid the foundations of the earth" (Job 38:4) and the like. These statements both approved of Job's innocence and refuted the erroneous doctrine of his friends. The doctrine expressed in Job agrees with what our Savior said concerning the man that was born blind. These are His words, "Neither has this man sinned, nor his fathers; but that the word of God be made manifest in him." It is said, "That death entered the world by sin", which means that if Adam would have never sinned, he would not have died, which means that his soul would never been separated from his body. But that does not mean that it would have been unjust for God to have afflicted him even if Adam had not sinned. After all, He does afflict other living creatures that cannot sin.

Divine Laws. I have just spoken of the right of God's sovereignty that is only based on nature. Next I shall consider what are the divine laws, or the dictates of natural reason. These laws concern the natural duties of one man to another and the honor that is naturally due to our divine sovereign. The former are the same Laws of Nature that I discussed in the 14th and 15th chapters of this treatise, which are equity, justice, mercy, humility and the rest of the moral virtues. All that remains, then, is to consider what precepts natural reason by itself dictates to men without the word of God, concerning the honor and worship of the Divine Majesty.

What are honor and worship. Honor is the inward thought and opinion that people have about the power and goodness of another. To honor God is to think as highly as is possible of His power and goodness. The external signs that appear in the words and actions of men that are called worship are the marks of peoples' opinions. Worship is one part of what the Romans understood by the term 'cultus', whose meaning is the labor that a person bestows on any thing in order to benefit from it. Some of the things we gain benefit from are subject to us and the profit they yield to us is a result, or natural effect, of the labor we bestow on them. But some things we benefit from are not subject to us and answer our labor according to their own wills. The first sense of bestowed labor on the earth is called culture and the education of children is a cultivation of their minds. The second sense of bestowed labor occurs when men's wills respond to our purposes, not by force, but by complaisance.[1] This is a kind of courting, that is doing whatever is pleasing to those from whom we hope to benefit. It is often done by such actions as pleasing or acknowledging the power of the other person. These activities are properly called worship, and '*publicola*' is understood as a worshipper of the people, and '*cultus dei*' as the worship of God.

Several signs of honor. Three passions arise from internal honor which consists of the opinion that something has power and goodness. Love is the passion that arises with reference to goodness, and hope and fear are the passions that relate to power. There are three kinds of external worship which are praising, magnifying and blessing. The subject of praise is goodness, and the subject of magnifying and blessing is power and the effect of these activities is our felicity. Praising and magnifying are signified both by words and actions. They are signified by words when we say a man is good or great, and they are signified by actions when we thank someone for his bounty and obey his power. The opinion concerning the happiness of another can only be expressed in words.

Natural and arbitrary worship. There are some natural sign of honor, both of attributes and actions. The words 'good', 'just', 'liberal', and the like refer to the honor of attributes, and prayers, thanks and obedience are natural signs of actions. There are other signs of honor that are a result of institution or the customs of men. These are sometimes in some times and places honorable, but in other times and places they are dishonorable. In still others they are indifferent. Gestures of salutation, prayer and thanksgiving are used differently in different times and places. The former kinds of signs are natural worship, the latter are arbitrary worship.

Commanded and free worship. There are two different kinds of arbitrary worship. They are commanded and voluntary. Commanded worship is the kind where the one who is worshipped requires it. Worship is voluntary when it is done when the worshipper thinks fit. When worship is commanded, the obedience itself is the worship and not the words or the gestures. But when the worship is voluntary or free, it consists in the opinion of the beholders. If the words or actions that are intended to honor seem ridiculous or contemptuous to the ones being worshipped, then worship is not occurring. These would not be signs of honor, because a sign if not a sign to the one that gives it, but only to the one to whom it is made, which is the spectator.

Public and private worship. There is public and private worship. Public worship is what a commonwealth performs as one person. Private worship is what a private person exhibits. In respect to the whole commonwealth, public worship is free; but in respect to private men, it is not so. Private worship in secret is free, but in the sight of the multitude, there is always some restraint, either from the laws or from the opinion of men, and this is contrary to the nature of liberty.

The end of worship. The end of worship among men is power. When a man sees that another is worshipped, he supposes this other to be powerful and so is readier to obey him, which makes the other's power even greater. But God has no ends and so the worship we do to Him proceeds from our duty and is directed according to our capacity. In doing so we follow those rules of honor that our reason dictates that the weak shall offer to more powerful men in the hope of some benefit, or from fear of some damage, or from thankfulness for some good that the powerful person has already provided.

Attributes of divine honor. I will begin with God's attributes so that we may know what the light of nature teaches us about the worship of God. First, it is clear that we should attribute existence to Him, for no one will have the will to honor something that he thinks does not exist.

Secondly, those philosophers who say that God is the world or the soul of the world, speak unworthily of Him and deny His existence. God is understood to be the cause of the world, but to say that the world is God is to say that there is no cause of the world, which in effect says there is no God.

Thirdly, since what is eternal has no cause, to say that the world is eternal and not created is just to deny that there is a God.

Fourthly, those who attribute ease to God, take away honor from Him, as they take away from Him the care of mankind. This would take away men's love and fear of Him, which are the roots of honor.

Fifthly, to say that God is finite is not to honor him in those things that signify greatness and power. To attribute to someone less than one can is not the sign of the will to honor God. By saying God is finite, we say less of Him than we can, because when something is finite, it is easy to add more.

Therefore, to attribute shape to God is not to honor Him, for all shapes are finite.

We do not honor Him when we say we can conceive or imagine Him, or have an idea of Him in our minds. Whatever we can conceive is finite.

We do not honor Him when we attribute parts or a totality to Him. These are the attributes only of finite things.

If we say He is in this or that place, we say that He is bounded and thus, finite.

If we say that He moved or rested, we attribute a place to Him.

If we say there are more gods than one, we imply they are all finite, for there cannot be more than one infinite.

We do not honor God when we ascribe the passions to him that partake of grief, such as repentance, anger, or mercy. Nor do we honor Him when we ascribe to Him the passion of want, such as appetite, hope or despair, or any other passive faculty. If we ascribe the passions metaphorically, we do not really mean that He has the passions, but we are just referring to their effects. Passions are powers that are limited by something else.

When we ascribe a will to God, it is not to be understood as a man's will, as a rational appetite, but rather as the power by which He effects everything.

When we attribute sight to a man we are talking about a tumult of the mind, raised by external things that press the organic parts of a man's body. These are not what we are attributing to God when we say he has sight or other acts of sense, such as knowledge or understanding. God does not have organic parts, and things that depend on natural causes cannot be attributed to Him.

By natural reason we can only attribute negative attributes, such as infinite, eternal, or incomprehensible, or superlative ones, such as most high, most great, and the like. We can also attribute to Him indefinite attributes, such as good, just, holy and creator. When we do this, we do not declare what He is, for that would be to circumscribe him within the limits of our fancies. Instead, we state these attributes to show how much we admire Him, and how ready we would be to obey Him. These are signs of humility and of the will to honor Him as much as we can. There is but one name that signifies our conception of His nature, and that is, I AM. There is but one name for His relation to us, and that is God, in which is contained, father, king and lord.

Actions that are signs of divine honor. It is a general precept of reason that the actions of divine worship are signs of the intention to honor God. These are first, prayers. It was not the carvers of images that made them gods, but rather they became gods when the people prayed to them.

Secondly, thanksgiving, which differs from prayer in divine worship in that prayers precede and thanks succeed a benefit. The end of both is to acknowledge God as the author of all benefits, in the past as well as in the future.

Thirdly, gifts, that is to say sacrifices and oblations[2] are signs of honor if they are of the best, as they are thanksgivings.

Fourthly, to swear only by God is naturally a sign of honor, for it is a confession that only God knows the heart, and that no man's wit or strength can protect a man against God's vengeance against those who perjure.

Fifthly, it is a part of rational worship to speak considerately of God, for it argues a fear of Him and fear is a confession of His power. It follows that the name of God is not to be used rashly and for no purpose, for that is to use it in vain. There is no purpose for using His name, unless it is as an oath and by order of the commonwealth to make judgments certain, or between commonwealths to avoid war. Disputing about God's nature is contrary to his honor. This is based on the supposition that in this natural kingdom of God, there is no other way to know anything except by natural reason, and this refers to the principles of natural science. These principles cannot teach us anything about God's nature, as they cannot teach us about our own natures, nor about the nature of the smallest living creature. So, when men dispute about the attributes of God on the basis of the principles of natural reason, they just dishonor Him. When we give attributes to God, it should be to signify our pious intention to do Him the greatest Honor we can and not to signify philosophical truth. Volumes of disputation about the nature of God have proceeded from a lack of consideration of what has just been said. The result is that these volumes tend not to honor Him, but to honor our own wits and learning, and are just inconsiderate and vain abuses of His sacred name.

Sixthly, it is a dictate of natural reason that in prayers, thanksgiving, offerings and sacrifices, that they all be the very best kind in order to signify His honor the most. For example, the words and phrases of prayers and thanksgiving should not be sudden, nor light, nor plebian, but should be beautiful and well-composed, for otherwise, we do not honor God as much as we can. While it was absurd for heathens to worship images as gods, it was reasonable for them to do so in verse and with vocal and instrumental music. It was also according to reason for them to offer gifts and beasts as sacrifices as actions of worship. These acts signified submission and were commemorative of received benefits and showed an intention to honor their gods.

Seventhly, reason dictates that we should worship God not only in secret, but especially in public and in the sight of other men. Otherwise, we lose the opportunity to procure others to honor Him and this is one of the most acceptable forms of honor.

Lastly, the greatest worship of all is obedience to His laws, which are the Laws of Nature. As obedience is more acceptable to God than sacrifice, to disobey His commandments is the greatest of all contumelies.[3] These are the laws of divine worship that natural reason dictates to private men.

Public worship consists in uniformity. Since a commonwealth is one person, it should exhibit one kind of worship to God. It does this when it commands the worship to be publicly exhibited by private men. This is public worship and its main property is to be uniform. Those actions that are done differently by different men cannot be said to be public worship. It cannot be said that there is any public worship or that the commonwealth has any religion when there are many sorts of worship that are allowed to proceed from different religions of private men.

All attributes depend on the civil laws. All words, and consequently the attributes of God, gain their meaning from the agreement and constitution of men. Thus, the words that are held to signify honor are those that men intend shall be so. Whatever may be done by the wills of particular men where there is no law but reason, may be done by the will of the commonwealth by civil laws. A commonwealth only has the will and only makes laws, according to the will of the one, or those, that have sovereign power. It thus follows that the attributes that the sovereign ordains for the worship of God as signs of honor ought to be taken and used by private men in their public worship.

Not all actions. Not all actions are signs by constitution,[4] as some are naturally signs of honor or contumely. The latter signs which men are ashamed to do in the sight of those they revere, cannot be made a part of divine worship by human power. The natural signs of honor, such as decent, modest and humble behavior cannot by excluded from signs of honor by the human power. But there are an infinite number of actions and gestures that have an indifferent nature. Of these, the ones that the commonwealth ordains to be publicly and universally used as signs of honor and part of God's worship should be so used by the subjects. The saying in Scripture, "It is better to obey God than men" has its place in the kingdom of God by contract, and not by nature.

Natural punishments. I have briefly spoken of the natural kingdom of God and of His natural laws. I will only add to this chapter a short declaration of His natural punishments. There is no action of man in this life that is not the beginning of such a long chain of consequences that no human capacity is great enough to provide a man with a view of the last one. This chain is made up of both pleasant and unpleasant events, and so one who will do anything for pleasure must also engage himself to suffer all of the pains that are annexed to it. These pains are the natural punishments of the actions that are the beginning of more harm than good. So intemperance is naturally punished with diseases, rashness with mischances,[5] injustice with the violence of enemies, pride with ruin, cowardice with oppression, negligent government or princes with rebellion, and rebellion with slaughter. As punishment is the consequence of the breach of laws, naturally punishments are the natural consequent of the breach of the Laws of Nature, and follow these breaches as their natural and not arbitrary effects.

The conclusion of the second part. This part has discussed the constitution, nature and right of sovereigns and the duty of subjects as derived from the principles of natural reason. This doctrine is very different from the practice of the greatest part of the world, especially of these Western parts that have received their moral learning from Rome and Athens. The moral philosophy that is required for the administration of them by a sovereign power is so deep that I am at the point of believing that my labor is as useless as the commonwealth of Plato. He also had the opinion that it is impossible for the disorders of the state and change of governments by civil wars to be removed until sovereigns should become philosophers. But on the other hand, consider that the science of natural justice is the only science necessary for sovereigns and their principal ministers. Opposed to Plato, the sovereigns and ministers do not have to study the mathematical sciences anymore than good laws encourage men to. Furthermore, neither Plato nor any other philosopher has put the theorems of moral doctrine that men need to learn how to govern and obey into an order where they are sufficiently or probably proven. Given all of this, I recover some hope that at one time or another, this writing may fall into the hands of a sovereign who will consider it himself. As it is short and I think clear, the sovereign will not need the help of any interested or envious interpreter in order to understand it. By the exercise of his entire sovereignty in protecting the public teaching of it, the truth of this speculation may be converted into the utility of practice.

Endnotes

1. Having a disposition to please
2. Religious offerings
3. Harsh insults
4. Conventions
5. Bad luck

Index